4|5

A MUSE AND A MAZE

A MUSE AND A MAZE

Writing as Puzzle, Mystery, and Magic

Peter Turchi

Trinity University Press
San Antonio, Texas

Published by Trinity University Press
San Antonio, Texas 78212
Copyright © 2014 by Peter Turchi

Book design ALSO

Printed in Korea

Trinity University Press strives to produce its books using methods and materials in an environmentally sensitive manner. We favor working with manufacturers that practice sustainable management of all natural resources, produce paper using recycled stock, and manage forests with the best possible practices for people, biodiversity, and sustainability. The press is a member of the Green Press Initiative, a nonprofit program dedicated to supporting publishers in their efforts to reduce their impacts on endangered forests, climate change, and forest-dependent communities.

The paper used in this publication meets the minimum requirements of the American National Standard for Information Sciences—Permanence of Paper for Printed Library Materials, ANSI 39.48–1992.

ISBN 978-1-59534-193-8 hardcover
ISBN 978-1-59534-194-5 ebook

CIP data on file at the Library of Congress.

18 17 16 15 14   5 4 3 2 1

This book is for
Laura and Reed,
for my mother and sister,
and for my students

To watch these shifting forms
fall into order and balance—
there is no greater joy than this.

— CAROLE MASO, *The Art Lover*

CONTENTS

THE CONTEMPLATION OF RECURRING PATTERNS

Endlessly retyped, [the novel looked] at every stage like a jigsaw puzzle as they labored … bits and pieces of it taped to every available surface in Gottlieb's cramped office. *That*, I thought, is editing.

— MICHAEL KORDA, on editor Robert Gottlieb's work with Joseph Heller on *Catch-22*

Every piece of writing is a kind of puzzle. This is true not only of a complex satirical novel but also of a Shakespearean sonnet, an autobiographical essay, a play or screenplay, a love letter, and an email to a colleague about a problem at work. Whom do we address? With what tone? How should we begin? What do we want the reader to think or feel or understand? Is it best to be direct or indirect, sincere or disarming? Should we start with a joke? A quotation?

There are many different kinds of puzzles, but generally speaking, a puzzle is an array of material or information that requires a solution. Let's say a woman has a job, she works hard, but at the end of the month she doesn't have enough money to pay her bills. Circumstances have presented her with a puzzle, a problem to solve. She could take on a second job, or stop eating out, or rob a convenience store—all possible solutions—but instead she decides to write a letter to her employer asking for a raise. The composition of that letter is another puzzle. Should it be a demand or a request? How should she support her argument? Should she mention that she's paying her mother's medical bills? It's a large company, very professional, so she decides she should simply state the circumstances, offering a few highlights of her excellent work and its benefits to the company. She deliberates over whether to issue an ultimatum ("More money, or off I go") or to acknowledge her employer's perspective ("These are difficult times, so if the budget won't allow it now, maybe next year?"). She decides not to mention that she knows two less-experienced men in her office are being paid higher salaries—not yet, anyway. Has she chosen well, arranged all the pieces successfully? She'll know as soon as she gets her response.

A short story or novel is a different kind of puzzle; and it is more than a puzzle.

The composition of a story is a puzzle for the writer, whose job is to decide what to include, what to exclude, and how to organize the parts. The problem is compounded by the fact that, as fiction writers, we begin to write without knowing precisely what we're trying to create. The work continually changes form, and emphasis, and purpose. Characters disappear, new characters are added; some scenes grow longer, others are reduced to summary. A pocket watch that just happened to be in a dresser drawer suddenly seems to indicate something larger. We can't truly solve the puzzle, or arrange the words and sentences and characters and events most effectively, until we finally feel confident that we understand what we're trying to create.

But while composing a piece of fiction is like assembling a puzzle, the finished work is not presented by the writer as a puzzle for the reader to solve. There may be puzzles within the story, elements of plot or character or imagery or meaning that require the reader's active participation, but the story as a whole is not a problem with a solution. Like Ariadne's thread allowing Theseus to journey into—and safely out of—the mythical labyrinth, a story means to lead the reader somewhere. But the destination isn't a monster, or a pot of gold, or a bit of wisdom. Instead, the destination is something—or several things—to contemplate. The best stories and novels lead the reader not to an explanation, but to a place of wonder. How do we know that? Because the books and stories and poems that mean the most to us are the ones we want to read again, to reexperience and reconsider.

Magic is an art very closely related to poetry. The poet manipulates words, and the magician manipulates objects. We are transcending reality in order to produce something poetic, something beautiful, something interior.

— SPANISH MAGICIAN JUAN TAMARIZ

The word "magic" is commonly used to refer both to a ritualized performance with a long history (the ancient Greeks wrote about magi, or magicians) and, more vaguely, to something transcendent that the speaker either can't or would rather not explain ("That night in Venice was magic, just plain magic"). The history of magic is richly populated with scientists and mathematicians, inventors and entertainers, gamblers, thieves, and con men. Professional magicians tend not to refer to what they do as "tricks," since that implies gimmickry—a trap door, a hollow pencil, a coin with a hole drilled through its center. The preferred term is "illusion," which can apply to effects facilitated by a mechanical device (a

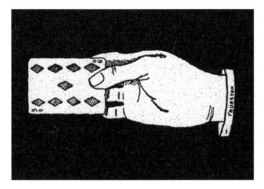

To begin with, the card is held between the tips of the middle finger and thumb.

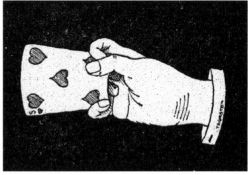

The first and little fingers now grip the card.

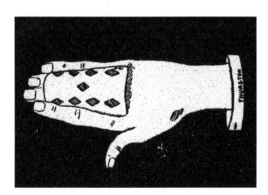

The two middle fingers are next bent and brought down under the card and round to the front of same, thereby causing the card to revolve between the first and fourth fingers, as though on an axis, and assume the position on the back of the hand clipped between the first and second and third and fourth fingers (*shown left*).

After considerable practice it will be found that all the movements I have just described will become practically one, and the card will apparently vanish from the hand.
— *Howard Thurston*

trap door, a hollow pencil, a drilled coin) as well as to those facilitated by skill and practice (a playing card palmed on the back of the hand, a deck cut to the exact same card ten times out of ten), and to those facilitated by surprising scientific and mathematical principles. Many card tricks are based on simple but non-obvious math.

A magical illusion is a puzzle for the magician who, like that woman hoping for a raise, imagines an intended effect (a rabbit produced from a hat that appeared to be empty) and then organizes his materials, movements, words, and gestures to create that effect for an audience. In theory, the illusion is a puzzle for the audience, too (Where did that rabbit come from?). But the sort of person inclined to watch a magic show is the sort of person who, while understanding that there must be a perfectly mundane explanation for how the illusion was created, simultaneously hopes to be moved to a state of wonder—in the same way that a reader who picks up a new novel hopes to be transported by mere ink on paper, the arrangement of words on a page.

The composer of a puzzle means to present a challenge, but also intends for his audience to solve it. A magician presents an illusion with the understanding that, while it can be "solved," or explained, his purpose is to disguise that solution so we can experience something that, however briefly, transcends rational understanding. It's tempting to say that a writer, then, is a kind of magician. A writer gives us a story not to provoke us to admire how it was produced, or to challenge us to tease out some hidden or coded message, but to invite us to think about something he or she has found worthy of extended consideration. But unlike a magical illusion, some of the most powerful effects of a story, poem, or novel actually do transcend rational explanation. Discussions of the writer's craft, of conscious decisions, can take us only so far. There's mystery in it for the writer as well as for readers.

Puzzles are not solved by the use of accurate reckoning alone . . . but also by a substantial use of insight thinking [an admixture of imagination and memory]. Insight thinking does not emerge fortuitously or haphazardly. It comes about only after the observation and contemplation of recurring patterns.

— MARCEL DANESI

The writer's craft is what we can study; and by looking carefully at the work that speaks most strongly to us we can, gradually, discern patterns, choices, and decisions we find effective.

Our curiosity, our interest in problems, means that many of us get pleasure from writing that yields more each time we read or see or hear it. Happily, there are plenty of stories and novels that offer up both immediate pleasure and the rewards that come from prolonged meditation. The challenge for writers is to arrange information—words, phrases, sentences, paragraphs, scenes, images—in ways that are intriguing, arresting, curiosity-arousing, and illuminating. In any particular story, novel, or poem (or essay, play, or screenplay), we need to regard how we're arranging that information, for whom, and why.

That's what this book is about.

This book is not so much a sequel but a companion to *Maps of the Imagination: The Writer as Cartographer*. Both books are, at least in part, about ways in which a piece of writing is designed. They both mean to invite writers to think differently about what we do. (That first-person plural pronoun is generally used to refer to writers, but also at times to readers, under the assumption that all writers read.) While the two books overlap in places, and some of the same authors are mentioned, I've tried to avoid unnecessary repetition. In *Maps of the Imagination*, it seemed useful to focus on the extended metaphor and to offer brief illustrations from a wide variety of writers. The topics contemplated here seemed better investigated by more detailed discussions. In several places I refer to visual artist Charles Ritchie, whose work and process served as initial inspiration. While the primary focus is on fiction, much of what is here could apply to any form of writing.

The chapters that follow consider the tension between puzzle and mystery; the gaps and contradictions that make fictional characters nearly as complex as actual people; the writer as a magician, directing the audience's attention away from himself and toward a created representative; the maze we find ourselves in when we try to follow the "narrative line"; and our desire, as readers and as writers, for challenge, as perverse as that sometimes seems. Appearing along the way are Jerry Seinfeld, Harry Houdini, Bruce Springsteen, *The Wizard of Oz*, Wassily Kandinsky, tangrams, famous Norwegians, reindeer hunters, and a disappearing elephant. You'll also encounter a variety of puzzles, which can be ignored or solved; the solutions appear in the notes to each chapter. If you'd like to try your hand at the tangrams, you can cut out the pieces on the last page of the book.

Art is often discussed as a form of play—and yet that playfulness, that sense of delight, is frequently absent from discussions of the writing process, and of what we tend to call "the work." But even T. S. "You must go by a way wherein there is no ecstasy" Eliot was a fan of the Marx Brothers. No matter how serious the tone, literature offers pleasure in its construction as well as in its content, and in the ways it connects us to others. While it's possible to forget, as we push ourselves to revise and improve, we write because both process and product give us—at least occasionally—delight. This book, then, is offered as a provocation, a companion, and a reminder of the joy writing offers.

DIRECTIONS FOR ATTAINING KNOWLEDGE OF ALL DARK THINGS

Creating order from chaos is the innermost room of a writer's desire.

— JOHN LE CARRÉ

SOLITARY PLEASURES

While fiction writers and their editors bemoan the relatively meager sales of literary fiction, and while poets wonder what they're complaining about, there are other kinds of books that a large percentage of the population buy and put to use, but are reluctant to discuss. On any given day, in bookstores but also in grocery stores and in airports, hundreds if not thousands of books are purchased, nearly all of them inexpensive paperbacks, which the reader will give the rapt attention that, we're told, ordinary men and women once gave the installments of Dickens's *The Old Curiosity Shop* or the latest J. D. Salinger story in *The New Yorker*.

These books that sell, well, wherever books are sold—and where aspirin, neck pillows, and beach balls are sold—are books of puzzles: crossword puzzles, double acrostics, word searches, cryptograms, and sudoku, the puzzle phenomenon that has had its grip on this country, among others, for several years. While puzzle books might seem to have nothing

The Card Players,
by Jonathan Wolstenholme

in common with fiction and poetry, many poets and fiction writers—however reluctant we may be to admit it—are also puzzle solvers and game players. (Some claim, adamantly, not to be; if you're one of them, we'll get to you soon.)

The puzzles and games that intrigue writers take many forms. Years ago, when I became the director of an MFA program in creative writing, and before email became our default mode of communication, I had

A MUSE AND A MAZE

occasion to talk with the program's academic board chair by phone almost every day. Our conversations would often go on for half an hour or more. One day, I recognized a sound in the background on the other end of the line. I started listening for it, and while I didn't hear it during every conversation, I heard it during nearly all of the longest conversations, a sound familiar from my youth: the clatter of cards being shuffled, followed by the soft snapping of a game being laid out.

When my sister and I were young, our parents and our mother's parents played bridge several times a week. We sometimes watched and, as we got older, sat in for a few hands, but for the most part our parents' and grandparents' card playing served as background music as we did homework or watched television or played our own games. The rhythm of shuffling, the quiet shushing of cards being dealt around the table, and then the irregular falling and snapping of cards being played was as much a part of our lives as the rumbling of the refrigerator motor or the grumbling of distant lawn mowers in summer. Accompanying the rhythms of the cards was the melody of our parents' and grandparents' conversation. Actually, there were several melodic lines: the necessary bidding ("One spade," "Pass," "Two hearts," "Pass"), the inevitable commentary on how the cards had been distributed ("Look at this mess," our grandfather might say. "Good Lordy, Miss Agnes") with stretches of silence as a hand was played, punctuated by "Ha! Chu devil" or "Hell tell the captain" (our father) or a disappointed "Shoot. Look at that" (our mother), then more boisterous conversation while our father tallied the score, someone shuffled, and our mother or grandmother refilled drinks or brought out a bag of cheese-flavored crackers shaped like cartoon fish. We had strict bedtimes in those days, my sister and I, and I still have vivid memories of lying in bed, on the verge of sleep, listening to the voices drifting up from our dining room, the game going on into the night.

That's a long way of saying that listening to my colleague playing solitaire summoned up fond old memories. Finally, one day, I acknowledged that I could hear the game. I said something like, "How are the cards?" She must have been surprised: she cut off a laugh, and stopped. I never heard her shuffle again. I imagine—though I never asked—that she suspected I might have taken her playing as a sign of inattention, or distraction. And maybe it was. But I have come to believe there is a clear link between the habitual consideration of the strategic arrangement of playing cards and the work we did together.

This colleague of mine was a poet, with a ferocious ear for form and music. She was also quite a remarkable organizer. For instance: for the program's semiannual residencies, we had to arrange workshops for about seventy students. The students were separated into seven groups. Each student's work was discussed once during each residency. Two faculty members led each workshop each day. Each student participated in one of these multiday workshops five times over two years. Most people would simply divide the students into groups and pair up the faculty more or less randomly. But my colleague treated the challenge as a puzzle, for which she created the following rules:

1. At any given residency, no faculty member could lead any particular workshop group more than once.
2. No two faculty members could be paired together more than once in each residency.
3. No student's work could be discussed in workshop twice by the same faculty member during that student's tenure in the program.
4. No student would have his or her work discussed on the first day of workshop or the last day of workshop twice during their five residencies.
5. All faculty would lead the same number of workshops. (This had various caveats related to other faculty responsibilities.)

Those rules were not arbitrary; the puzzle had a serious purpose. It seemed unfair for a student to have his or her work discussed on the first day more than once, because on the first day the groups were often just getting up to speed, and on the last day they were sometimes running out of energy. It seemed ideal for a student to have his or her work discussed by as many different faculty as possible, so the writer could hear many different perspectives. And so on. Still, most people wouldn't have bothered, in part because not everyone steps back to see the pattern in a particular problem, in part because the puzzle could be difficult to solve. Underlying the puzzle was a critical component of my colleague's pedagogical beliefs: while, as administrators, we couldn't control everything, the things we could control would be designed to treat everyone equally. Her attention to fairness in the organization of the groups helped keep the focus on the work being discussed, rather than on whether someone was being favored or disadvantaged by the arrangement of the workshops. Rule-bound logic governed the structure of the discussions, and the clarity of that structure was particularly important because what was being discussed—drafts of poems and stories—was unquantifiable, immeasurable. Those discussions deserved everyone's full attention, so we made it our goal to eliminate distractions regarding the organization of the groups.

Is it too much to say that my colleague's habitual contemplation of solitaire (and, I later learned, a variety of puzzles in newspapers and magazines) encouraged her to see administrative challenges as puzzles to be solved? Is it so far-fetched to think that a poet who would write a book-length series of sonnets might be inclined to see how other kinds of forms might contain and productively shape less poetic material?

I'm not filling a deep emotional hole here. I'm playing a very difficult game, and if you'd like to see someone who's very good at a difficult game, that's what I do.

— JERRY SEINFELD, on writing comedy

The scheduling puzzle that confronted us every six months reminded me of a particular Saturday morning in a particular college lecture hall. That day, I had dutifully penciled in bubbles for the verbal section of the GREs, then for the quantitative section. But when I got to the analytical problems,[1] I was a happy young man. According to the test, suddenly I was traveling down a country lane, trying to get to town; where the road forked, I found a pair of identical twins, one of whom always lied, one of whom always told the truth.[2] I was in my element. "Four men enter an elevator on the first floor. On each even floor they pass as they rise, one woman and one man get on; on each odd floor they pass, two men get off. When will the elevator hold the same number of women as men?"

[1] No longer a part of the test. Alas.

[2] The challenge being, then as now, to ask just one question of one of the twins in order to know which road to take.

Even now, it's hard to express the giddy pleasure I felt entering that absurd world where people get on and off elevators by gender, where foxes on rafts crossing rivers can always be counted on to eat chickens but not boys,[3] where five pilots have five different colored planes and fly to five different cities on five different days of the week, where identical twins stand around forks in country lanes for no apparent reason other than to annoy out-of-towners (why a country lane? why twins?). The world had been turned into a narrative Wonderland—and into puzzles. Ridiculous as the premises seemed, some anonymous authority—the Test Master, say—was promising that it all made sense, and that in some strange, alternative universe, life's problems had answers. It was my colleague's gift to see the puzzles in our own universe.

3 You remember: A boy has to get a fox, a chicken, and a sack of corn across a river. He has a small raft, and it can only carry him and one other thing. If the fox and the chicken are left together, the fox will eat the chicken. If the chicken and the corn are left together, the chicken will eat the corn. How does the boy get them all across the river?

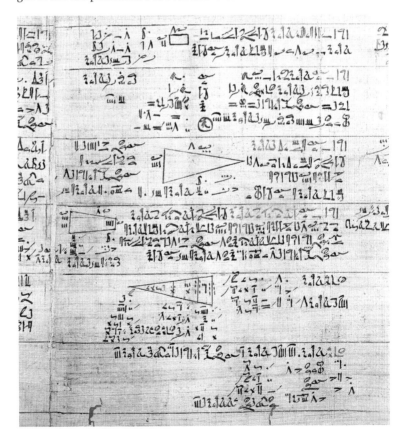

Detail of the Rhind Mathematical Papyrus

A MUSE AND A MAZE

Sudoku as most of us know them were created (under the name "Number Place") by an Indianapolis architect named Howard Garns in the 1960s. They were refined and became popular in Japan in the 1980s and around the world after a New Zealand judge persuaded the *Times* of London to begin publishing the puzzles in 2004. While the sudoku craze is relatively recent, Garns either consciously adapted or unknowingly re-created a type of puzzle that appeared in France in the nineteenth century, which was itself based on Latin Squares, which date back at least to the early eighteenth century.

Latin Squares are in turn related to Magic Squares, which were discovered by multiple cultures, independently, between two thousand and five thousand years ago. One of the earliest surviving manuscripts, known as the Rhind Mathematical Papyrus, named for the Scotsman who bought it in Egypt in the mid-nineteenth century, and as the Ahmes Papyrus, for the scribe who copied it, is a collection of mathematical problems and puzzles enchantingly titled *Directions for Attaining Knowledge of All Dark Things*. The document dates to approximately 1650 B.C.E., but Ahmes writes that he is copying an "ancient text"; the content is assumed to be a few hundred years older. In addition to a study of fractions, it includes a variety of problems, or puzzles, with practical applications. While those of us who solve puzzles might feel compelled to hide our book and pencil under the sofa when company comes, or to laugh nervously and say something about "wasting time," Magic Squares were once considered to have powerful mystical qualities, and were carried as talismans to ward off evil. No

Edna, Walt, Elizabeth, Louise, and Alexander are all poets who happen to write in forms. When Walt is shortlisted for the National Book Award, the old friends get together for a drink before the ceremony. Match each of the five poets with his or her chosen form, first book, and drink.

Their preferred forms are haiku, sonnet, limerick, villanelle, and sestina. Their first books are *Two Cheeks* (1985), *One Moon* (1987), *My Thoughts* (1990), *Surging Tides* (1996), and *Mist Shifts in Fits* (2001). Their favorite drinks are gin, an apple martini, malbec, scotch, and bottled water.

Elizabeth writes haiku.

The author of *One Moon* is not Alexander.

The first book by the poet who drinks bottled water was published earlier than the first book by the writer of haiku.

The sestina writer drinks scotch.

The poet who drinks gin does not write limericks or villanelles.

We might refer to these five poets as the one who drinks apple martinis, Edna, the author of *My Thoughts*, the limerick writer, and the bottled-water drinker.

Walt's first book was published earlier than the poet's who drinks apple martinis.

Of Edna and Walt, one drinks scotch and the other wrote *Surging Tides*.

Louise's first book is more recent than the limerick writer's.

Either the author of *Surging Tides* or the author of *Mist Shifts in Fits* drinks bottled water.

less a writer, statesman, and scientist than Benjamin Franklin amused himself with puzzles very similar to what we call sudoku.

What's the appeal? We can imagine why an architect might have been interested in the seemingly infinite arrangement of virtually identical boxes.[4] But what about others? A surprising number of people say they find the puzzles relaxing, and refreshing, because they don't have to think. They call sudoku mindless. But nearly everyone also admits that they have run into at least a few sudoku they can't do. If you're in a room with someone working a sudoku, it isn't unusual to hear an occasional vulgar exclamation; and if you check the in-flight magazine in the seat pocket in front of you, there's a good chance it contains a sudoku half-finished, scratched out or simply abandoned. No puzzles are truly "mindless"—we have to think to do them. But in standard sudoku we have to think about only one thing—the organization of nine distinct indicators, the digits 1 through 9—and whether their arrangement satisfies a few simple rules. We know we will have rendered void the world of our diversion if we fill a box on a standard sudoku grid with the number 15, or a picture of a duck.

Puzzles focus our attention on a select body of knowledge and a single task. To that extent—and to the extent that each puzzle has one or more correct answers—they represent closed systems and, in the case of sudoku, a kind of pure knowledge, a miniature world in which some decisions are right, others are wrong, and ultimately there can be no question about which are which. (If we make an error, we can either start over or go on to another puzzle, one that is different yet essentially identical.) It can be refreshing to mentally inhabit, even for a few minutes, a world in which a goal and the means of reaching it are perfectly clear, and where our reward is complete comprehension of the whole. Of course, us being us, as soon as we attain that comprehension, we lose interest. We turn the page.

[4] The actual number of distinct 9x9 grids was calculated by Bertram Felgenhauer and Frazer Jarvis to be 6,670,903,752,021,072,936,960.

		2			7			
					3	6		
9	6					1	4	
			8			2	9	3
8				1			7	
			5					
			3					6
			9					
		4		2	8	9		

3	2	1
1	3	2
2	1	3

A Latin square is a square divided into rows and columns, the resulting boxes filled with symbols (numbers, letters, pictures) so that each symbol appears once and only once in each row and column.

Mr. Logan … showed me a folio French book filled with magic squares … in which, he said, the author had discovered great ingenuity and dexterity in the management of numbers; and,

though several other foreigners had distinguished themselves in the same way, he did not recollect that any one Englishman had done anything of the kind remarkable. I said it was perhaps a mark of the good sense of our English mathematicians that they would not spend their time in things that were merely "difficiles nugae" [laborious trifles], incapable of any useful application.

— BENJAMIN FRANKLIN

7	12	1	14
2	13	8	11
16	3	10	5
9	6	15	4

The rows and columns of a magic square are filled with distinct numbers so that all of the rows, columns, and main diagonals add up to the same total, or Magic Constant. A 3x3 square is typically filled with the numbers 1–9, a 4x4 square the numbers 1–16, etc. In the square above, which is depicted in a tenth-century Indian temple, the sum of each row, column, and main diagonal is 34.

A popular diversion in England during the mid-nineteenth century was word squares, in which each word appears both horizontally and vertically. At left is an order-6 word square. Smaller squares are easier. It probably wouldn't take you long to create an order-4 word square beginning with the word "cube."

B	I	S	H	O	P
I	L	L	U	M	E
S	L	I	D	E	S
H	U	D	D	L	E
O	M	E	L	E	T
P	E	S	E	T	A

Sudoku are not for everyone. Puzzle solvers have their biases. An avid fan of the *New York Times* weekend crosswords might speak scornfully of those who attempt only the easier Monday through Thursday puzzles; Monday through Thursday crossword fans might belittle those who go no further than jumbled words and their cartoon punch lines; jumbled-word solvers can be heard to speak disdainfully of sudoku fans; and any of the above might heap abuse on those calm, methodical people content to circle "hidden" words. But then, diagramless crossword fans don't think much of the puzzles with black squares, avid followers of composers like Thomas Snyder ("Dr. Sudoku") have no time for the computer-generated sudoku that fill the airport and grocery store shelves, and people who prefer chess problems know better than to bother with any of them. Peering down on all of this are the aficionados who collect Oskar van Deventer's mechanical puzzles or who have dog-eared copies of Martin Gardner's books. This attitude translates as *My puzzles*

Elizabeth Kingsley is credited with having created the first acrostic, published in the *Saturday Review* in 1934. While the puzzles are published under various related names (crostics, anacrostics, double-crostics, e-crostics, etc.), they typically work like the one below, created by Michael Ashley. The solver answers as many of the clues as possible, one letter per numbered blank. Next, these letters are transferred to the correspondingly numbered squares in the diagram. This begins the spelling out of a quotation reading from left to right, with the black squares separating the words. The solver can work back and forth between the diagram and the answer words to complete the puzzle. The first letters of the answer words spell out the author and title of the work the quotation is taken from.

1F	2B	■	3E	4I	5K	6X	7C	8D	9P	■	10B	11P	■	12B	13H	14X
■	15J	16W	17K	18Q	19A	20C	21S	22N	23U	■	24D	25I	26K	27Y	28N	29M
30T	31L	32X	33E	34C	35H	36R	■	37B	38Y	39E	40R	41N	42U	43J	44A	45Q
■	46A	47P	48L	49H	50Q	51B	52X	53K	54M	■	55V	56E	57K	58Q	■	59A
60Q	61K	■	62A	63M	■	64K	65V	66P	67G	68Q	■	69P	70T	■	71E	72J
73P	74K	75H	76F	■	77X	78O	■	79V	80T	81C	■	82V	83G	84L	85S	■
86J	87V	■	88Y	89Q	90C	91A	92S	93K	94W	95D	96U	■	97V	98M	99B	100G
101X	102H	103Q	■	104O	105Q	■	106U	107T	108K	109K	■	110I	111J	■	112T	113L
114J	115C	116A	117B	118M	119G	■	120C	121K	122A	123X	124Q	125B	126G	127S	128V	■
129N	130W	131K	132G	■	133V	134P	135G	136K	■	137P	138F	■	139G	140O	■	141T
142H	143I	144K	145G	146X	147R	148W	■	149X	150E	151K	152A	153D	154T	■	155X	156L
157V	158G	159E	■	160A	161T	162X	■	163W	164Q	■	165N	166D	167A	168V	■	169P
170I	171Q	■	172F	173P	174V	■	175P	176E	177I	178Q	■	179I	■	180X	181Q	182N
183V	184E	■	185U	186P	187E	188R	■	189W	190U	■	191T	192B	193Y	194O	■	195N
196S	■	197Q	198T	199V	200A	201X	202S	203R	■	204J	205O	■	■	■	■	■

A. Nom de crime of Robert Leroy Parker (2 wds.)

___ ___ ___ ___ ___ ___ ___ ___ ___ ___ ___
62 44 19 167 152 59 116 122 46 91 200 160

B. Man Booker Prize winner for *Amsterdam* (2 wds.)

___ ___ ___ ___ ___ ___ ___ ___ ___
192 99 51 117 12 125 10 37 2

C. Joseph Conrad's young seafarer (2 wds.)

___ ___ ___ ___ ___ ___ ___
34 81 20 120 115 7   90

D. The Brown Bomber

___ ___ ___ ___ ___
95 153 166 24 8

E. Classic litigation novel with troubling East Wind (2 wds.)

___ ___ ___ ___ ___ ___ ___ ___ ___ ___
39 184 3   33 159 56 176 150 187 71

F. Life of the party, say

___ ___ ___ ___
76 1   138 172

G. Author of 2001 bestseller, later a major movie (2 wds.)

___ ___ ___ ___ ___ ___ ___ ___ ___
132 139 119 158 100 83 145 135 67 126

H. Call for Marlon?

___ ___ ___ ___ ___ ___
142 49 75 102 35 13

I. A court might hand this down

___ ___ ___ ___ ___ ___ ___
177 143 179 4   110 170 25

J. Capital of Cyprus

___ ___ ___ ___ ___ ___ ___
114 72 15 43 111 204 86

K. 1976 novel about Colonel "Bull" Meecham (3 wds.)

___ ___ ___ ___ ___ ___ ___ ___ ___ ___ ___ ___
26 74 136 5   131 53 57 64 109 93 61 151 121

___ ___
17 144

L. A. A. Milne-featured snack food

___ ___ ___ ___ ___
156 31 48 113 84

M. Common concern of dramatists and con artists

___ ___ ___ ___ ___
63 98 118 29 54

N. Hare raiser?

___ ___ ___ ___ ___ ___ ___ ___
165 129 41 108 22 195 182 28

O. Frequently

___ ___ ___ ___ ___
104 78 205 194 140

P. 2005 bestseller narrated by Death (3 wds.)

___ ___ ___ ___ ___ ___ ___ ___ ___ ___ ___ ___
137 173 11 175 134 186 66 73 9   69 47 169

Q. Narrated by ivory transporter with "a passion for maps" (3 wds.)

___ ___ ___ ___ ___ ___ ___ ___ ___ ___ ___ ___ ___
181 103 60 171 58 164 105 89 124 197 178 68 50

___ ___
18 45

R Giving the once over

___ ___ ___ ___ ___
188 36 40 147 203

S Altercations: hyph.

___ ___ ___ ___ ___ ___
92 21 202 127 196 85

T. Lawrence's Brangwen family saga (2 wds.)

___ ___ ___ ___ ___ ___ ___ ___ ___ ___
191 107 198 154 141 30 70 112 161 80

U. Type of mall or pass

___ ___ ___ ___ ___ ___
190 42 23 185 96 106

V. A Cool Million satirist (2 wds.)

___ ___ ___ ___ ___ ___ ___ ___ ___ ___ ___ ___ ___
87 199 55 168 65 133 157 174 183 82 97 128 79

W. Coiner of the term "cyberspace"

___ ___ ___ ___ ___ ___
148 130 94 163 16 189

X. Classic muckraking novelist of 1906 (2 wds.)

___ ___ ___ ___ ___ ___ ___ ___ ___ ___ ___ ___
162 101 155 77 32 180 201 14 52 6   149 146 123

Y. Title character of 1815

___ ___ ___ ___
27 193 38 88

offer intellectual stimulation; your puzzles are childish. But there are also people who think, *My puzzles are fun; your puzzles are work;* those who think, *While I'm too intimidated to say so, I don't even know how to start those puzzles you do*; and those who feel confident that *All of you people are wasting your time.*

That last group includes those who claim to be completely immune to puzzles. But any investment manager, political campaign strategist, teacher creating a test, lawyer framing a case, carpenter framing a house, baseball manager making out a lineup, chef planning a menu, designer laying out a magazine or website, or busy parent trying to coordinate children's school and soccer schedules is actively involved in puzzle solving. Each task has a goal, elements to put to use (lumber, players, vegetables), and rules or constraints (time, money, left- and right-handed batters who also need to field), and success or failure is usually fairly clear (either all the children are clothed when they get on the bus, or not). So that last attitude actually translates as something like, *I don't have time for those frivolous puzzles of yours; I'm busy solving real ones.* The truth is, we all practice for life by solving puzzles of one kind or another nearly from birth. (Who comes when I cry? How soon? To help, or to scold?) We could even say that each of us represents one solution to a puzzle, a unique combination of twenty-three pairs of chromosomes.

Readers, too, have biases. There are awkward moments around the globe every day when two strangers meet, claim to enjoy reading fiction, but discover that one is thinking Follett while the other is thinking Beckett. The fan of *The Great Gatsby*, *Sometimes a Great Notion*, and *Great Expectations* might fancy herself "better read" than the fan of *The Good Mother* and *Good in Bed*, but then Mark Twain referred to "the Sir Walter Scott disease," Henry James said Mark Twain's work appealed only to "rudimentary minds," Faulkner called Twain "a hack," Nabokov referred to Faulkner's novels as "corncobby chronicles," Nietzsche called Dante Alighieri "a hyena that wrote poetry on tombs," Gertrude Stein called Ezra Pound "a village explainer," Joseph Conrad called D. H. Lawrence's novels "filth," Lord Byron called Keats's poetry "driveling idiotism," Virginia Wolff said James Joyce's *Ulysses* was "the work of a queasy undergraduate scratching his pimples," and Tolstoy told

Chekhov, "Shakespeare's plays are bad enough; yours are even worse." Fans of whatever they consider "experimental" fiction might feel obliged to belittle "conventional" fiction, readers of "literary fiction" might feel obliged to distance themselves from "best-sellers," and on and on. But the factions setting up camp and lobbing impotent grenades fail to acknowledge that one individual reader might appreciate Samuel Beckett, Edith Wharton, *and* Henning Mankell, and might have read both David Foster Wallace and Irving Wallace. (David Foster Wallace was himself a fan of Stephen King's work, an awkward complication for those who seem to think each of us is just one kind of reader.)

Rather than attacking books we don't feel are worth our time, worrying about whether we appreciate the "right" books, or being embarrassed by books we enjoy, all we need to consider, as writers, are which books interest and engage us, and what aspects or elements of that work— however diverse it may be—might inform our own. Even the books we don't choose to spend time with tell us something about what we value.

THE PUZZLE OF THE ART

Semiotician Marcel Danesi tells us that puzzles are more than tests of knowledge or adeptness; to solve them, we rely most of all on "insight thinking," which he defines as "the ability to see with the mind's eye the inner nature of some specific thing." He continues,

> The psychologist Robert Sternberg argues...that insight thinking is anchored in three forms of reflective memory: (1) *selective encoding*, or the use of information that may have originally seemed irrelevant but that may become crucial in due course, (2) *selective comparison*, or the discovery, often through analogical and metaphorical thinking, of a nonobvious relationship between new information and information already in memory; and (3) *selective combination*, or the discovery of nonobvious pieces of information that can be combined to form novel information and ideas.

Insight thinking, then, involves storing information that, for one reason or another, we believe could be useful; recognizing relationships between that stored information and what is currently in front of us; and realizing combinations of information that aren't explicit. Sternberg's use of "nonobvious" distinguishes insight thinking from the more common remembering and recognizing we do every day ("I've gotten food in restaurants; this looks like a restaurant; I think I can get food here"). Mathematician Charles Sanders Peirce called insight an "informed hunch" resulting from abductive thinking—a sort of educated guess based on knowledge and experience. Another way to put it, Danesi suggests, is that insight thinking is a combination of memory and imagination: "The very process of reasoning in mathematics and science relies upon the ability of the human imagination to [as Jacob Bronowski said] 'make images and to move them about inside one's head in new arrangements.'"

This is a type of puzzle solving familiar to every writer. Every well-told story is a strategic arrangement, one that withholds or conceals certain information while providing or revealing other information, and which is intended to guide the reader clearly in some ways while also, simultaneously, creating uncertainty, curiosity, tension, and suspense. The nature of that uncertainty is key. Sadly—because it discourages some people from reading—literature is sometimes taught as an annoying game that could be called "Guess What the Writer Meant." As Flannery O'Connor said, "People talk about the theme of a story as if the theme were like the string that a sack of chicken feed is tied with. They think that if you can pick out the theme, the way you pick out the right thread in the chicken feed sack, you can rip the story open and feed the chickens. But this is not the way meaning works in fiction."

Robert Boswell has compared meaning in fiction to lightning bugs in a yard—they can be attracted, but not manufactured. The words, phrases, sentences, images, and scenes in poetry and fiction are arranged deliberately to create a particular effect, to lead the reader on that journey toward contemplation. It's one thing to tell us that a man is on an island; something else to tell us that he's been stranded for a year, and will do anything to get home; something quite different to tell us that he's being held captive on that island; something different still when we learn his captor is a beautiful woman; and that something starts to become *The Odyssey* when we're told that our mortal hero is being held prisoner by the goddess Calypso, that Athena will intervene to enable his departure, that he'll make it back home, but that he will suffer mightily along the way—and all that is conveyed in dactylic hexameter. In the opening of Homer's epic, suspense about whether Odysseus will make it to Ithaca is virtually eliminated; instead, the focus is placed on his trials and adventures along the way and after he arrives.

Decisions about what information to release when, and how, are important to all writing. While it became an enormous commercial success, *Butch Cassidy and the Sundance Kid* is a very unusual western. The opening of the film had to prepare viewers for a story that portrays outlaws as heroes, despite the fact that they spend most of the movie running from the law, all the way to Bolivia, where they are murdered. Among other things, the screenwriter, William Goldman, had to convey that the two men are very well known by reputation, and feared; yet he also had to indicate that their time is ending, and to prepare the audience to accept the fact that the main characters would die in the final scene. So the film opens with various shots of a bank closing for the day, with an emphasis on heavy doors and locks and security. When a dismayed Butch Cassidy asks what happened to the old bank, which was beautiful, a guard says

Paul Newman as Butch Cassidy, contemplating a newly barred bank it kept getting robbed. "That's a small price to pay for beauty," Butch responds, introducing the film's bittersweet tone, humor wedded to loss. The next scene focuses on the face of a blond-haired man sitting at a card table as the man he'd been playing accuses him of cheating. When Butch comes in and addresses the blond-haired man as Sundance, his accuser immediately turns anxious; and when the accuser asks, "How good are you?" Butch dives out of the way as Sundance shoots the holster off the man's waist, then shoots the man's gun out of the holster and across the floor. In addition to demonstrating the Sundance Kid's particular expertise, the scene establishes the character, who was not nearly as well known a historical figure as Butch Cassidy, and simultaneously the actor who plays him, as at the time Robert Redford had nothing like the fame of Paul Newman. The scene also introduces the bond between the two, apart from the rest of the gang, which prepares the viewer for their long journey together. The casual moviegoer is unlikely to think about what information is being presented, and how, and why; but those decisions have their intended effect, nonetheless.

Joseph Heller said that one of his motivations for writing *Catch-22* arose from two conversations he had with veterans of World War II. One of them told raucous, entertaining stories about his time in the service; the other said he couldn't see how anyone could find humor in war. While the novel is known for its comedy and manic, Who's-on-first-style dialogue, Yossarian, the main character intent, above all else, on staying alive, has suffered a terrible shock. His insistence on self-preservation isn't simply instinctive; it's a response to a horrific death he witnessed. While his discovery of Snowden's catastrophic wound offers at least a partial explanation for Yossarian's behavior, it also causes potential problems for the writer. If the death were described in all its gruesome detail at the beginning of the novel, it would be difficult to persuade the reader to think anything about Yossarian's situation is funny; but if the death were withheld until late in the novel, it would seem like a cheat—a crucial bit of information unjustifiably denied to the reader. So instead Heller tells us early, almost casually, that Yossarian witnessed a death, then mentions it again at least half a dozen times, adding information each time, until finally we get the entire story (which still has a surprising turn). As a result, we accept the comic tone of the early chapters even as we anticipate something darker. Heller's selection and arrangement of information about Snowden's death is one of the novel's defining structural features.

Art lives from constraints and dies from freedom.

— LEONARDO DA VINCI

The correlation between certain types of puzzles and, say, forms of poetry is fairly straightforward.

Sudoku—a puzzle that adheres to the following constraints:
- It must be a nine-by-nine grid.
- The grid must be further divided into nine three-by-three squares.
- Each cell in the grid must be filled with the numbers 1–9.
- No number may be repeated in any horizontal line.
- No number may be repeated in any vertical line.
- No number may be repeated in any three-by-three square.
- The puzzle composer omits certain numbers, and those omissions allow for one unique solution.[5]

5 This describes standard sudoku, the kind that appear in most newspapers; there are many variants.

Villanelle—a poem that adheres to the following constraints:
- It must have nineteen lines.
- The nineteen lines must be further divided into six stanzas.
- The first five stanzas must be tercets.
- The final stanza must be a quatrain.
- The poem must have two refrains.
- The poem must have two repeating rhymes.
- The repeating rhymes must be in the first and final lines of the first tercet.
- The rhymes must repeat alternately in tercets two through five.
- The quatrain must include both repeated lines and both rhymes.

Night in Three Panels,
by Charles Ritchie

Of course, this isn't to say that the tasks faced by the puzzle composer and the poet are essentially identical. The puzzle composer's only responsibility, in the case of sudoku, is to create a functional puzzle (though some composers are much more ambitious). The poet's task is not simply to fulfill the requirements of the form but to use it to create something unique and beautiful. The point is that, to the extent the formal poet begins with "rules," or constraints, she has a container to work in and against. While fiction writers may not have the benefit of pre-defined forms (there are no rules for the short story that come near the specificity of the rules for the villanelle), every writer has the option, in every story or novel, to create his own rules, his own form.

If [my method of organizing my research into thirty folders] sounds mechanical, its effect was absolutely the reverse. If the contents of the seventh folder were before me, the contents of twenty-nine other folders were out of sight. Every organizational aspect was behind me. The procedure eliminated nearly all distraction and concentrated only the material I had to deal with

A MUSE AND A MAZE

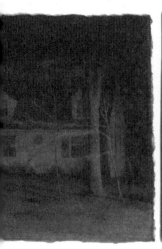

in a given day or week. It painted me into a corner, yes, but in doing so it freed me to write.

— JOHN McPHEE

Visual artist Charles Ritchie's work is tightly bound by constraints. For a large part of his artistic life, he has focused primarily on what he can see from his home studio in Silver Spring, Maryland, on the outskirts of Washington, DC. He has recorded a few simple objects dozens, even hundreds of times. They include the houses and trees he can see through his windows, those windows themselves, a streetlamp, an astronomical chart, a vase, and a few chairs. Over time, these objects have become iconic. The repetition of subjects has also allowed him to record both minute and dramatic changes.

Other constraints he chose include working almost exclusively in black and white ("Contrast and atmosphere can accomplish so much on their own," he says. "Why encumber them if it's not necessary?"); with the exception of his self-portraits, depicting no living creatures ("too loaded"); omitting as much as possible, often by depicting objects in fading light ("Night filters things out," he says, "it creates powerful negative space."); and executing his images on a scale so small that they are

essentially private, available to one viewer at a time. Many are no larger than a postcard. He means to offer the viewer "an invitation to crawl into an intimate yet immense universe."

These constraints can be amended, bent, or even ignored whenever he chooses; but as general guidelines, they have provided the form for his art. His constraints are not necessarily evident to a viewer of the work, any more than the constraints that went into the creation of an equitable workshop are evident to the student in the workshop. The viewer of one of Ritchie's images has no need to know what informs the choices he's made. From the artist's perspective, the purpose is to provide boundaries, a container for creative expression. In order to focus our attention on a problem, or task, we can impose restrictions that free us to focus on its essence.[6]

6 For more on constraints in fiction, including a discussion of the Oulipo, see "A Rigorous Geometry" in *Maps of the Imagination*.

WHERE WE DWELL: THE VIRTUE OF OBSESSION

Well, I'm like that [repressive and obsessive] all the time. It's sort of where your OCD comes in handy. You're a dog with a bone and you'll just gnaw on it until it's right.... But the level of intensity and the demand that it accompanies—thank God, everybody was young men at the time because it demanded your twenty-four-hour fealty. Because I had no life, I didn't think you should have one either [*laughs*]. And so it was all music, music, music, music, music.... We've learned how to ... bring the same sort of intensity and get the job done with a little bit less craziness. But at the time it was important, and madness is not to be underrated.

Madness in the appropriate place and at the service of an aesthetic ideal can help you get to higher ground sometimes.

— BRUCE SPRINGSTEEN

Several years ago, Charles Ritchie chose to devote his few weeks at an artist's colony to printmaking, something he hadn't done much of on his own. When he opened his studio to visitors, the prints he made were tacked to the walls. None of them had turned out the way he hoped. Someone else might say that his experiment in printmaking had failed. But Ritchie saw the images as opportunities to contemplate which aspects of the printmaking process he could control, and how, and which aspects he couldn't. More than that, he saw the "failed" prints as opportunities to reconsider what he thought he had wanted in the first place.

Back home, he transferred one of his images, roughly the size of a record album cover, onto a copper plate, in order to make prints. Preparing the plate meant re-creating the image in reverse, and in negative, using a doctor's scalpel to shape the copper to hold the ink. The process took nine months. That patience and perseverance, combined with his dedication over decades to his chosen constraints, is evidence of an artistic obsession, one increasingly at odds with the pace of modern life. None of us can observe the entire world that intently; daily we find ourselves paying partial, casual, or superficial attention. This sort of specialization is common in the sciences, where, according to the naturalist E. O. Wilson, even today one could devote a productive career to the thorough study of everything living at the base of a single tree. But in art, many of us fear repetition, or what might appear to others to be repetitious. In the same way that a scientist or mathematician might devote herself to a single problem, question, locale, or species, though, we might devote ourselves to a particular circumstance, a particular type of character, a particular moral dilemma, or a particular form. The virtue of obsession is the power of a narrow focus combined with ongoing investigation and deep contemplation. Like Thoreau's writing about Walden Pond and Wordsworth's poems about the English Lake District, the product of devoted attention encourages us to rediscover the virtues of a meditative relationship with our world.

The refusal to rest content, the willingness to risk excess on behalf of one's obsessions, is what separates artists from entertainers.

— *John Updike*

We've all heard—and possibly given—the advice "Write what you know." But that implies that one knows quite enough. And while it may be true, as William Maxwell said, that at a very young age he had all the material he would ever need as a writer, having that material wasn't enough; devoting obsessive attention to it was what yielded *So Long, See You Tomorrow*, among other books. So the better advice might be, Know what you write. And know it as deeply, as comprehensively, as possible. Then acknowledge the remaining mystery.

I dwell in Possibility –
A fairer House than Prose –
More numerous of Windows –
Superior – for Doors –

— EMILY DICKINSON

It may go without saying that there is a dark side to obsession. Simply being obsessed is no virtue, and obsessive-compulsive disorder can be crippling. In his memoir *Elsewhere*, novelist Richard Russo tells the story of his mother's paralyzing obsessions, and the extent to which he recognizes something similar in himself: "Somehow, without ever intending to, I'd discovered how to turn obsession and what my grandmother used to call sheer cussedness . . . to my advantage. Call it whatever you want— except virtue." Obsessive devotion to work may not be a virtue in the moral sense, but it benefits the writing. To complete a book of sudoku a day would be to miss most of the finer things in life, and we routinely remind ourselves of the dangers of watching too much television, spending too many hours on Facebook or Twitter, or indulging an addiction to a simple game. Late-twentieth- and early-twenty-first-century technology seems to have exposed a cultural vulnerability to obsessive game playing (from FreeCell to Minesweeper, from Temple Run to Candy Crush Saga, to whatever has replaced all of those by the time you read this), and while someone can no doubt argue persuasively for the intellectual, psychological, neurological, and physical benefits of same, it seems likely that on our deathbeds we will regret having spent so much of our time passing time. Even writing every day is not necessarily a virtue if we do it thoughtlessly, or mechanically. The various challenges to write a poem a day or a novel in a month might provide motivation to type, but combining words is an intermediate goal, not the ultimate one; we want to express something, we want to communicate, we want to produce something meaningful to ourselves and to others. Cal Ripken Sr., father of the famous baseball player, used to tell the young men he coached, "Practice doesn't make perfect; perfect practice makes perfect." In art, the ongoing engagement with both material and process is our practice.

I'd always lose the audience there.... I was obsessed with figuring it out. The way I figure it out is I try different things, night after night, and I'll stumble into it at some point, or not. If I love the joke, I'll wait.

— JERRY SEINFELD, on getting a joke right

There is no shortage of examples of writers obsessed with their material. Edmund Spenser devoted over a decade to *The Faerie Queene*, and Walt Whitman continually revised *Leaves of Grass*, essentially making a book of his life's work. John Updike was obsessed with marital politics, and with particularly American themes; three of his novels are reconsiderations of *The Scarlet Letter*. In novel after novel, Thomas Bernhard wrote about despair, suicide, and the impossibility of perfecting a work of art. As readers, we're glad Mark Twain kept yearning for his youth, so wrote *The Adventures of Tom Sawyer*, *Adventures of Huckleberry Finn*, and *Life on the Mississippi*. We're glad Proust didn't grow weary of his lifelong project, but instead wrote into the night even as his illnesses were killing him. But obsession isn't uniquely linked to longer works. Kathleen Spivack writes of Robert Lowell, "Elizabeth Hardwick, Stanley Kunitz, and other friends of Lowell's sometimes were fed up with his constant questioning and revision of each line. He was obsessed with a poem while working

on it and demanded the same attention, or obsession, from others."
Marianne Moore published her poem "Poetry" in six different versions
ranging from three lines to thirty-nine. Tim O'Brien has examined and
reexamined, in his stories as well as in novels, the effects on the individual of war in general and of Vietnam in particular.

To truly dwell in the possibility of our work is to favor the considered
life, the penetrating gaze. Our obsessions spring from a source we can't
identify; or their origin is obvious yet inescapable; or we choose them.
We might feel confined by them, or enraptured; in either case, they focus
our interest and attention the way a magnifying glass focuses the heat
of the sun.

> Most writers who produce an extensive body of work do so
> as a result of obsessions that they have.... As we grow older
> the meanings of our obsessions gradually change, and ma-
> ture as we mature. Some of the pain goes out of them and
> understanding enters, perhaps. So, we return to our obses-
> sions and we reshape them. We reshape ourselves as we write.
> — ROSS MacDONALD

CULTIVATING THE PUZZLE INSTINCT

We don't typically think of obsession as something that can be willed.
To be obsessed is to be possessed, consumed, overtaken. Can artistic
obsession be learned, or taught?

In terms of content, probably not—though it isn't uncommon to be
led to recognize an obsession. The writer looks at a draft of a new story
only to find it feeling familiar—or gives it to a trusted friend who says,
"This is like that story you showed me last year, except this time the
sisters are cousins. Which, come to think of it, is a lot like your story
from two years ago, where the sister characters are the two neighbors."
As the friend goes on, excitedly making connections, explaining how
every story the writer has ever written can be boiled down to yet another
depiction of her relationship with her sister, the writer begins to despair.

But reductive reading could make anyone's work look bad. From that perspective, John Cheever wrote about suburban alcoholics, Jane Austen wrote love stories, and Poe was a madman writing about madmen. Rather than be disappointed or embarrassed when we feel we're repeating ourselves, we need to investigate further. We need to work to recognize the difference between mere repetition and meaningful variation. We need to commit to an intensity of gaze that will allow us to see beyond what we've already comprehended. Our obsessions and constraints define us. We must cultivate them.

This isn't to say that a writer needs to be obsessed by some particular content. Ultimately, we each follow our own interests, or what we might think of as the Muse, unpredictable as she seems to be. So while we might cultivate, through conscious exploration, situations, problems, characters and/or themes, we might also, or alternately, explore aspects of process, form, and style. Milan Kundera says that when a critic pointed out that he tended to write his novels in seven sections, he seized the revelation as an opportunity to further develop his structural inclinations. Don DeLillo considers the physical appearance of words in a sentence.[7] From Dante and Petrarch, Wordsworth and Shakespeare, John Berryman and Robert Lowell, there is no end of examples of poets who have chosen the sonnet as a vehicle for exploration. By sustaining an investigation of any aspect of content or form, we can learn to dwell in our work. To dwell—to reside—to inhabit.

For Occupation - This -
The spreading wide my narrow Hands
To gather Paradise -

— EMILY DICKINSON

Sustained attention requires consciously resisting the temptation to keep moving, to get through a piece, to be finished. This may never have been popular—we are, most of us, eager to see results, to move forward—and deliberately dwelling might seem like a particularly antiquated notion

7 "There's a rhythm I hear that drives me through a sentence. And the words typed on the white page have a sculptural quality.... The rhythm of a sentence will accommodate a certain number of syllables. One syllable too many, I look for another word. There's always another word that means nearly the same thing, and if it doesn't then I'll consider altering the meaning of a sentence to keep the rhythm, the syllable beat. I'm completely willing to let language press meaning upon me. Watching the way in which words match up, keeping the balance in a sentence—these are sensuous pleasures. I might want *very* and *only* in the same sentence, spaced a particular way, exactly so far apart. I might want *rapture* matched with *danger*—I like to match word endings. I type rather than write longhand because I like the way the words and letters look when they come off the hammers onto the page—finished, printed, beautifully formed."

A MUSE AND A MAZE

now, when so much in our world emphasizes speed: faster connections, faster movement, faster responses.

To learn to dwell in our work is to use drafts to explore, with the understanding that our movement toward the final draft of a story or poem or novel is likely to include not only lateral movement but backward movement, and circular movement, and movement we can't confidently describe. Because to insist to ourselves that each draft carry a story toward closure is, necessarily, to limit the possibilities. Every choice must then at least seem to be an improvement on what's currently on the page, part of a straight-line progression, rather than an alternative to what's on the page, movement within a larger plane. We need to allow ourselves to pursue hunches, to discover, in the words of Robert Sternberg, nonobvious pieces of information and, even more important, nonobvious relationships between new information and information already in our memory. Like Joseph Heller and Robert Gottlieb taping bits of manuscript to every surface in the editor's office, and Charles Ritchie affixing those attempts at printmaking to the wall of his studio, we need to give ourselves time to make images and move them around inside our heads, and on paper, in new arrangements.

> Old men ought to be explorers
> Here and there does not matter
> We must be still and still moving
> Into another intensity . . .
>
> — *T. S. Eliot*

Dwelling is not the same as standing still. Emily Dickinson didn't simply stare out the window all day. To dwell is also to occupy, to linger over.

BUILDING BRIDGES

A few years ago, a team of biochemists at the University of Washington decided to enlist the help of nonscientists to solve a complicated problem. Their goal is to learn about proteins, and even to create new proteins to fight disease. The problem is that while proteins form according to certain apparent rules, there are so many potential combinations and arrangements of components that not even high-speed computers can efficiently consider all the possibilities. Protein creation is a story with infinite possibility, and no clear path to the end.

The biochemists enlisted help from the university's Center for Game Science to turn protein creation into an online puzzle video game called Foldit. The website includes some introductory information, but no background in science is necessary. Given a few basic rules, the user—the player—is invited to solve a series of puzzles, which progress in difficulty. The puzzles are designed to teach protein-building strategies, and are constantly revised in order to do that more effectively. Users can then move on to more complicated tasks, competing with players around the globe.

News stories about Foldit tend to say that the game is enlisting lay-people to help create proteins and potentially cure diseases, but that's not quite accurate. As the site itself explains, the goal of the game is actually to collect information about how people address the problem of solving protein-making puzzles—and then to build those problem-solving strategies into the computer programs currently being used. A video game is being used to cultivate obsession toward a particular end.

Foldit puzzle 697

In a similar way, exercises and imitations and focused revisions help initiate a writer into the complexities of prose and poetry. With patience, we can train ourselves to write not only with an end product in mind but for the rewards of a single draft, the possibilities of a sentence, the subtle but significant variation in a constellation of characters we've seen in our work before. And if we happen to have obsessions that seem unwriterly—if we find ourselves spending hours sewing, or building rock walls, addressing administrative challenges, studying old maps, practicing magic tricks, or solving puzzles—we might do well to consider how that could inform our writing, in content or in practice.

My wife believes my puzzle-solving is a sign of idleness. So do I, most of the time. And while I'd like to think that whatever hours I've devoted to crosswords and cryptographs and double acrostics and logic problems and sudoku will pay off in years of additional mental alertness, when I

A MUSE AND A MAZE

consider my current state of mental alertness, the outlook seems dim. But writing this book—like writing any book—has been a long process, one requiring obsessive attention as well as the extended pursuit—and, sometimes, abandonment—of many hunches. Those hours of pursuing solutions, of refusing to settle for *nearly* finishing a puzzle, is an exercise in persistence that pays benefits when applied to significant challenges.

I don't believe that studying math will eventually yield knowledge of all dark things, but some combination of observation and contemplation—specifically, seeing patterns in how marriages and families tend to work—eventually led me to understand what was going on during those childhood bridge games. My mother's parents, Dutch/Germans whose families had been in this country for many generations, did not approve of my first-generation Italian American father. My mother was very close to her parents, so she found herself caught between a young, hot-tempered husband and a quiet, frowning father. The appropriately named card game provided a way for her to bring her husband and her parents together and allowed them hours of casual conversation, week after week. The result was an intimacy that might otherwise have been impossible. By her own admission, our mother wasn't very good at cards, and the long days of working and taking care of two children sometimes had her nodding off mid-hand, spilling clubs and hearts onto the table. But in one way she was the canniest player: she had arranged the game, and she knew what it was really about.

Four writers, close friends, have each completed their first books and are invited to meet a famous and influential editor. She's read all their work and was surprised to find that she admires it all equally. After meeting them, she realizes that if she publishes any one or two of these writers, their friendship will suffer terribly. So the editor presents them with a puzzle.

The editor sends the first writer to another room. She instructs the other three to arrange their chairs in a line so that each writer can only see the writer(s) in front. No peeking. (And there are no mirrors in the office.) Then she explains that she's going to give each writer—including the one in the other room—a book to balance on his or her head. Two have red covers, two have black covers. The writers can't see the books on their own heads, and the writer in the other room can't see or be seen by the other three. The writers can't talk (or pass notes, send texts, use hand signals—you get the point).

The deal: if the first writer who speaks can tell the editor the color of the cover on his or her own head, she'll publish all four of their books. If the first writer who speaks is wrong, she won't publish any of them.

You need to know: the four writers, unlike a lot of writers, are perfectly logical; and they know each other well enough to trust one another to respond logically.

How do the writers get published?

HOW, FROM SUCH WRECKAGE, WE EVOLVE THE EVENTUAL EFFECT

Now, it is quite easy to obtain mystery and disorder ... the difficulty is to keep organization in the midst of mystery.

— JOHN RUSKIN

BENJAMIN FRANKLIN'S SECRET

Like many a sheepish puzzle fan before and after him, the author of *Poor Richard's Almanack* was not being entirely honest when he suggested that Magic Squares weren't worthy of his time. In his autobiography,

Franklin confesses, "In my younger days, having once some leisure which I still think I might have employed more usefully, I had amused myself in making these kind of magic squares," and goes on to claim that, as an adult, in the course of a single evening, he composed a 16 x 16 magic square—one that is considered remarkable to this day.

200	217	232	249	8	25	40	57	72	89	104	121	136	153	168	185
58	39	26	7	250	231	218	199	186	167	154	135	122	103	90	71
198	219	230	251	6	27	38	59	70	91	102	123	134	155	166	187
60	37	28	5	252	229	220	197	188	165	156	133	124	101	92	69
201	216	233	248	9	24	41	56	73	88	105	120	137	152	169	184
55	42	23	10	247	234	215	202	183	170	151	138	119	106	87	74
203	214	235	246	11	22	43	54	75	86	107	118	139	150	171	182
53	44	21	12	245	236	213	204	181	172	149	140	117	108	85	76
205	212	237	244	13	20	45	52	77	84	109	116	141	148	173	180
51	46	19	14	243	238	211	206	179	174	147	142	115	110	83	78
207	210	239	242	15	18	47	50	79	82	111	114	143	146	175	178
49	48	17	16	241	240	209	208	177	176	145	144	113	112	81	80
196	221	228	253	4	29	36	61	68	93	100	125	132	157	164	189
62	35	30	3	254	227	222	195	190	163	158	131	126	99	94	67
194	223	226	255	2	31	34	63	66	95	98	127	130	159	162	191
64	33	32	1	256	225	224	193	192	161	160	129	128	97	96	65

The rows and columns of Franklin's magic square add to 2,056. While the main diagonals do not, the bent diagonals—for example, 200, 39, 230, 5, 9, 234, 43, 204, 181, 86, 151, 120, 124, 155, 90, 185—do. Each half row and half column adds up to 1,028. Furthermore, Franklin explained, "a four-square hole being cut in a piece of paper of such a size as to take in and show through it just 16 of the little squares, when laid on the greater square, the sum of the 16 numbers so appearing through the hole, wherever it was placed on the greater square (for example, 246, 12, 244, 14, 11, 245, 13, 243, 22, 236, 20, 238, 43, 213, 45, 211), should likewise make 2056." And does.

We might remember Benjamin Franklin best as a statesman, or as a mythic figure flying a kite in a thunderstorm, but he was also a puzzle composer and solver. His close observation of the world around him and his curiosity about what he saw led to his inventing the lightning rod, making discoveries related to meteorology and evaporative cooling, and proposing a solution to a curious puzzle regarding transatlantic mail delivery. When he served as deputy postmaster, Franklin looked into a complaint that the mail from England took substantially longer to get from Britain to New York than it did to get from Britain to Rhode Island. He learned that captains of the mail ships were sailing directly against the Gulf Stream, which he named and charted. When the ships avoided the current, they reached New York two weeks faster.

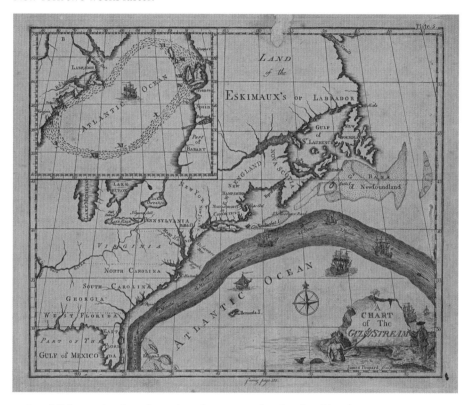

In addition to books of puzzles, there are other kinds of books we might read and dispose of quickly, only to buy another when our desire, our appetite, can no longer be suppressed: genre novels. Genre novels work, to varying degrees, both to satisfy our expectations of form and to stand apart as unique creations. The plotting of a classic detective story appeals to our rational side, not only at the end, when whodunit, why, and howitdone are made clear, but all along the way. The detective story offers the reassurance of order, of the ability of the human mind to make

Benjamin Franklin's map of the Gulf Stream

sense of what, at some point, seemed senseless. The classic detective story offers a world of answers and logic, a world in which problems can be not avoided, but solved.

I've been saying "detective story" and not "mystery" in part to identify a specific subgenre, but also to avoid confusion. To define two key terms, it might be useful to hear from an unlikely literary resource: Gregory F. Treverton's *Reshaping National Intelligence for an Age of Information*.

> The Cold War legacy of intelligence was a vast capacity to solve strategic puzzles, ... ones that could, in principle, have been answered definitively if only the information had been available: How big was the Soviet economy? How many missiles did the Soviet Union have? ...
>
> Different from a puzzle is a mystery, which is a question that cannot be answered with certainty even in principle. Russia's inflation rate this [coming] year is a mystery. ... No one [knows the answer]. The mystery is real. ...
>
> Today's chaotic world still throws up plenty of puzzles to be solved. Whether China sold M-11 missiles to Pakistan is a puzzle. So is whether France bribed Indonesia to give a contract to a French company. Yet most of the critical questions facing American foreign policy are mysteries: Will North Korea fulfill its nuclear agreement with the United States? ... Will China continue to grow rapidly, or will it fragment?

By these definitions, most of the narratives commonly called "mysteries" are, in fact, puzzles—which is to say that everything we need to know can be known, and by the end of the story or novel *is* known. True mysteries are questions we are compelled to contemplate but cannot expect to answer with certainty. The examples of mystery Treverton offers are questions about the future that will, ultimately, have answers—they were only mysteries when he was writing. This might make it seem as if every mystery can eventually become a puzzle, if only we wait long enough or, looking to the past, if we do enough research. But we will never know exactly what George Washington was thinking and feeling as he crossed the Delaware, no matter what references he might have made in letters or in conversations that someone recalled later. We'll never know if Abraham Lincoln heard a strange sound behind him that April night in Ford's Theater, or what mixture of pride, satisfaction, and ego was felt by the hairy guy (or gal) who made the first wheel.

A fundamental distinction between what is often referred to as genre fiction and what is often referred to as literary fiction is that in genre fiction questions of plot (what happened), character (who did it), and even human motivation (why the character did it) are treated as puzzles— questions that can be answered—while literary fiction is more inclined not only to tolerate but to focus on true mystery.[8] In E. M. Forster's *A Passage to India*, we never know exactly what happened in the Marabar Caves; in Graham Greene's *The Quiet American*, the reader is left to sort out Thomas Fowler's professed and unstated motivations for aiding in the murder of Alden Pyle. The first type of fiction is interested in telling stories in which virtually everything can be explained. The second is interested in telling stories about a more complicated world, one that more closely resembles the one we live in.

That isn't to suggest that either type of fiction is easy to create. A pleasing detective story needs to engage readers in a sufficiently complicated and intriguing problem and resolve it in satisfying fashion. A story that means to reveal or acknowledge mystery needs to define that mystery clearly, and provide a satisfactory shape, including a sense of closure, or completion, despite the fact that the central mystery cannot be resolved. A story filled with unfocused mystery—a story in which we don't know if the main character is male or female, or young or old, or human; or if the setting adheres to the physics of the world as we know it; or if the tone is meant to be serious or satirical; or if the main character is meant to be sympathetic, or there's anything in particular he wants—is likely to collapse under the weight of uncertainty. Beginning writers sometimes make the mistake of creating "mystery" by making situations and even sentences either vague or impenetrable; the result isn't mystery, but a mess. Mystery may be a condition ("Their meeting was shrouded in an air of mystery"), but for writers it is also a tool.

To consider how fiction can operate along a scale of puzzle to mystery —or, more accurately, along a scale of almost pure puzzle to an effective combination of puzzle and mystery—we'll start with a detective story.

8 These terms are unsatisfactorily vague and, in certain company, the cause of passionate debate. For this discussion, I'll suggest that genre fiction is written by an author aware of certain conventions, for readers aware of those conventions, and largely aims to satisfy both those readers and the conventions. That said, there are books we might call westerns or science fiction or detective novels or even romance novels that mean to challenge us, to lead us to consider some aspect of the world in a new way. We sometimes say books like these transcend their genre. Similarly, there are stories and novels that look like literary fiction but which intend only to please the reader and to satisfy the conventions of, say, the coming-of-age story; they are, like other genre fiction, intent primarily on entertainment. So many books blur the line that there is no clear line. Is Toni Morrison's *Beloved* a ghost story? Is *Wuthering Heights* a romance novel? Is Cormac McCarthy's *All the Pretty Horses* a western? Is Larry McMurtry's *Lonesome Dove*? More important: outside of publishers' sales meetings, when is it necessary or useful to attach labels to books?

Long before he created a strangely charismatic bear, a chronically depressed donkey, and an eternally tiny piglet, A. A. Milne wrote *The Red House Mystery*. Published in 1922, it has, remarkably, never gone out of print. Milne quite consciously worked within the conventions of a particular subset of detective stories: when a man is killed on the estate of wealthy Mark Ablett, pipe-smoking Anthony Gillingham suggests to his friend Bill Beverly that they assume the roles of Sherlock Holmes and Dr. Watson. Anthony Gillingham is perfectly observant and clever, and faithful Bill Beverly is always a step behind. Over the course of a few days they determine who is responsible for the murder and how and why he did it. At the end of the book, Gillingham and Beverly head back to their lives, whatever those may be—we know almost nothing about their educations and occupations, their marital status, or their families. The pleasure the book offers is in the banter between Gillingham and Beverly, the small bits of suspense, and the variations on such familiar elements as a secret passageway, a mysterious stranger, a disappearing gun, and a man rowing into the middle of a pond late at night to drop a weighted canvas bag into its depths.

In an introduction to the book, Douglas G. Greene writes that, in this subgenre of detective story, "The author provided all the clues to the reader and the detective at the same time, and the game for the reader was to avoid surprise at the identity of the murderer. The corpse was provided to supply the puzzle. That the victim was once a living, breathing human being with hopes and fears was irrelevant." Milne seems to have been well aware of the frivolity of the enterprise; at one point his narrator tells us, "How could [Bill] help feeling that this was … merely a jolly kind of detective game?"

If we enjoy books like *The Red House Mystery*, we enjoy them as entertainments, diversions; something to be consumed. Unless we're studying the genre or attempting to create a similar book ourselves, they are not likely to repay contemplation. The novel is a closed system. It does not open out into the world, informing us or provoking introspection, and does not intend to. It doesn't mean to disturb us, or to confide in us, or to express an understanding of our lives. It means to amuse us for a little while. It is, in essence, a prose puzzle.

One of *The Red House Mystery*'s famous detractors was Raymond Chandler, who believed the detective novel could and should be something more. In the spirit of Mark Twain's attack on James Fenimore Cooper's "literary offenses," Chandler poked holes in several essential aspects of Milne's plot. "However light in texture the story may be," he wrote in "The Simple Art of Murder," "it is offered as a problem of logic and deduction. If it is not that, it is nothing at all. . . . If the problem does not contain the elements of truth and plausibility, it is no problem; [but] if the logic is an illusion, there is nothing to deduce . . . the whole thing is a fraud." After offering similar criticism of other "classic" detective stories, he adds, "These stories . . . do not really come off intellectually as problems, and they do not come off artistically as fiction. They are too contrived, and too little aware of what goes on in the world. . . . if the writers of this fiction wrote about the kind of murders that happen, they would also have to write about the authentic flavor of life as it is lived."

Chandler is arguing two points at once. One is about the need for a piece of fiction to have internal logic, intellectual integrity. The other is about substance, and his clear preference for fiction that captures "the authentic flavor of life as it is lived." Even if the logic posed by Milne's book was sound, Chandler wanted the detective novel to be something more than a puzzle. Reasonable as that might seem, sales of *The Red House Mystery* for nearly a century serve as evidence that consistent logic, plausibility, and realism don't matter to a large number of readers so long as something persuasive, entertaining, or compelling is offered in their place.[9] Still, Chandler's argument is important. While he may not have said it in quite these terms, he was trying to explain why he believed some detective stories not only aspired to be but should be considered literature, while others were laborious trifles.

9 And again: each of us is more than one reader. Or, we are each many kinds of readers. The fact that we enjoy T. S. Eliot's *Four Quartets* doesn't mean we can't also enjoy Arthur Conan Doyle's *The Sign of the Four*, though the reasons for our pleasure might be quite different.

IT'S ALL PRETTY UNSATISFACTORY: MURDER BY MATHEMATICS

The realist in murder writes of a world in which gangsters can rule nations and almost rule cities, in which hotels and apartment houses and celebrated restaurants are owned by men who made their money out of brothels, in which a screen star can be the fingerman for a mob, and the nice man down the hall is a boss of the numbers racket; a world where a judge with a cellar full of bootleg liquor can send a man to jail for having a pint in his pocket, where the mayor of your town may have condoned murder as an instrument of moneymaking, where no man can walk down a dark street in safety because law and order are things we talk about but refrain from practicing; a world where you may witness a hold-up in broad daylight and see who did it, but you will fade quickly back into the crowd rather than tell anyone, because the hold-up men may have friends with long guns, or the police may not like your testimony, and in any case the shyster for the defense will be allowed to abuse and vilify you in open court, before a jury of selected morons, without any but the most perfunctory interference from a political judge. . . . It is not a very fragrant world, but it is the world you live in, and certain writers with tough minds and a cool spirit of detachment can make very interesting and even amusing patterns out of it.

— RAYMOND CHANDLER

Literature has that name because it shows life as it really is. Literature's objective is the truth, unconditional and honest. . . . no matter how awful he may find it, [the writer] is obliged to overcome his squeamishness and sully his imagination with the filth of life.

— *Anton Chekhov*

Raymond Chandler suggests that an overreliance on plot emphasizes the artificiality of a story, reducing it to a "problem of logic." Within the world of detective fiction, Chandler singled out Dashiell Hammett as a writer who worked to recognize complex reality. Hammett is perhaps most famous for *The Maltese Falcon*—and for the fact that, before becoming a writer, he worked as an operative for the Pinkerton Detective Agency. Chandler says,

> Hammett . . . was one of a group . . . who wrote or tried to write realistic mystery fiction. . . . A rather revolutionary debunking

of both the language and material of fiction had been going on for some time. . . . Hammett gave murder back to the kind of people that commit it for reasons, not just to provide a corpse. . . . He put these people down on paper as they are, and he made them talk and think in the language they customarily used for these purposes. . . . He did over and over again what only the best writers can ever do at all. He wrote scenes that seemed never to have been written before.

Mystery writer and scholar Ross MacDonald discovered *The Maltese Falcon* in a tobacco shop when he was young:

It wasn't escape reading. As I stood there absorbing Hammett's novel, the slot machines at the back of the shop were clanking and whirring, and in the billiard room upstairs the perpetual poker game was being played. Like iron filings magnetized by the book in my hands, the secret meanings of the city began to organize themselves around me like a second city. For the first time that I can remember I was consciously experiencing in my own sensibility the direct meeting of art and contemporary actuality—an experience that popular art at its best exists to provide—and beginning to find a language and a shape for that experience.

It isn't that narrative puzzles are bad and narrative mysteries are good; rather, every well-constructed piece of fiction has elements of a puzzle, and every piece of fiction that means to provoke readers to a state of wonder or contemplation has at least some element of mystery. The meeting of art and actuality, or artifice and reality, can be seen as the combination of the strategic arrangement of information and the acknowledgment of true, unsolvable, mysteries. The composition of the work, and the elements that give it shape, satisfy our desire for order; mystery, Chandler's "life as it is lived," MacDonald's "actuality," and Chekhov's "filth of life" challenge that sense of order, and connect the work to the world as we experience it in potentially more meaningful and moving ways.

In Hammett's novel *The Thin Man*, Nick Charles is a former detective who refuses to take on the case of an eccentric inventor's murdered secretary but who serves as the novel's detective nonetheless. His wife, Nora (modeled after Hammett's lover, the playwright Lillian Hellman), offers quips and advice. She also asks the questions that allow Nick to explain the work of a real detective, as opposed to the detectives in lesser fiction, and allow Hammett to encourage his readers to look beyond plot. Late in the novel, in their hotel suite in New York, Nora is working on a jigsaw puzzle:

> "You used to be a detective. Find me a brownish piece shaped something like a snail with a long neck." [Nora] put a finger on her puzzle. "The piece I want goes in there."
>
> I found the piece she wanted and told her, almost word for word, what had been done and said at Mimi's.

Nora wants a piece to the jigsaw puzzle; she also wants to know what happened at Mimi's. That quickly, puzzles are equated with plot. But toward the end of the novel, as we reach "the solution," Nora is disturbed that the pieces don't fit together with absolute certainty. "'When murders are committed by mathematics,' [Nick says], 'you can solve them by mathematics. Most of them aren't and this one wasn't.'" And later,

> "Now are you satisfied with what we've got on him?"
>
> "Yes, in a way. There seems to be enough of it, but it's not very neat."
>
> "It's neat enough to send him to the chair," I said, "and that's all that counts. It takes care of all the angles and I can't think of any other theory that would . . ."
>
> "Have it your own way," she said, "but I always thought detectives waited until they had every little detail fixed in—
> .... What do you think will happen to Mimi and Dorothy and Gilbert now?"
>
> "Nothing new. They'll go on being Mimi and Dorothy and Gilbert just as you and I will go on being us and the Quinns will go on being the Quinns. Murder doesn't round

out anybody's life except the murdered's and sometimes the murderer's."

"That may be," Nora said, "but it's all pretty unsatisfactory."

The novel ends on that line—and so echoes the ending of Ernest Hemingway's "The Killers" ("I can't stand to think about him.... It's too damned awful." "Well, you better not think about it."). Hammett recognizes the need to bring a story to satisfying closure yet insists on acknowledging what can't be known, the ways in which the world resists our complete comprehension. Our wariness of neat solutions, our desire to grapple with deeper mysteries, is what draws us to serious fiction.

X AXTF X ZNLPE ABXOU QT KVTOUBXNLT QT Q ZQO

In a work of art there is a kind of merging between . . . the precision of poetry and the excitement of pure science . . . and the greater one's science, the deeper the sense of mystery.

— VLADIMIR NABOKOV

A re-creation of the Turk

The stories and novels classified as "mysteries" in bookstores did not begin as the sort of parlor game that so frustrated Raymond Chandler. Edgar Allan Poe is widely recognized as the father of the modern detective story. He published "The Murders in the Rue Morgue" in 1841, eighty-one years before *The Red House Mystery* and forty-six years before the first Sherlock Holmes story. Soon after, he published "The Gold-bug," which includes a coded message, or substitution cipher. Poe's particular puzzling interest was in what he called "Secret Languages"; for six months he ran an ad in a Philadelphia newspaper inviting readers to submit ciphers for him to solve. He is credited with popularizing cryptograms, a type of

10 The title of this section is a cryptogram, a simple substitution cipher in which each letter of the alphabet is consistently replaced by a different letter of the alphabet.

puzzle that still appears in some daily newspapers.[10] Some of the more complicated and intriguing examples of encryption are the work of the Navajo code talkers in World War II and the writing on *Kryptos*, Jim Sanborn's sculpture standing in front of the Central Intelligence Agency's headquarters in Langley, Virginia, which was installed in 1990 and, over twenty years later, remains unsolved.

Kryptos,
by John Sanborn

Poe also took an impassioned pleasure in debunking certain popular myths, as when he investigated and wrote at length about a much-celebrated "chess-playing machine" called the Turk. (Benjamin Franklin played chess against the Turk, in Paris.) Long before IBM created a computer to challenge the world's greatest chess masters, the Turk appeared to be an automaton capable of playing human opponents at a very high level.[11] Attempting to uncover the secrets of the Turk required careful observation, intuition, deduction, induction, analysis, and testing of hypotheses—actions and qualities displayed in "The Murders in the Rue Morgue," the story that introduces amateur detective C. Auguste Dupin, who possesses a wide breadth of knowledge, a keen analytical mind, and imagination. Ross MacDonald said Poe was living in the age of reason but descending "into the maelstrom of the unconscious. It was with a kind of desperation—a desperation we continue to feel—that he held on to rational explanations. The murdered girl in the chimney (in "Rue Morgue"), Dupin assures us, was only the victim of an animal. But in spite of this explanation the story leaves a residue of horror. The forces of terror and reason remain in unresolved conflict."

So while Poe predates Arthur Conan Doyle and A. A. Milne, his detective stories represent a more complicated combination of puzzle and mystery. Even more so than in Hammett's novels, in Poe's stories we might say that the narrative's puzzle is its plot, and its mystery resides in the characters' motivations and responses—their psychology. More generally, we might think of a literary work's composition, the effective arrangement of its parts, as its puzzle, and the irreducible, inexplicable aspects of its content as its mystery. While a short story may not have a strictly pre-defined form to fill or respond to, its own individual arrangement is its form and can provide pleasure through symmetry, repetition, proportion, patterns of imagery, motifs, extended metaphors, and so on.

[11] As almost anyone might have guessed, a human was behind the Turk's genuinely impressive chess playing—a particularly nimble chess master who sat hidden in the ingeniously designed cabinet on a silently rolling seat, so that doors on both sides could be opened to reveal the automaton's machinery and allow viewers to see completely through the cabinet, albeit one section at a time. In addition to being confined for long periods, the chess master had to regard the board from beneath, moving the pieces using magnets, demonstrating impressive dedication to a hoax. As Teller, of the magician duo Penn and Teller, has said, "You will be fooled by a trick if it involves more time, money, and practice than you (or any other sane onlooker) would be willing to invest."

POSING THE QUESTION CORRECTLY

I was . . . a young doctor, and had been educated in a very severe and critical school of medical thought, especially coming under the spell of Dr. Bell of Edinburgh, who had most remarkable powers of observation. He prided himself that when he looked at a patient he could tell not only their disease, but very often their occupation and place of residence. Reading some detective stories, I was struck by the fact that their results were obtained in nearly every case by chance. (I except of course Edgar Allan

Poe's splendid stories. . . .) I thought I would try my hand at writing a story where the hero would treat crime as Dr. Bell treated disease, and where science would take the place of chance. The result was Sherlock Holmes.

— SIR ARTHUR CONAN DOYLE

Several of Anton Chekhov's most famous statements about an artist's responsibility appear in a series of letters he wrote in 1888, when he was an unusually wise man of twenty-eight. Chekhov was writing in the shadow of the great moralist and didact Leo Tolstoy. Chekhov respected Tolstoy, especially as a young man, but ultimately parted from the older writer's philosophy and aesthetic. Most significantly, he claimed to "lack a political, religious and philosophical worldview," and declined to use his fiction to tell readers how they should live. Chekhov wrote,

> I have always insisted that it is not up to the artist to resolve very specific questions. . . . Only the individual who has never written and never dealt with images can say that there are no questions in his sphere, just a solid mass of answers. . . . You are right to demand that an artist take a conscious attitude to his work, but you confuse two concepts: *resolving a question* and *posing a question correctly*. Only the second is required of the artist. . . . The judge must pose the questions correctly; let them be resolved by the members of the jury, each in accordance with his own taste.

In that same letter, he makes clear that the correct posing of the question is a significant responsibility: "An artist observes, selects, guesses, arranges—these actions alone must be prompted by a question. If he did not ask himself a question at the very start, there would be nothing to guess and nothing to select. . . . if an author were to boast to me that he had written a story without having thought through his intentions first, on inspiration alone, I would call him mad."

According to Chekhov, then, the artist (a) asks himself a question, (b) thinks through his intentions, (c) observes, (d) selects, and (e) arranges. In short, he is encouraging the writer to be a kind of puzzle maker—the crucial difference being that the completed puzzle leads readers to a provocative question. Ideally, that question is of interest and consequence to the characters, to the writer, and to the reader. This might seem like common sense now, but Andrei Turkov reminds us, "The characteristic absence [in Chekhov's work] of any overt moralizing, of the 'pointing finger' and clear 'hints' to the reader—who was left the right to judge for himself what the writer had depicted—was taken by the critics not as a particular and original literary style, but as a major conceptual and literary defect.... He was accused of indifference [and]... social insensibility."[13] Chekhov himself wrote, "I am afraid of those who look between the lines for a social stance.... When I write, I place my complete trust in the reader; I presume he will add the missing subjective elements himself."

Vpybsxasxoatovtyjawxaeutfupsgjustcjvagkfajurscj? Rtntctfupsghaetfjarvtcuuskfajurscj. Rlrptbtcjvagjrbhatxsorurertc.

— *afdacarscajes*[12]

As Conan Doyle recognized, a doctor approaching a patient is like a detective approaching a crime scene. They both investigate, eliminate misleading information, identify relevant evidence, and then, ideally, solve the problem. Like the creator of Sherlock Holmes, Chekhov was trained as a doctor—a man of science. His fiction and plays benefited directly from his practice observing and analyzing. Early in his career he wrote a number of stories and sketches about crime, the titles of which would not have been out of place in the pulp magazines that flourished soon after his death: they include "Thieves," "Murder," "Bad Business," and "The Drama at the Hunt." A story called "Criminal Investigator" begins with a county doctor and a criminal investigator "riding to perform an autopsy one wonderful spring day." The investigator asserts that "there are many mysterious, dark forces in the world... even in our everyday life, dear doctor, you can stumble on events that cannot be explained." The doctor disagrees, saying, "There is no action without a reason." To make his case, the investigator tells the story of a beautiful young woman who predicted her own death. The doctor responds by suggesting that the woman committed suicide, and goes on to explain not only why she did it, but how. The story leads us to believe that he's correct, and so supports the notion that all actions can be logically explained.

12 Another substitution cipher, this one made a bit more difficult by removing the spaces between words. For a hint, see the solutions for this chapter.

13 Even today, art that allows for ambiguity, or that opts not to take an explicit stance toward its material, runs the risk of being seen as "defective." These arguments often arise in response to abstract public sculpture, to fiction presented from the point of view of an unlikeable character, and to satire. Randy Newman's song "Short People" angered a lot of people who thought it expressed the songwriter's disapproval of the vertically challenged, and even today some members of his concert audiences who clamor to hear "Rednecks" seem not to understand the lyrics' ultimate implications. He's on much safer ground with "You've Got a Friend in Me."

The story's interest lies in a dramatic twist: we learn that the beautiful young woman was the investigator's wife, and by saying that her death could not be explained, the investigator was actually expressing his confusion and grief. Even so, the story doesn't offer much in the way of mystery, suspense, or insight beyond the obvious irony that the professional investigator can't examine his own life clearly. As a detective story, "Criminal Investigator" reads like a pale imitation of the kind of tale Conan Doyle perfected. As an examination of character, it comes off as far too self-assured, even smug. The reader is in the position of watching a character solve a puzzle, but the doctor provides the solution almost immediately, with no trouble at all. As an indication of the work Chekhov would go on to produce, though, "Criminal Investigator" serves as evidence that the author was already less interested in plot—the entire story unfolds as the two men ride to work—than in human psychology.

Chekhov came to see writing stories and plays as an opportunity to depict aspects of the world, and specifically human behavior, that could not or should not be explained away so easily. Unlike Conan Doyle, who continued to illustrate, in each new Sherlock Holmes story, how the rational mind could make sense of the most apparently senseless circumstances, Chekhov went on to pit the rational mind against the emotional and irrational in more challenging ways and to interrogate characters who confidently professed to have ultimate knowledge. Rather than making the know-it-all doctor the source of insight, a more mature Chekhov would focus our attention on the tormented young mother, her deeply conflicted husband, and the doctor who mistakenly believes in his own superiority. In that way, Chekhov's development illustrates the movement toward the kind of psychological realism that continues to prevail over a century later.

Chekhov's "A Doctor's Visit" can be read as a reconsideration of "Criminal Investigator" in which he rejects the notion that serious questions can be so easily answered. In the later story, a young woman isn't dead, but ill, and the cause of her illness is the apparent problem to be solved. The story is set into motion by a "long, incoherent telegram"—a piece of writing that fails to make sense. The doctor, or professor, is unavailable, so he sends his assistant. The game is afoot.

Korolyov, the assistant, is "charmed with the evening, the farmhouses and villas on the road, and the birch trees, and the quiet atmosphere all around." But in the story's fourth paragraph, Chekhov invites us to step back. He tells us Korolyov "did not know the country, and he had never taken any interest in factories, or been inside one, but he had happened to read about factories ... [and] he always thought how quiet and peaceable it was outside, but within there was always sure to be impenetrable ignorance." With that, we're notified that our main character's understanding is limited and that he suffers from a particular bias. We have been deputized, put in the role of detective. We don't know what case we're being asked to solve, but we know that we're on the lookout for something Korolyov doesn't see.

The young woman's governess tells Korolyov, "She has been, one may say, ailing from childhood." Elevated to a lifelong condition, the illness moves from the physical to the psychological and metaphorical.

Korolyov's first impression of his patient, Liza, is that she is "big and tall, but ugly like her mother ... a poor, destitute creature." He examines her, says her heart is fine, and concludes she must have suffered an attack of nerves, and it's over. At that the girl begins sobbing, and Korolyov's impression changes: "He saw a soft, suffering expression which was intelligent and touching; she seemed to him altogether graceful, feminine, and simple; and he longed to soothe her, not with drugs, not with advice, but with simple, kindly words." This moment of sympathy extends to the patient's mother: "What despair, what grief was in the old woman's face! She, her mother, had reared her and brought her up, spared nothing ... and now she could not make out the reason of these tears, why there was all this misery." This sort of compassionate understanding is nearly always virtuous and redemptive in Chekhov, and here Korolyov transcends himself as the story's explicit and metaphorical concerns merge.

But Korolyov soon affects a professional distance: he becomes bored; he tells mother and daughter, "I find nothing special the matter ... it's ... an ordinary trouble." He prepares to leave, but the mother asks him to stay the night. After dinner he takes a walk, and thinks

> what he always thought when he saw a factory. They may have performances for the workers, magic lanterns, factory doctors, and improvements of all sorts, but all the same, the

workers . . . did not look in any way different from those he had known long ago. . . . As a doctor accustomed to judging correctly of chronic complaints, the radical cause of which was incomprehensible and incurable, he looked upon factories as something baffling . . . and all the improvements in the life of the factory workers he looked upon not as superfluous, but as comparable with the treatment of incurable illnesses.

His thoughts continue along these lines until the watchman strikes the hour, and he thinks the sounds are uttered by "the Devil himself, who controlled the owners and the workers alike, and was deceiving both." Here we seem to have an answer to the story's deepest problem: Liza is ill, sick at heart, because of the inhumanity not just of this particular factory, but of all factories. The Devil, representing man's worst impulses, is to blame. The story is verging on the didactic, and its setting, plot, and characters suddenly seem to have been summoned into existence simply to provide an opportunity for Chekhov to make this political and moral statement. The story is no longer a mystery but a puzzle, and it has been solved.

But Chekhov knew that making a diagnosis was not the same as providing a cure. Korolyov hears the patient awake and goes in to check on her. She tells him she is wretched every night, that she needs not a doctor but a friend, that she is lonely and frightened. Korolyov thinks "she needed as quickly as possible to give up the five buildings and the million if she had it . . . it was clear to him, too, that she thought so herself. . . . But he did not know how to say it . . . it is awkward to ask very rich people what they want so much money for, why they make such a poor use of their wealth . . . even when they see in it their unhappiness." And so he makes a "roundabout" speech, in which he tells Liza that her sleeplessness does her credit, that this represents improvement over their parents' generation, and that things will be clearer for their children.

Liza, who has given her discomfort many nights' thought, can't be persuaded by such vague consolation. "What will our children and grandchildren do?" she asks. "I suppose they will give it up and go away," he tells her, and when she asks where—a question with urgent implications for her, but only theoretical ones for him—he tells her, "Where? . . . Why, where they like.... There are lots of places a good, intelligent person can go to." With that, out of patience and ideas, he says goodnight. The next morning, as he drives off, "Korolyov thought neither of the workers ... nor of the Devil, but thought of the time, close at hand, when life would be as bright and joyous as that still Sunday morning; and he thought how pleasant it was on such a morning in the spring to drive with three horses in a good carriage, and to bask in the sunshine."

The story has posed its crucial question in Liza's voice. "What will our children and grandchildren do?" is an only slightly encoded version of "What should I do?" What appeared to be an answer—that Liza's "illness" is unease caused by her awareness of the inhumanity and injustice of the factory—has been turned into a question: Once we recognize that dilemma, what should *we* do? Korolyov's answer is that we should congratulate ourselves for recognizing the problem, let future generations solve it, and, in the meantime, enjoy the spring day. The narrator provided us with distance from him at the outset so that we could doubt him; and now we see that his answer is unsatisfactory. Liza is "pale and exhausted," sorrowful and intelligent, "with an expression as though she wanted to tell him something"—and Korolyov drives off. We, however, are left looking at Liza, and forced to consider what we would say to her. A question has been framed and one answer rejected.

In his mature work, while Chekhov allows his characters moments of insight, those insights are almost always limited. When he allows them epiphanies, they are often false epiphanies—that is, the character believes he's understood something essential, a solution of some kind, but the story quickly undermines it. An epiphany is often used by lesser writers as the final piece of a puzzle. In the best Chekhov stories, that piece doesn't quite fit; the critical question remains unanswered.[14]

DISTURBING STRANGENESS

A satisfying plot, I believe, involves not a diminution of mystery but rather a fundamental enlargement.

— TIM O'BRIEN

14 Reflecting on his death, Chekhov's wife, Olga Knipper, wrote: "Awareness of grief, of the loss of such a man as Anton Pavlovich, came only with the first sounds of awakening life, with the arrival of people; and what I experienced and felt, standing on the balcony and looking now at the rising sun, now at nature melodiously awaking, now at the fine, peaceful face of Anton Pavlovich, which seemed to be smiling as if he had just understood something—that, I repeat, still remains for me an unresolved mystery. There had never been such moments as those before in my life, and there never will be again." *"What I experienced and felt... remains for me an unresolved mystery."* She was with Chekhov when he died. Who could know better her experiences and feelings? Yet any of us who have lost someone close to us understands how, despite all the facts at hand, mystery persists.

ANIMAL CRACKERS

A crossword in which the clues are embedded in a story, created by Emily Cox and Henry Rathvon for the American Crossword Puzzle Tournament:

"Well, your **4D** there'd be days like this," cracked the monkey with a wink of his **8D**.

We were standing near the **14D** in the bow of my **47A**, the "**62D**," named for my Oregon home back in the **46A**. It seemed like **49A** since the **74A** of our voyage. I knew I should have **50A** the animals in orderly **59D** at the start. Now I had to **63A** the deck to lizards who said "I feel like **21A** bucks" and **69A** who asked "What **5D** is **73D**?" My crew, like some loony zoo from Dr. **30A**, had become addicted to the **19A** form of humor. The hyenas were the worst of a bad **51D**:

"What did **58A** Garbo tell her banker?" asked one.

"I want to be a **70D**," shot back the other.

"How do salamanders learn?" laughed the first.

"They **67A** questions!" came the retort.

"Do Bangkok lovers **40A** the knot?"

"Are fortune-tellers' dupes called **62A** suckers?"

"As Rudolph said to Santa, you **16D** me!"

And so forth, till I wanted to hurl myself down a bottomless **32D**. I sighed heavily—scarcely *sans* **36D**. I wished I were off in Lebanon sitting under some **38D** **59A**, or touring the markets in London's **55D** (2 wds.), instead of hearing every beast from **29D** (2 wds.) Z get into the **42A** of mangling people's **80A** and professions:

"What country was Wharton's Ethan **1A**?"

"Did tennis star Tony smash bugs with his racket or use a **2D** Motel?"

"Is jazz singing **75A**-mentary?"

"Is Peter **6D** related to MC *Hammer*?"

"Speaking of actors, does Anne eat corned-beef **33D**?"

"Do jilted farmers get John **65D** letters?"

"Are benched hockey players off-**18A**?"

And then there was the onboard bickering. The tropical fauna (who sublimely **77A** hot climes) insisted I keep the **39A** (2 wds.)—up to **76A** degrees and more—until I feared the rowers would suffer **43A**. The canned rations were getting worrisomely **27A**. The wolves, who had a convenient **34D** (hyph.) kitchen in their private **68D**, seemed bent on making a Greek **54D** of the lambs. (I knew it was an **12D** putting them so close together.) Meanwhile the wildcats squabbled over chess.

"You fiddled with your kingside **7D**," cried one. "You dirty **32A**!"

"Captain," winked a pelican, "don't you think a wading bird gives you a great **48D** to view?"

"Sure, your two gams are swell," I conceded,

"But I have other avian concerns." Just then the **20A** was tangled in the rigging, cawing "This is another fine **11A** you've got me in!" And the herring **71A** was telling the **72A**, "Move over, little raptor. It's my **44D** to fly!"

"Say, Captain," laughed that first hyena. "I'd like to **35D** 1-800-diet. Would that be a **15A** (hyph.) call?"

"**56A** enough," said his mate, "that number's fake!"

"What a dugong shame," spouted one of the **23A** (2 wds.). "I've kidnapped a dolphin for immoral **35A**."

"But **26A** well that ends well," quipped the painting panda, dabbing her brush from **37D** to canvas. (The panda also plays bongo **79A** in our boat's band, and **30D** her sore paws in **64D** salts when she's done.)

On top of all this madness, we were lost. At sea where no sonar systems or **22D** could locate us, I felt I could have been on the **9D** Ice Shelf, in the **31D** Canal on one of those flat-bottomed **13D**—or foundering in Hades' own river **78A** for all I knew. (They say **41A** landed at Ararat, but I was hoping for at least a rocky peak in **66D** Park, Colorado.)

"With **52D** luck," said the boa to her cousin the water **11D**, "we'll **16A** (2 wds.) course and **56D** soon we'll reach dry land."

"And then we'll **17A**-strate some music," sang the killer whales. "An **6A** buffa, perhaps?"

"Too soon to **60D** in celebration," said I. "The round **45D** of Earth is still one blue expanse of **3D**. I suggest we pass the time with a nice Hollywood **1D** like *Von* **57A** *Express* or *Hello,* **61D***!*. Or we could play a game. If everybody **10D** (2 wds.), we'll try poker, or maybe bingo or beano or **25A**."

"Okay, **28A**," barked a saluting Lhasa **24D** (who seemed to think we were in the Army). "But first a question, sir. All we animals come in twos except the **58D**. Why are there *three* of those civet-like creatures?"

"Oh," said I, getting my punning revenge at last. "They're having a **53A** à **40D**."

As anyone who has tried it can attest, creating an engaging puzzle involves more than simply arranging pieces of the whole in some disorienting way. Cutting a picture in half, for instance, doesn't make for much of a jigsaw puzzle; neither does simply keeping at it with the scissors until there are a thousand tiny rectangles. The creation of a puzzle, like the creation of a story or poem, requires choosing a form, working within the conventions of that form (or finding a way to communicate departures from them to the solver/reader), engaging the solver's/reader's interest or curiosity, and making sure the puzzle/story/poem has a satisfactory degree of internal logic or consistency. Serious puzzle composers also work to make the result more than just another representative of its type. The computer-generated sudoku and crossword puzzles that fill cheaply produced paperback books are essentially interchangeable, but there is a large realm of puzzles that aim both to satisfy our essential expectations and to be, in some way, uniquely interesting.

Crossword puzzles are relatively new; the first was published in 1913, and they didn't become popular until more than a decade later. The first book published by Simon & Schuster, in April 1924, was *The Crossword Puzzle Book*, and by the end of that year the publisher's four books of crossword puzzles had sold more than a million copies. Devotees of crosswords tell us that the puzzles enrich our vocabulary and frame of reference and have been proven to ward off senility—though it seems virtually every type of puzzle, and many games, make similar claims, as if they needed to provide some medical benefit.

Georges Perec, author of *A Void* and *Life: A User's Manual*, and one of the founding members of the Oulipo, the international workshop of potential literature, also created crossword puzzles. He wrote about how the two stages of crossword puzzle creation draw from different sides of the brain:

> The filling of the diagram is a tedious, meticulous, maniacal task, a sort of letter-based arithmetic where all that matters is that words have this or that length, and that their juxtapositions reveal groupings that are compatible with the perpendicular construction of other words; it is a system of primary constraints where the letter is omnipresent but language is

absent. Contrariwise, the search for definitions is fluid, intangible work, a stroll in the land of words, intended to uncover, in the imprecise neighborhood that constitutes the definition of a word, the fragile and unique location where it will be simultaneously revealed and hidden. . . .[15]

What, in the end, characterizes a good crossword definition is that its solution is obvious, as obvious as the problem had seemed insoluble as long as it was not solved. Once the solution is found, one realizes . . . one did not know how to see it, the whole problem being to see in another way. . . . What is at stake, in crosswords as in psychoanalysis, is this sort of quavering of meaning, this "disturbing strangeness," the uncanniness through which the language's unconscious seeps out and reveals itself.

[15] At the American Crossword Puzzle Tournament, finalists in the top three divisions each compete to solve "the same" puzzle. That is, the answers are the same; the clues are entirely different.

The "quavering of meaning" and "disturbing strangeness" echo Ross MacDonald's description of the power of "The Murders in the Rue Morgue" ("But in spite of this explanation the story leaves a residue of horror. The forces of terror and reason remain in unresolved conflict.") and the unease the reader feels at the end of "A Doctor's Visit" when Korolyov drives away from Liza as if he's done his job. Perec's discussion of crosswords also suggests how a work's form can stand in useful contrast to its content. A sonnet or villanelle adheres to or responds to a long-established pattern, and its adherence to or response to that pattern offers a certain kind of pleasure, a pleasure that comes from shapeliness and organization. The content, however, might very well "disturb" us, in the sense that it means to disrupt our expectations, to lead us to feel or see or understand something new. Similarly, a narrative built on the basic framework of a detective story (or a quest, a romance, etc.) is in conversation with the reader's expectations.

THE MANIPULATION OF INFORMATION

[Lolita] was like the composition of a beautiful puzzle—its

composition and its solution at the same time, since one is a mirror view of the other, depending on the way you look.

— VLADIMIR NABOKOV

This notion of fiction as a combination of puzzle and mystery is by no means limited to stories about detectives and doctors. Truman Capote's novella *Breakfast at Tiffany's* is a perhaps surprisingly rich illustration. If you're familiar with only the film starring Audrey Hepburn and George Peppard, give yourself the pleasure of reading Capote's charming tale for which, the author said, he needed to learn an entirely new prose style. The story is a recollection, by an unnamed narrator, of the time when he first moved to New York and, along with many others, fell under the spell of an immensely appealing but ultimately mysterious young woman, Holly Golightly. (Nearly all of the characters have equally implausible names—Sally Tomato, Rusty Trawler—and the novella walks a fine line between wistful romance and plain goofiness. Capote uses a comic tone, among many other devices, to mask the narrator's yearning, and so transfer that yearning to the reader.)

The novella opens when Joe Bell, a bartender, calls the narrator to say he has something the narrator needs to see. This slight suspense (what is it?) is quickly defused (the narrator assumes it must have something to do with Holly) but leads to another question: where is Holly now? It turns out that Joe has three photographs—not of Holly, but of an African wood carving that, Joe and the narrator agree, depicts her. They speculate as to her whereabouts ("You know so much, where is she?" "Dead. Or in a crazy house. Or married. I think she's married and quieted down and maybe right in this very city."), and that speculation gradually leads the narrator to begin the story that promises to answer the questions, Who is Holly Golightly? And why does she loom so large in the memory of these two men?

MISSING DIGIT?

1								
	2			1	5	3		
		3	4					6
4			5					3
	5				6	1	2	
		6		3				7
7				6				4
					4	9	7	
		9						

Thomas Snyder's puzzles include sudoku unlikely to be generated by a computer thanks in part to the wit of their presentation.

The instigating question about Holly's whereabouts is one of many the narrative raises but never answers. (Others include: Exactly who is our narrator? And what's he doing, these days, aside from telling us this story?) These are puzzles (somewhere, in the world of the fiction, someone knows where Holly is, or what happened to her; and the narrator could tell us where he lives and what he does, if he chose to), the solutions to which are withheld not to frustrate us but to indicate that those answers—those questions—are not what the novella is about. Neither will the narrative provide an explanation of Holly's appeal; instead, it will attempt to re-create it. Ultimately, the power someone like Holly has—a power beyond generosity, or glamour, or beauty, or sexual attraction—is mysterious, and Capote has no intention of lessening that mystery.

Early in *Breakfast at Tiffany's*, the narrator engages in a bit of snooping in order to learn more about his intriguing neighbor:

> I discovered, from observing the trash-basket outside her door, that her regular reading consisted of tabloids and travel folders and astrological charts; that she smoked an esoteric cigarette called Picayunes; survived on cottage cheese and melba toast; that her vari-colored hair was somewhat self-induced. The same source made it evident that she received V-letters by the bale. They were always torn into strips like bookmarks. I used occasionally to pluck myself a bookmark in passing. *Remember* and *miss you* and *rain* and *please write* and *damn* and *goddamn* were the words that recurred most often on these slips; those, and *lonesome* and *love*.

The bits of trash are partial information, but together they create a portrait of Holly. Most interesting are those scraps of wartime Victory letters that, like the fragments of parchment from which we know Sappho's poetry, convey meaning despite their being incomplete. Later, we come to infer that those letters are from Holly's brother, Fred; and those key words the narrator notices create a kind of tone poem summarizing their relationship. We never see an entire letter from Fred, and we don't need to; a carefully selected group of pieces of the puzzle tell us quite enough. We get the pleasure of assembling them, or intuiting what's left unsaid.

Mystery can also be created, provocatively, through an abundance of information, particularly when it's conflicting. Capote builds anticipation about Holly until, finally, he has to present her in a scene. The writer's challenge is to maintain the air of mystery even as we're looking at the enigmatic character, something Capote accomplishes through multiplicity of detail. What color is her hair? "The ragbag colors of her boy's hair, tawny streaks, strands of albino-blond and yellow, caught the hall light." What general impression does she create? "For all her chic thinness, she had an almost breakfast-cereal air of health, a soap and lemon cleanness, a rough pink darkening in the cheeks. Her mouth was large, her nose upturned. A pair of dark glasses blotted out her eyes. It was a face beyond childhood, yet this side of belonging to a woman. I thought her anywhere between sixteen and thirty; as it turned out, she was shy two months of her nineteenth birthday." By the time we get to the fact of her age, we have so much dynamic information that we never think of her merely as an eighteen-year-old, any more than we think of her as simply pretty or blond. She's much more complicated than that.

A perhaps even greater challenge to maintaining the mystery of Holly is her voice, as her speech—her diction and syntax and allusions—will necessarily expose her intelligence and insight. In keeping with Holly's physical description, Capote makes her voice a unique mélange. Her first conversation with the narrator begins, "I've got the most terrifying man downstairs. . . . I mean, he's sweet when he isn't drunk, but let him start lapping up the vino, and oh God quel beast! If there's one thing I loathe, it's men who bite." She continues,

> I think he thinks I'm in the bathroom, not that I give a damn what he thinks, the hell with him, he'll get tired, he'll go to sleep, my God he should, eight martinis before dinner and enough wine to wash an elephant. Listen, you can throw me out if you want to. I've got a gall barging in on you like this. But that fire escape was damned icy. And you looked so cozy. Like my brother Fred. We used to sleep four in a bed, and he was the only one that ever let me hug him on a cold night. By the way, do you mind if I call you Fred?

The pidgin French, the colloquial vulgarity and surprising figures of speech, coupled with occasional flights into higher diction and self-consciousness, make Holly's dialogue lively and unpredictable, unsettled and fractured—all of which hints at her deeper character. So it's no surprise when she takes off her dark glasses and, through the narrator, we see her eyes are "a little blue, a little green, dotted with bits of brown." Even as she stands in front of us, exposed, Holly is irreducible.

Structurally, Capote manipulates the release of information both for the sake of compression, to get the maximum effect from scenes, and to disrupt a merely chronological recollection of the past—and he does both so subtly that the reader is never jarred from the fluid, apparently logical narrative. The first scene he recollects from his past with Holly, the night he first saw her, begins when he hears Mr. Yunioshi, on the third floor of the brownstone they share, calling down to "Miss Golightly," who is at the bottom of the stairs (and whose first words introduce that multifaceted voice: "Oh darling, I *am* sorry. I lost the goddamn key"). Holly and Yunioshi argue briefly; she reconciles by saying that, if he promises not to be angry, "I might let you take those pictures we mentioned." The implication is underscored by Yunioshi's "audible change of breath," the punch line provided when he asks, "When?" and she laughs and says, "Sometime."

The scene—our introduction to flirtatious, careless Holly—seems to be over. But the narrator, who has been overhearing all of this, opens his door a crack, looks down, and provides the aforementioned description of her hair and apparent age. And then we learn "She was not alone." She's accompanied by Sid Arbuck, a short, "vast" man who nuzzles her neck as she opens the door, a man who clearly expects entrance to her chambers in return for the dinner he just bought. But Holly turns him away ("The next time a girl wants a little powder-room change . . . take my advice, darling: *don't* give her twenty cents!"), simultaneously confirming our sense of the kind of girl she is and complicating it. She expects money, but she's no prostitute. More to the point structurally: by situating his narrator on the second floor, and by playing the first part of the scene entirely through dialogue, Capote is able to compress three scenes into one—the conversation with Yunioshi, the narrator's solitary gaze as he sees Holly for the first time, and the rejection of Sid Arbuck are three acts in a very brief play, the undeniable star of which is Holly.

Capote manipulates information even more dramatically and deftly in the novella's long climactic sequence. In one eventful day he and Holly go to Central Park; they decide to go horseback riding; the narrator's horse runs away with him, and it takes Holly and a mounted policeman to stop them; they go back to his apartment, where he takes a bath to soothe his bruises; police detectives arrive and arrest Holly for involvement with gangster Sally Tomato; Joe Bell brings copies of the evening newspapers; the narrator reads about what Holly has been up to; then he goes to Joe Bell's bar and begins making phone calls to try to get her out of jail. It might seem that the focus of the sequence is Holly's being arrested. But all of that business about the Mafia and Sally Tomato is comic window dressing, a bit of drama in the background that we are never asked to take seriously, and which is important to the novella primarily because it forces Holly to leave New York.

The heart of the sequence is the narrator's moment of wild abandon with Holly (after the horse chase he says, for the only time, "I love you," and she kisses him on the cheek), their deepest intimacy (when the narrator is in the bath, Holly is naked, too, though theirs is a chaste relationship). But he introduces it, misleadingly, as the day Holly "had the opportunity to save my life," intentionally steering our attention away from the emotional poignancy, a wistful combination of desire and loss that is both at the novella's center and nearly always pushed into the background. After the horse chase, the narrative cuts directly to the headlines and to a gossip column quoted at length. Only after reading it do we learn that, after the horseback adventure, they went to his apartment, where Holly was arrested; and then we see Joe Bell bring the newspapers that have already been quoted. This disruption of chronology breaks up a potentially monotonous progression (and then, and then, and then); more than that, it creates jolts of surprise followed by the satisfaction of explanation. More generally, rearranging information allows Capote to control the rhythm of the narrative without allegiance to the sequence of events. This may seem like a very modest sort of manipulation, but Capote's energetic and unpredictable movement through time in the novella creates a sense of excitement when, in fact, nothing much of dramatic consequence occurs. The novella is not, ultimately, about events; it's about an extraordinary young woman who captivated our narrator for a year or so, who looms large in memory, and who, if the narrative succeeds, captivates us as well.

At one point the narrator is in Holly's bedroom ("strewn, like a girl's gymnasium") as she searches for shoes, a blouse, a belt. "It was a subject to ponder," he tells us, "how, from such wreckage, she evolved the eventual effect." Capote's narrative, composed of compounded and rearranged scenes, partial memories, even scraps of trash, suggests some of the mechanics behind the magic.

To say that fiction relies on the conscious management of information might seem cold, manipulative; but the goal *is* something like magic—an orchestration of artifice intended to evoke genuine emotional response.

THE POETRY OF PROBLEMS

The Game of Chess is not merely an idle amusement. Several very valuable qualities of the mind, useful in the course of human life, are to be acquired and strengthened by it.... For life is a kind of Chess, in which we have often points to gain, and competitors or adversaries to contend with, and in which there is a vast variety of good and ill events that are, in some degree, the effect of prudence, or the want of it. By playing at Chess, then, we may learn ... Foresight ... Circumspection ... [and] Caution.

— BENJAMIN FRANKLIN, "The Morals of Chess"

Chess, long considered the ultimate game of abstract reasoning, has been the focus of any number of battles pitting Man against Machine: the wide variety of chess players and celebrities who took on the Turk; chess grandmaster Garry Kasparov vs. Deep Thought, Deep Blue, and Deeper Blue; and, say, a precocious twelve-year-old in the backseat of a car deeply engaged in a handheld computer chess game.

Georges Perec's *Life: A User's Manual*, told in ninety-nine chapters and an epilogue, is set in a Parisian apartment building in which one inhabitant, Bartlebooth, assembles fiendishly difficult jigsaw puzzles created from paintings he made as a young man. Perec wrote, "It would have been tedious to describe the building floor by floor and apartment by apartment; but that was no reason to leave the chapter sequence to chance. So I decided to use a principle derived from an old problem well known to chess enthusiasts as the Knight's tour; it requires moving a knight around the 64 squares of a chess-board without its ever landing more than once on the same square.... For the special case of *Life: A User's Manual* a solution for a 10 x 10 chess-board had to be found.... The division of the book into six parts was derived from the same principle: each time the knight has finished touching all four sides of the square, a new section begins." Perec's 10 x 10 Knight's Tour was diagrammed by Steve Hodges and redrawn by Daniel Thomasson, who highlighted the error, or departure from the strategy, between chapters 65 and 66.

According to Matthew Gidley, "Perec overlaid the knight's tour onto the ten-by-ten Graeco-Latin bi-square. Each box in which the knight landed gave coordinates referring to the 'schedule of obligations.' These lists provided the objects, emotions, places and periods in time which would feature within each chapter. One movement of the knight equalled one chapter. Secondly, Perec superimposed all of this onto the drawing of the townhouse to determine the location where the action would take place. The result was a sprawling, panoramic history of the house and its inhabitants, past and present."

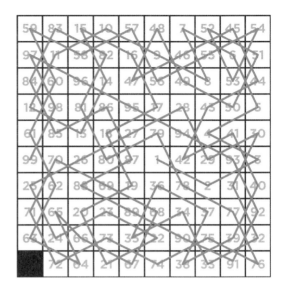

Chess problems are not (usually) moments or situations taken from actual matches; they are most often specially devised exercises. Rudimentary chess problems help beginners learn basic strategy, while more sophisticated problems challenge even experienced players. The creator of the problem establishes a situation (the specific white and black pieces and their positions on the board), a goal (usually to put the king in check or mate), and other constraints (most often, the number of moves allowed). "Problems," Nabokov wrote, "are the poetry of chess. They demand from the composer the same virtues that characterize all worthwhile art: originality, invention, harmony, conciseness, complexity, and splendid insincerity." While that consideration of "splendid insincerity" may sound uniquely Nabokovian, the creator of any puzzle or problem is, simultaneously, providing clues to the solution and trying to lead the solver astray. One of the pleasures of puzzles involves misdirection. Just as a magician withholds or conceals certain information (say, a pocket attached to a large sheet of paper) in order to create a particular effect (the sheet is torn into tiny pieces, stuffed into a fist, and an intact paper hat is produced), puzzle makers steer us toward false solutions, engaging us in a game of wits. These same tactics can even be found in a well-constructed jigsaw puzzle, as Georges Perec explains in the opening pages of *Life: A User's Manual*:

> The art of jigsaw puzzling begins with wooden puzzles cut by hand, whose maker undertakes to ask himself all of the questions the players will have to solve, and, instead of allowing chance to cover his tracks, aims to replace it with cunning, trickery, and subterfuge. All the elements occurring in the image to be reassembled ... serve by design as points of departure for trails that lead to false information. The organized, coherent, structured signifying space of the picture is cut up not only into inert, formless elements containing little information or signifying power, but also falsified elements, carrying false information.... From this, one can make a deduction which is quite certainly the ultimate truth of jigsaw puzzles: despite appearances, puzzling is not a solitary game: every move the puzzler makes, the puzzle-maker has made before; every piece the puzzler picks up, and picks up again, and studies and strokes, every combination he tries, and tries a second time, every blunder and every insight, each hope and each discouragement have all been designed, calculated, and decided by the other.

While Perec exaggerates the power of the puzzle maker (the puzzle solver could instead choose to ignore the puzzle, set fire to it, or mash it into paste and feed it to hippos), the essential notion—that the composer keeps his audience in mind and anticipates their reactions—holds true, as does the notion that a dedicated puzzle solver is engaged in conversation with the composer.[16] A puzzle presents a problem, and even if we pick one up for relaxation, we're choosing to engage with difficulty or conflict. A puzzle whose solution is immediately apparent isn't refreshing or enjoyable; it's "too easy." We feel neither exercised nor rewarded. The deception or distraction in a composition takes the place of the

16 In the documentary *Wordplay*, puzzle solvers as diverse as Jon Stewart, pitcher Mike Mussina, and Bill Clinton are shown talking back to the *New York Times* Sunday crossword as they work on it.

multiple possibilities, distractions, and arbitrariness of life. A fiction writer might not think she's deliberately misleading her reader, but she is, almost undoubtedly, trying to get her reader to imagine the various things that could happen (as opposed to the more limited number of things that do happen), the choices her characters could make, all the

The Chess Players,
by Jonathan Wolstenholme

possible stories that could follow from what's been set in place. If we can't imagine Elizabeth Bennet marrying Mr. Bingley or Mr. Collins—if *Pride and Prejudice* failed to help us anticipate what either of those marriages would do to Elizabeth—Jane Austen's novel would lose much of its tension and dramatic interest.

In addition to originality, invention, and conciseness, chess problem composers talk about illustrating one or more themes and, perhaps surprisingly, about aesthetic value. Marcel Duchamp famously said, "I have come to the conclusion that while all artists are not chess players, all chess players are artists." To some people, it comes as a surprise to hear puzzle makers, problem composers, scientists, and mathematicians talk about art and beauty. While the first goal is to create a functional puzzle or problem, or—in math and science—to solve a problem, the next goal is to achieve a combination of clarity, economy, and—in the case of puzzles—cleverness. That combination of qualities makes a composition ingenious, surprising in its simplicity. In math, in physics, and in computer science, among other fields, there are ugly solutions and elegant ones.[17]

[17] A solution can be elegant, though, only if it's also correct.

PATTERN RECOGNITION

In *Speak, Memory*, his autobiography, Nabokov describes his process for composing a chess problem, which serves as a metaphor for his composition of a novel:

> I would experience, without warning, a spasm of acute mental pleasure, as the bud of a chess problem burst open in my brain, promising me a night of labour and felicity. It might be a new way of blending an unusual strategic device with an unusual line of defence; it might be a glimpse, curiously stylized and thus incomplete, of the actual configuration that would render at last, with humour and grace, a difficult theme that I had despaired of expressing before; or it might be a mere gesture . . . suggesting new harmonies and new conflicts. . . .
>
> It is one thing to conceive the main play of a composition and another to construct it. The strain on the mind is formidable. . . . This or that knight is a lever adjusted and tried, and readjusted and tried again, till the problem is tuned up to the necessary level of beauty and surprise. . . . Competition

Will Shortz, puzzle editor of the *New York Times*, has been creating puzzles for National Public Radio since 1987. He recalls as one of his favorites a puzzle in which he lists two things in an unstated category. The solver is required to name the one other item in the same category that comes between the first two alphabetically. To solve "Florida and Hawaii," for instance, the solver would determine that the category is "United States" and then identify Georgia as the correct answer.

1. Thursday / Wednesday
2. Earth / Mars
3. Cleveland / Coolidge
4. Africa / Asia
5. Comet / Dancer
6. Neptunium / Niobium
7. Ecclesiastes / Exodus
8. Sagittarius / Taurus
9. Catcher / First base
10. Flush / Full house
11. Bashful / Dopey
12. Drummers drumming / Geese a-laying

"There are several reasons I like this puzzle," Shortz says. "One is that it's very accessible—anyone can try it. You don't have to be a puzzle whiz. Second, it plays with your mind in a weird way. It's kind of funny to think what comes between Thursday and Wednesday, for example, since we usually think of those things chronologically. And third, it's completely different from any puzzle that's come before it, at least as far as I know. I can't think of any earlier puzzle with an alphabetical constraint like this."

in chess problems is not really between White and Black but between the composer and the hypothetical solver (just as in a first-rate work of fiction the real clash is not between the characters but between the author and the world)....

But whatever I can say about this matter of problem composing, I do not seem to convey sufficiently the ecstatic core of the process ... the event is accompanied by a mellow physical satisfaction, especially when the chessmen are beginning to enact adequately, in a penultimate rehearsal, the composer's dream.

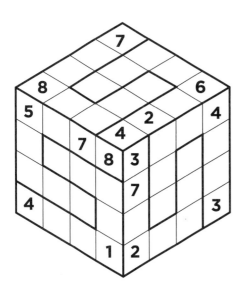

To solve this 3D grid sudoku by Thomas Snyder, place the digits 1–8 into the empty cells in the grid (a single digit per cell) so that each digit appears exactly once in each of the six outlined regions and the twelve "rows." A "row" follows the opposite, parallel sides of each quadrilateral.

While other writers might not feel they are engaging in competition with their readers, to the extent that the writer means to lead her reader somewhere new, along a route that contains at least a few surprises, even the friendliest writer anticipates and makes use of the reader's expectations. We all recognize the gap between conceiving "the main play of a composition," or the essence of a story, and actually constructing it. Just as puzzle composers have many ways of conversing with puzzle solvers, writers have many different ways of conversing with their readers.

The puzzles Nabokov embedded in his novels for his readers to solve go well beyond plot, and in many cases they are never explicitly stated. His particular game-playing depends on a like-minded reader. But while *Pale Fire* might seem far removed from *Bonfire of the Vanities*, every novel and story and poem—every piece of written communication—relies on certain assumptions about the reader, and what he or she will recognize and understand.

Exploit pattern recognition: I magically produce four silver dol-
lars, one at a time, with the back of my hand toward you. Then
I allow you to see the palm of my hand empty before a fifth coin
appears. As *Homo sapiens*, you grasp the pattern, and take away
the impression that I produced all five coins from a hand whose
palm was empty.

— TELLER

William Gibson's *Pattern Recognition* begins as a novel about a woman
consulting for a corporate client: "It's about a group behavior pattern
around a particular class of object. What I do is pattern recognition.
I try to recognize a pattern before anyone else does." Cayce Pollard's
particular talent is recognizing what will generate talk on the streets,
cultural and consumer excitement, and she operates so instinctively that
she refuses to provide any explanation of her judgments; she's paid to say
yes or no. Her current task is the rebranding of one of the world's largest
manufacturers of athletic shoes. She's been asked to pass judgment on a
new logo, a symbol intended to speak wordlessly, internationally. At the
same time, she's caught up in an online community devoted to something they call "the footage"—bits of film released via the Internet by an
unknown person for unknown reasons. Some speculate that the bits of
footage are from a complete work; others believe they're from a work
in progress; others debate whether the pieces are part of a single whole.
"The footage" is a puzzle Cayce and others would like to solve. Also early
in the novel, Cayce realizes that someone has broken into the apartment
that she's borrowing—and that a woman who works for another company knows far more about her than she can explain.

   On the level of plot, then, Gibson establishes a number of puzzles that
are eventually solved. But the theme of pattern recognition is conveyed
in the prose as well. Gibson makes use of sentence fragments, or partial
sentences, assuming the reader will recognize common syntactical patterns. He also mixes real and fictitious place names and product names,
and familiar and newly coined slang and acronyms. Cayce refers to England, where she's working, as a "mirror-world" of the United States,
where she lives, with some things identical, some familiar but not quite

the same (coins, the heft of a phone). Gibson reminds us that every work of fiction is a mirror-world (the term draws us, inevitably, to *Alice's Adventures in Wonderland*, written by the mathematician and puzzle composer Lewis Carroll). As we read, we compare the world of the fiction to the world we live in. We look for similarities, note differences. This is true not only when we read realistic fiction, where we expect a more direct correspondence to "reality," but when we read science fiction, fantasy, historical novels, and post-realistic fiction. How does what we read look like other things we've read? If we recognize *Pattern Recognition*'s allusions to *Alice in Wonderland*, what parallels do we draw? How do they inform our reading? If we're familiar with other William Gibson novels, we might feel a similarity in voice and tone. If we're not, we consciously or subconsciously draw connections of our own, quite possibly even to books and stories William Gibson has never read. As another character tells Cayce,

> Musicians today, if they're clever, put new compositions out on the web, like pies set to cool on a window ledge, and wait for other people to anonymously rework them. Ten will be all wrong, but the eleventh may be genius. And free. It's as though the creative process is no longer contained within an individual skull, if indeed it ever was. Everything, today, is to some extent the reflection of something else.

Musical sampling, mash-ups, remixes of songs, and fan fiction may have us more aware than ever that every creative work is completed, or interpreted, by its audience, but the human tendency to see the self reflected in the world goes back at least as far as Narcissus—and of course the myth of Narcissus, which was familiar when Ovid retold it, is a story that means to reflect a recognizable human trait. We read fiction, in part, to see our world reflected. Richard Adams's *Watership Down* might be about rabbits, but we care about those rabbits only because they have very human concerns. On the other hand, we might refer to a situation as a Catch-22 because we recognize the phenomenon Joseph Heller labeled in his best-known novel when we see it in our daily lives. As readers we're able to understand—to decode—a new book or story or poem thanks in part to our life experience, and in part to all of the other books and stories we've read.

As writers, we assume our readers will be familiar with certain patterns, or conventions, though those might be very general. In Gibson's novel, when we find out that someone has broken in to the apartment Cayce is using, we anticipate that the break-in will be connected to her job and/or to her interest in "the footage." Why? Because our experience with fiction has conditioned us to expect that significant but apparently disparate events will ultimately be connected. This sort of pattern recognition occurs in the most conventional fiction—consciously or not, we all respond to the cues in a Hollywood film that tell us a certain character isn't to be trusted—as well as in the most innovative or challenging fiction. "Difficult" fiction often seems difficult because of the way it delays or refuses to provide the kinds of connection—the patterns—we're used to. The puzzle is unfamiliar, and its rules may not be immediately apparent.

Carole Maso's collage novel *The Art Lover* is written in many short sections—some less than a page. The book has three distinct sets of characters, the text is often accompanied by unexplained images, and the captions to some of the images are often obscured or fragmentary, such as clippings torn from a newspaper. It takes even the most attentive reader a while to understand that the first character we're introduced to, Allison, and her family, are characters in a novel being written by Caroline, another character in the book, whose father has recently died; and it isn't until late in the book that Maso introduces the true story of the death of her friend, the artist Gary Falk. Carole Maso is reflecting her real-life loss in the story of the writer Caroline, who is in turn mirroring her loss of her father in the story of Allison. At times it might feel that, like Alice, we're falling through the looking glass. But the book is arranged in six chronological sections, and very early our attention is drawn to significant images, including a starburst and fiddlehead ferns. Because we don't have the traditional continuity of plot and character to guide us, we read Maso's novel alert for repetitions of those images and indirect references to them. In this way, a writer can rely on something like insight thinking on the part of the reader. As readers, we're encouraged to focus on information—details, images—that might merely be part of the setting in another novel but which will serve another role here; we're forced to compare characters and to consider a variety of potential metaphors; and we're asked to combine what we're told to understand something larger. The repetition of images, the formal arrangement of material, and the relationships among the three sets of characters are pieces of a puzzle, and they serve to organize the book. While *The Art Lover* doesn't look quite like most novels we read, and might initially seem frustrating, it offers distinct patterns the reader is led to recognize.

Benjamin Franklin was wrong (and no doubt knew it): mathematical novelties aren't useless. Latin Squares were not invented, or created, to give us something to do during plane rides. They were famously explored by a contemporary of Franklin's, the Swiss mathematician Leonhard Euler, and they have been particularly useful in controlling variables in experiments. Among other achievements, in 1736 Euler solved a prob-

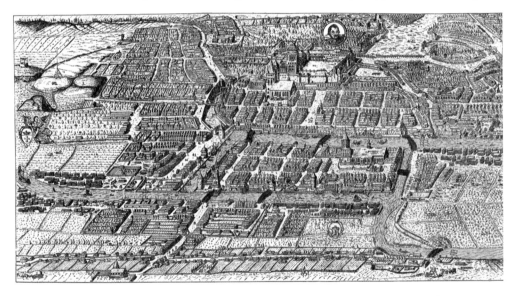

lem known as the Seven Bridges of Königsberg. The city that was once Königsberg, Prussia, is beside the Pregel River and at that time included two large islands, which were connected to each other and the mainland by seven bridges. One day, some thoughtful person—probably a writer, procrastinating—wondered whether it was possible to walk a route that crossed each bridge exactly once and return to the starting point. (You can try it for yourself by using a pencil to draw a continuous line on the illustration, crossing each bridge just once and returning to where you begin.) Trial and error seemed to indicate that it wasn't possible; but Euler abstracted the problem to one of nodes (the bits of land) and links (the bridges). This allowed him to determine under what circumstances it is possible to make a single complete circuit among any given number of nodes and links and under what circumstances it is not. His solution is the first theorem of graph theory and eventually led to the establishment of topology, a branch of mathematics concerned with the property of networks.

In other words: a mathematician took a situation in the real world, turned it into a puzzle, solved it, looked for a larger pattern, or recurrent circumstance, and then applied his understanding of that circumstance to other real-world situations. This is how the kinds of puzzles contemplated not only by mathematicians but by biologists, physicists, astronomers, ecologists, and economists are not merely amusing, or trifling, but useful. They serve as models of experience. In the same way, a poem or novel or story reflects a real-world situation, character, problem, or idea in a way that allows us to consider it, and perhaps even understand it, differently. When Chekhov wrote that the artist's job is to pose the question correctly, he was essentially saying that the artist, like Euler, must stand back and see the essence of the problem or the issue at hand; then he must find a way to frame it that focuses the reader's attention on that essence.

All writers are puzzle makers. As models of our experience, stories and novels aim not to reduce that experience, or to simplify it, but to reflect its pleasures and sorrows, and to bring its mysteries into sharp focus.

SEVEN CLEVER PIECES

So, how do the pieces of a life fit together?

— JAN KJÆRSTAD

Around 1760, a London engraver and cartographer carefully affixed one of his maps to a thin sheet of mahogany and, using a fine-bladed saw, proceeded to cut it to pieces.

John Spilsbury wasn't intent on destruction; he had cut carefully along the borders of each country. He called the result a "dissected map" and hoped it would serve as an educational tool, a sort of geography game, for children. He could not have guessed that, 250 years later, inexpensive jigsaw puzzles would be available in virtually every grocery store and drugstore, or that they'd be commonplace in hospitals and hospices and beach houses. He might also be surprised to learn that the quality of physical interaction and connectivity he had given to his map is preserved even in many online jigsaw puzzles, still composed of pieces shaped as if they had been cut from wood.

It may be equally hard for us to imagine that roughly a century ago jigsaw puzzles were, for a brief period, the Cabbage Patch Dolls, the Beanie Babies, the Harry Potter novels, or the Angry Birds of their day. In 1908 a *New York Times* headline read "New Puzzle Menaces the City's Sanity."

Jigsaw puzzles weren't just popular; they were the focus of parties in high society, they spawned clubs and rental libraries, they were sold by subscription, and entire factories were converted in order to mass-produce them. Like so many consumer goods, they became an indicator of class and social standing, as high-quality jigsaw puzzles were (and are) hand-cut from wood, some with unique and even customized shapes,

John Spilsbury's "dissected map" of Europe

while inexpensive puzzles were eventually die-cut from cardboard by the thousands. Gender roles were a factor as well, as the craze began with women and children constructing puzzles largely cut by women, in home workshops; by 1909 large manufacturers were taking over, including Parker Brothers, which hired women to cut a minimum of 1,400 pieces by hand each day. While the original craze passed by 1910, the passion returned during the Great Depression, when over ten million puzzles were sold in a week.[18]

18 Other tremendously popular diversions during the Depression included miniature golf and the board game Monopoly. Difficult times drive at least some of us to new forms of amusement.

A MUSE AND A MAZE

While some jigsaw puzzles are still designed as educational tools for children, the great majority are made for idle diversion. (Those early fans of jigsaws enjoyed an additional challenge: no picture of the completed puzzle was included. They discovered the image they were constructing as they gave it shape.) And yet somehow a jigsaw puzzle has become a common metaphor for any kind of assembly, particularly one that involves patiently putting many pieces in their proper place to form a whole.

So, how do the pieces of a life fit together? Or, to put it another way, do they fit together at all?

— JAN KJÆRSTAD

About the time jigsaw puzzles were captivating Americans and, back across the Atlantic, the British, thirty-year-old Graham Greene set off on an extraordinary adventure: a four-week walk through the interior of Liberia. In *Journey Without Maps*, his account of the trip, he says he was in search of "something lost": "The 'heart of darkness,' if one is romantically inclined, or more simply, one's place in time, based on a knowledge not only of one's present but of the past from which one has emerged. . . . A quality of darkness is needed, of the inexplicable. . . . One sometimes has a curiosity to discover if one can from what we have come, to recall at which point we went astray."

Early in the book, Greene writes about the night he saw a young woman sitting at one end of a bar, drinking and crying. The section begins, "A reminder of darkness: the girl in the Queen's bar. . . . I hadn't the nerve to say anything [to her] and find out the details. . . . Besides, it's always happening all the time everywhere. You don't weep unless you've been happy first; tears always mean something enviable."

In the next few paragraphs Greene is moved to reflect on three other memories of darkness: a trip he took to Berlin, where he saw "a man and woman . . . copulating . . . under a street lamp, like two people who are supporting and comforting each other in the pain of some sickness";

his first memory, of a dead dog his nurse picked up out of the street and put at the bottom of the baby carriage he was riding in; and his first awareness of "the pleasure of cruelty," which he discovered at the age of fourteen, related to adolescent lust. "There was a girl lodging close by I wanted to do things to," he tells us. "I could think about pain as something desirable and not something dreaded. It was as if I had discovered that the way to enjoy life was to appreciate pain."

Then, without transition, he returns to the scene of the girl at the bar: "She embarrassed everybody. They cleared a space. . . . I thought for some reason even then of Africa, not a particular place, but a shape, a strangeness, a wanting to know. . . . The shape, of course, is roughly that of the human heart." Pain, darkness, the origin of man, the relationship of tears to happiness, the inexplicable, and the desire to understand both oneself and others are all bound together in those unsettling opening images. The crucial tension is between "wanting to know" and resisting the urge to talk to the young woman who was crying—or rather, between whatever explanation she might have offered and something both more fundamental and more mysterious about human suffering.

At the very outset, in an epigraph to his book, Greene acknowledges an essential dilemma at the core of his quest for understanding. The quotation comes from miscellaneous notes and reminiscences by Oliver Wendell Holmes:

> The life of an individual is in many respects like a child's dissected map. If I could live a hundred years, keeping my intelligence to the last, I feel as if I could put the pieces together until they made a properly connected whole. As it is, I, like all others, find a certain number of connected fragments, and a larger number of disjointed pieces, which I might in time place in their natural connection. Many of these pieces seem fragmentary, but would in time show themselves as essential parts of the whole. What strikes me very forcibly is the arbitrary and as it were accidental way in which the lines of junction appear to run irregularly among the fragments. With every decade I find some new pieces coming into place. Blanks which have been left in former years find their complement

among the undisturbed fragments. If I could look back on the whole, as we look at the child's map when it is put together, I feel that I should have my whole life intelligently laid out before me.

Holmes is explicitly addressing the challenge of autobiography. "Who am I?" he is asking. "Who have I been? How have I become who I am?" With a change in pronouns, these questions are also essential to biography; and they are often just beneath the surface of fictional narratives.

When we sit down to write a story or novel and begin to imagine our characters, we typically work to gain a deep understanding of them. We strive to "assemble" their lives. We're likely to find "new pieces coming into place"; we find connections among the blank spaces and the fragments; we may even, eventually, find the "whole laid intelligently out before" us.

To gain such a comprehensive view of characters, the people in a fictional world, might seem like the ultimate goal. But the crucial elements of Holmes's quotation are its conditional statements: "I find *a certain number* of connected fragments"; "I *might*" put them in their natural connection; "*If* I could look back on the whole . . . *I feel I should* have my whole life intelligently laid out before me." If only we could stand back far enough, if only we had enough time, if only we could find the right point of view, if only we could determine what shape allows all the pieces to fit—if only we could do all of that, we would understand. All the pieces of the dissected map of the self would find a place, all the blanks would be filled. The image would be complete.

Inherent in Holmes's assertion is the belief that it can't be done.

Jigsaw puzzles feature prominently in Orson Welles's *Citizen Kane*. Kane's disenchanted wife, Susan, passes the time assembling puzzles of outdoor scenes, yearning to escape the mansion he claims to have built for her. As in *The Thin Man*, assembling a jigsaw puzzle is used as a metaphor for assembling a story: in this case, the life of Charles Foster Kane. Mystery has gathered around Kane's dying word, "Rosebud," and a woman suggests

Susan Alexander
passing time, puzzling
over her husband

The jigsaw puzzle
of objects and artifacts
left behind by
Charles Foster Kane

to Jerry Thompson, the investigative reporter trying to learn all he can about the man, "If you could have found out what Rosebud meant, I bet that would have explained everything." This counterargument to Holmes has something in common with claims made by over-reaching counselors and psychotherapists: if only you can recognize why you're angry at your mother, if only you correctly interpret your dreams, your problems can be solved. Through a moment of dramatic irony, *Citizen Kane* manages to have it both ways. We, the viewers, see the name "Rosebud" on Kane's boyhood sled as it burns in an incinerator, but none of the characters in the film do—at least none who are aware that the name was Kane's final utterance. Like Nick Charles in *The Thin Man*, Thompson knows from experience that the human psyche is not so neatly packaged: "Maybe Rosebud was something he couldn't get or something he lost," he says. "Anyway, it wouldn't have explained anything. I don't think any word can explain a man's life." As in a Chekhov story, the viewer is given what appears to be a final piece to the puzzle, then left to decide what, if anything, it resolves.

Once one image is placed against another, once a particular song is paired with a particular set of images, you see how they interact, how they come to life. It's something like the pieces of a DNA sequence coming together.

— MARTIN SCORSESE, on his documentary about George Harrison

To the extent that a piece of fiction focuses on character, we might think of it as a fictitious biography or autobiography. A key to writing a biography is to find the story of the life—to make sense of the whole. The biographer, like the fiction writer, sees a shape, sees a way to understand the character, and then sets about ordering information, emphasizing some things, deemphasizing or even eliminating others, in order to present the reader with a particular understanding of the person.

At least, that's one way a biography can work. So we have biographies of Thomas Jefferson the statesman, Jefferson the architect, Jefferson the author of the Declaration of Independence, Jefferson the inventor, Jefferson the American hero, Jefferson the slave owner, and Jefferson the hypocrite, among many others. As interesting as any of those books might be, the fiction writer recognizes there's something wrong; the clear view of the subject we're offered is the product of simplification and distortion.

The more interesting story, the truer story, is the one that attempts to capture all those fascinating, perhaps not clearly related, even contradictory aspects of the man. That story would engage the reader in the challenge of understanding, refusing to resolve the contradictions, refusing to reduce the highly complex individual to a simpler one. If what we want is a deeper truth, a biography that allows for the possibility that Jefferson was, in addition to many other things, a great statesman, a brilliant writer, and a slaveholder who fathered children with one of his slaves—a biography that acknowledges a complicated life—we have to surrender some of the comforting reduction those other versions offer. The patience and willingness to embrace complexity seems particularly important these days, when much of the rhetoric of business and politics is devoted to reducing and simplifying people and problems. Easy understanding comes at a high price. One of the things fiction and poetry can do is to remind us of the value of refusing to rush to judgment, the need not just to recognize, but to accept, complexity and mystery.

Characterization is achieved ... through a process that opens up and releases mysteries of the human spirit. The object is not to "solve" a character—to expose some hidden secret—but instead to deepen and enlarge the riddle itself.

— TIM O'BRIEN

A great deal of fiction is about the tension between who a character is and who he wants to be; between who he is and who he believes himself to be; or about a character in transition, such as the standard coming-of-age story. When fiction emphasizes the tension between a character's two or more selves, when it dwells on the fact that multiple selves exist simultaneously, when it refuses to settle for a single or fully explicable depiction of character, it makes use of what we might call unresolved characterization.

Unresolved characters result when a piece of writing emphasizes the challenge of trying to assemble the pieces and on recognizing the unfilled spaces. The narrative draws our attention to the fact that some pieces are missing, never to be found, as well as to the fact that some pieces seem not to fit. The focus is on stress fractures in the surface of character, places where the tectonic plates of personality shift, collide, and reveal something new. Unresolved characterization is an attempt to represent what Graham Greene calls that "strangeness, or wanting to know" without "solving the problem." Unresolved characterization frames the questions that define a character.

There is a large body of fiction that does this, and it includes some of the greatest American novels, including *Moby-Dick*, *The Great Gatsby*, and *Lolita*. It also includes books as varied as Joseph Conrad's *Heart of Darkness*, James Salter's *A Sport and a Pastime*, and Alison Bechdel's graphic memoir *Fun Home*. We focus, in *The Great Gatsby*, on who a man says he is, what he does, who he was, who he wants to become, and why; we focus, in *Lolita*, on the tension between what a man has done, why he says he's done it, who he says he is, and what we think of him—and on a girl, the man's fantasy of who that girl is, or might be, who he thinks he knows she is, and who she became. In all of those books, the main character, the first-person narrator, is ostensibly telling the story of a mysterious figure, a mythical or fantastic or heroic or tragic character; at the same time, and with different degrees of consciousness, the narrator is investigating and revealing him- or herself. In every case, the presumed subject of the narrative—Ahab, Jay Gatsby, Delores Haze, Kurtz, Philip Dean, Bechdel's father—remains elusive. In most cases, as the narrators tell their tales, they too are exposed as curiously complicated, mysterious, perhaps not entirely trustworthy. Even after we read the final page, these characters remain unknown in some essential way. The story or novel actively provokes and prolongs our wondering.

To call these characters "unresolved" is not to suggest that something about the writing is incomplete. An unresolved character is not one the author has failed to explore or understand. Rather, an unresolved character is one that the author has explored deeply, depicted in some detail, come to understand—and then explored more deeply. That sense of wonder can be provoked by absences—things that haven't been explained for us—and by ambiguity and contradictions: multiple, competing understandings of character. Like Holly Golightly, such characters resist being pinned to the page. The writer's goal is to present a person in fiction with something approaching the complexity, the irreducibility, of people in life—the people who most fascinate us.

Twilight, by Charles Ritchie

Because Charles Ritchie's primary subject has been his neighborhood as seen from his home studio, and because he typically works very early in the morning, many of his images depict scenes perceived in dim light, either at night or in the very first light of day. Twilight occurs between daylight, when we can see clearly, and night, when, without the moon or artificial light, we can see almost nothing. In twilight, we strain to perceive. We can't be absolutely certain whether we're seeing what's actually in front of us or if we're seeing what we know is there, or think is there, or imagine could be there. "If night obscures, and day reveals," Ritchie has said, "the transition between them explores nuances of presence and absence."

One of Ritchie's largest drawings is *Blue Twilight*. The houses in *Twilight* reappear, toward the bottom of the image, but they're dwarfed by an enormous tulip poplar. In its equal illumination of the scene, the image presents a distorted or extended twilight.

The print of *Blue Twilight*—the result of those nine months spent etching the image, in reverse, into copper, using a scalpel—allows for a

Blue Twilight drawing,
by Charles Ritchie

Blue Twilight print,
by Charles Ritchie

more natural gradation of light. Stare as hard as we might at the bottom of the image, those houses won't come into full focus. We know they're there, we try to see them, but we can't, quite. The visual information ends; we've reached the limits of sensory understanding. As a result, we're forced to contemplate anew what we can only glimpse in twilight.

We tell ourselves we know people well (some people, at least). Our sense of them is based on what we can see clearly, or what we think we see. Visually and psychologically, we might be able to detect more about them than they can see themselves, but there will always be parts of their interior lives that remain inaccessible.

STRATEGIC OPACITY

Shakespeare found that he could immeasurably deepen the effect of his plays, that he could provoke in the audience and in himself a peculiarly passionate intensity of response, if he took out a key explanatory element, hereby occluding the rationale, motivation, or ethical principle that accounted for the action that was to unfold. The principle was not the making of a riddle to be solved, but the creation of a strategic opacity. This opacity, Shakespeare found, released an enormous energy that had been at least partially blocked or contained by familiar reassuring explanations.

— STEPHEN GREENBLATT

19 As I write this, a former National Football League player charged with murder is in jail awaiting trial. In the days immediately following his arrest, several newspaper columnists argued that the team that signed him should have known what was coming, as the player had admitted to smoking marijuana in college. Others suggested that his alleged act could be explained by the fact that his father had died several years earlier. This sort of hasty, nonsensical connecting of dots goes on all the time.

Greenblatt's statement is helpful to consider but potentially misleading. The key isn't to take out a true "explanatory element," so simply withhold a piece of information; rather, it's to reveal information that makes impossible the "familiar reassuring explanation," the sort of easy answer provided by pop psychology and genre fiction.[19] To see complex characters brought fully to life and yet left unresolved, and to see strategic opacity at work in the depiction of an individual, it will be useful to look at an example or two in detail.

Jay Gatsby, the golden boy, the millionaire party host, is a projection, one as vivid and insubstantial as any image carried by light onto a silver screen. What F. Scott Fitzgerald's novel examines, brilliantly, are the distortions in that projection, its inaccuracies and inconsistencies as well as its shallowness. The novel's narrator, Nick Carraway, is deeply and rewardingly fascinated by what's wrong with the picture—the doubts and insecurities that make it impossible for young James Gatz to play the role of Jay Gatsby successfully and which, ultimately, reveal Jay Gatsby to be a misguided creation.

When Midwestern Nick takes a job in New York, he finds himself living alone in a commuting town, West Egg. He's invited to have dinner with his cousin, Daisy, where he learns her friend, the golfer Jordan Baker, knows Nick's neighbor—the owner of the mansion next door. That very night, when he returns home, Nick sees a man he assumes must be Gatsby "emerge from the shadow" and then "vanish."

Every reader of the novel knows that the title character is presented as two people: wealthy Jay Gatsby, host of lavish parties, and the former Jimmy Gatz, son of poor farmers, intent on making good. Late in the narrative, Nick imagines the moment of transformation:

> It was James Gatz [of North Dakota] who had been loafing along the beach that afternoon in a torn green jersey and a pair of canvas pants, but it was already Jay Gatsby who borrowed a rowboat....He'd had the name ready for a long time....His parents were shiftless and unsuccessful farm people—his imagination had never really accepted them as his parents at all....So he invented just the sort of Jay Gatsby that a seventeen-year-old boy would be likely to invent, and to this conception he was faithful to the end.

But that transformation doesn't quite take. The novel is ultimately less interested in *how* James Gatz became Jay Gatsby than in *why*, and Gatz/Gatsby's own answer is not the most revealing one. A different book might focus on Gatsby's unveiling, the climactic showdown in the New York hotel room when Tom Buchanan aims to expose the truth. (Many lesser books do just that. This sort of "moment of truth" routinely appears in fiction that is more puzzle than mystery.) But just as Truman Capote refuses to reduce Holly Golightly to an eighteen-year-old blonde, and as Graham Greene resists any easy explanation for why a woman in a bar is crying, Fitzgerald insists that we consider Gatsby from many angles, to try to understand what he wants and whether it's worth the wanting. We could say Nick Carraway plays the role of Gatsby's biographer, trying to "put the pieces together until they make a properly connected whole." There are many gaps and, as Nick learns, many possible ways to assemble the pieces. By the end, Nick believes he's solved the puzzle—he feels he knows who Gatsby is and what he represents. But the novel allows us to see both less and more than Nick sees.

Who is Jay Gatsby? The novel offers many answers. They take the form of descriptions, facts or apparent facts, and assessments provided by other characters:

- "A man of about my age."
- "A regular Belasco." [David Belasco was an actor and playwright known for creating elaborate realistic effects on stage.]
- "A person of some *undefined* consequence."
- "Simply the proprietor of an elaborate road-house."
- "Fine fellow ... Handsome to look at and a perfect gentleman ... A man of fine breeding."
- "A penniless young man without a past."
- A man who "dispensed starlight to casual moths."
- A "regular tough underneath it all."
- "A strained counterfeit of perfect ease."
- "An ecstatic patron of recurrent light."
- "Mr. Nobody from Nowhere.... I picked him for a bootlegger the first time I saw him, and I wasn't far wrong."
- A lieutenant in the First Division, promoted to be a major, with decorations from every Allied government, including Montenegro.
- A student janitor at St. Olaf.
- A "poor son-of-a-bitch."
- Trimalchio. [In *The Satyricon*, Trimalchio, a former slave married to a chorus girl, devotes himself to lavish feasts and self-indulgence.]

Even when we see him firsthand, through Nick, Gatsby is enigmatic, an apparition:

> [He had] one of those rare smiles with a quality of eternal re-assurance in it, that you might come across four or five times in life. It faced—or seemed to face—the whole eternal world for an instant, and then concentrated on *you* with an irresistible prejudice in your favor.... It understood you just so far as you wanted to be understood, believed in you as you would like to believe in yourself, and assured you that it had precisely the impression of you that, at your best, you hoped to convey. Precisely at that point it vanished—and I was looking at an elegant young rough-neck, a year or two over thirty, whose elaborate formality of speech just missed being absurd.

So Gatsby isn't just James Gatz with money—even in the present, he's at least two people. And even he seems to recognize a flaw in the presentation: "He talked a lot about the past, and I gathered that he wanted to recover something, some idea of himself.... His life had been confused and disordered since then, but if he could once return to a certain starting place and go over it all slowly, he could find out what that thing was." This is Gatsby's crisis on the last night of his life—a crisis of identity. It resembles the crisis of adolescence, the crisis of middle age, and the perhaps quieter, ongoing crisis of living.

That last quotation comes from Nick's recollection of his final conversation with Gatsby, the night before he is murdered. In it we can hear clear echoes of Oliver Wendell Holmes: "He wanted to recover something, some idea of himself.... His life had been ... disordered"—or dissected, like that child's jigsaw puzzle—"but if he could once return to a certain starting place and go over it all slowly, he could find out what that thing was." Again, the conditional phrase underscores both the yearning and the impossibility of the task. Gatsby cannot recover that clear view of himself, the one that has been shattered, and that would have been shattered even if Daisy had agreed to leave Tom. Without the dream of some fantasy life with Daisy, Jimmy Gatz/Jay Gatsby doesn't know who he is. Having devoted himself to an illusion, he is profoundly lost.

While we eventually learn about his past, and we know something about how he acquired his wealth, Gatsby remains distant; and, on closer inspection, we realize that most of what we think we know about Gatsby's desires and motivations is conjecture, speculation asserted as knowledge by Nick.

Gatsby doesn't appear in a scene in the first quarter of the novel. Up until that point, we've seen him—Nick has seen him—only from afar, standing behind his house briefly in the dark. Much of the opening of the book isn't even about Gatsby—it's about Daisy and Tom and Jordan and, ultimately, about Nick. In telling this story, Nick Carraway is trying to stand back far enough, to see clearly enough, to assemble another whole: his own life. Specifically, Nick is trying to document, for himself and for us, what happened, why he feels the way he does about it, and what it means. He believes it changed him.

But who *is* Nick Carraway? Nick's voice is so persuasive, and his perspective is so central to the novel, that we can be forgiven if, on first reading, we regard Nick as he'd like us to regard him: as the one sane, grounded, moral voice amid what he keeps calling "riotous" people in a "riotous" summer. We live in the world as we imagine it, and our imagining influences everything we see. Nick alone is cautious and deliberate and responsible and trustworthy—or so he'd like us to think.

But Nick Carraway is a bachelor, a Yale graduate who returned to his native Midwest until, he tells us, he became restless, and decided to go east to learn the bond business. Why? Because everyone he knows is in the bond business, he says; because, at the age of twenty-nine, Nick has no idea what to do with himself. Nick is miserable in New York, and he leaves at summer's end. He accuses Tom and Daisy of drifting restlessly, but that same shoe fits him.

From the famous first lines of the novel to its more famous last lines, Nick Carraway presents himself as a figure of authority, a guide, the one person who truly understands these people he means to tell us about; but Nick is a kind of genteel slacker, a well-educated young man without clear aim or ambition. In addition to the extraordinary prose style provided by his creator, Nick's virtues as a narrator include the facts that he has strong and sometimes contradictory opinions and that he is engaged in deep internal conflicts, at least some of which he appears not to recognize.

One of the many things Nick doesn't want us to think about, and that *he* doesn't want to think about—he provides the information only after Daisy raises the subject—is that he came east in part because of a rumor circulating about his engagement to an old friend. Nick doesn't reveal much about his relationships with women, and he would rather we not look too closely at them. His avoidance of the topic in a narrative prompted by romantic desire is curious, and draws the careful reader's attention.

Nick asserts that his cardinal virtue is honesty. He says that, interestingly enough, by way of explaining why he can't enter into a serious relationship with Jordan Baker. "I'd been writing letters once a week and signing them: 'Love, Nick' … there was a vague understanding that had to be tactfully broken off before I was free.… I am one of the few honest people that I have ever known." But just two pages earlier he told us: "I … had a short affair with a girl who lived in Jersey City and worked in the accounting department, but her brother began throwing mean looks in my direction, so … I let it blow quietly away." The fact that he was writing his friend back home letters signed "Love, Nick" didn't stop him from having an affair with that girl in accounting, so his rationalization regarding Jordan is questionable at best. If he were a courtroom witness, it wouldn't take much of a lawyer to point out other, similar contradictions in Nick's story. He simultaneously acknowledges his interest in Jordan and all but denies it.

> Jordan Baker instinctively avoided clever, shrewd men, and now
> I saw that this was because she felt safer on a plane where any
> divergence from a code would be thought impossible. She was
> incurably dishonest … [but that] made no difference to me.

That's an interesting assertion, coming from a man who prides himself on his honesty. Elsewhere he tells us, "I wasn't actually in love, but I felt a sort of tender curiosity"; "I thought I loved her"; and "I'd had enough of all of them for one day, and suddenly that included Jordan, too" (the implication being that, until then, he hadn't had enough of her). Toward the end of the novel he tells us, "Angry, and half in love with her, and tremendously sorry, I turned away."

What's significant about Nick's inability to decide on or admit to his true feelings toward Jordan is that he doesn't recognize his confused and contradictory statements. He doesn't seem aware of the pattern he's revealed whereby he enters into a relationship only to back out because neighbors gossip about marriage, or a woman's brother looks at him cross-eyed; he doesn't recognize that the woman who most appeals to him, the one he banters with and who shares his horror at displays of emotion, is Daisy; and he doesn't realize that his inability to commit himself to a relationship with a woman, and his inability to decide where to live and what profession to pursue, is directly tied to the loneliness and deep romanticism that he ascribes to Gatsby.

Nick's feelings about Gatsby, too, are greatly conflicted.

"I'm inclined to reserve all judgments," he tells us; but he goes on to say, "Gatsby . . . represented everything for which I have an unaffected scorn." And yet, "If personality is an unbroken series of successful gestures, then there was something gorgeous about him . . . an extraordinary gift for hope, a romantic readiness such as I have never found in any other person and which it is not likely I shall ever find again." And "Gatsby turned out all right at the end."

When Gatsby explains that he was a student in Oxford for five months, Nick tells us he had "one of those renewals of complete faith in him that I'd experienced before." He has "complete faith" in a man who represents everything for which he feels "unaffected scorn"? Nick's image of Gatsby is in flux—the jigsaw pieces keep moving, or even changing shape. Not much later he says, "I disliked him so much by this time that I didn't find it necessary to tell him he was wrong." Still later—after feeling scorn for him, after reaffirming "complete faith" in him, after disliking him—Nick expresses one of his most explicit contradictions:

> I didn't want to leave Gatsby. . . . "They're a rotten crowd," I shouted across the lawn. "You're worth the whole damn bunch put together."
>
> I've always been glad I said that. It was the only compliment I ever gave him, because I disapproved of him from beginning to end.

A MUSE AND A MAZE

If Nick so strongly disapproves of his neighbor, why, when Gatsby has been killed, does Nick say, "I found myself on Gatsby's side, and alone.... It grew upon me that I was responsible, because no one else was interested.... I wanted to go into the room where he lay and reassure him: 'I'll get somebody for you, Gatsby. Don't worry.'"

Nick takes on that responsibility out of loyalty, and out of a sense of friendship he finds it very difficult to admit to.

Jay Gatsby is an unresolved character because our views of him are limited and contradictory.[20] Nick's view of Gatsby is given greatest authority, and it's compelling, but the novel reminds us that other characters see him in other ways. Depending on where we stand, we might see Gatsby the bootlegger, Gatsby the wealthy available bachelor, Gatsby the romantic dreamer, or Gatsby the lost boy in a suit of gold. Like Meyer Wolfsheim, Nick makes his own Gatsby for his own purposes. Even then, his view is conflicted.

Nick's conflicted view of Gatsby is one of the indications that he, too, is unresolved.

The key to understanding the complexity of Nick's story isn't the novel's introduction, in which he tells us that others confide in him, or the conclusion, in which he compares Gatsby to Dutch sailors approaching the New World; those are consciously crafted statements, ideas Nick has formed and polished. What's most revealing is a confession that slips out almost as an aside:

> I began to like New York, the racy, adventurous feel of it at night, and the satisfaction that the constant flicker of men and women and machines gives to the restless eye. I liked to walk up Fifth Avenue and *pick out romantic women from the crowd and imagine that in a few minutes I was going to enter into their lives, and no one would ever know or disapprove.* Sometimes, in my mind, I followed them to their apartments on the corners of hidden streets, and they turned and smiled back at me before they faded through a door into a warm darkness. At

20 In earlier drafts of the novel, Fitzgerald told the reader less about Gatsby's past but had Gatsby explain himself more explicitly. In the draft published as *Trimalchio* by Cambridge University Press, Gatsby says things like "It's all so sad," and "I might be a great man if I could forget that once I lost Daisy.... I used to think wonderful things were going to happen to me," and "Daisy's all I've got left from a world so wonderful that to think of it makes me sick all over," and perhaps worst of all, "I thought for awhile I had a lot of things, but the truth is I'm empty, and I guess people feel it. That must be why they keep on making up things about me, so I won't be so empty. I even make up things myself." By adding biographical information and removing self-analysis, Fitzgerald deepened the mystery around the character.

the enchanted metropolitan twilight I felt a haunting loneliness sometimes, and felt it in others—poor young clerks who loitered in front of windows waiting until it was time for a solitary restaurant dinner—young clerks in the dusk, wasting the most poignant moments of night and life. Again at eight o'clock . . . I felt a sinking in my heart . . . there was laughter from unheard jokes. . . . Imagining that I, too, was hurrying towards gaiety and sharing their excitement, I wished them well.

In hindsight, we understand that the romantic person from the crowd whose life he enters without disapproval, the one who actually turns and smiles at him, the one who helps him temporarily forget his "haunting loneliness," isn't his cousin Daisy or Jordan Baker; it's Gatsby. While Nick tells himself he is disgusted and repulsed by being drawn into Gatsby's affairs, he is in fact thrilled.

Nick transfers his own romantic yearning to Gatsby. This is what allows him to articulate Gatsby's unspoken thoughts, to imagine his feelings in past and present. Nick lives vicariously through Gatsby, and so stands in unconscious judgment of his own romantic inclinations. When he's in the apartment Tom's rented for his trysts with Myrtle, Nick tells us,

Each time I tried to go I became entangled in some wild, strident argument which pulled me back, as if with ropes, into my chair. Yet high over the city our line of yellow windows must have contributed their share of human secrecy to the casual watcher in the darkening streets, and I was him too, looking up and wondering. *I was within and without, simultaneously enchanted and repelled* by the inexhaustible variety of life.

Even before he's met Gatsby, Nick is already "enchanted and repelled"—by life. When he says, "The city seen from the Queensboro Bridge is always the city seen for the first time, in its first wild promise of all the mystery and the beauty in the world," he's not only foreshadowing the novel's closing lines, he's also revealing that he *is* those Dutch sailors; and, by extension, he is Gatsby: enchanted by wild promise, repelled by the inevitably disappointing reality that follows.

The promise of mystery and beauty is what Nick sees in Gatsby. When Jordan tells Nick that Gatsby bought the house in order to be across the bay from Daisy, we're told, "He came alive to me, delivered suddenly from the womb of his purposeless splendor." Gatsby comes alive for Nick at that moment because Gatsby stands across the bay longing for Daisy in the same way that Nick walks up Fifth Avenue imagining following the ideal mysterious "romantic woman."

Nick runs away from the threat of engagement in the Midwest, he runs away from the mean-looking brother in Jersey City, he runs away from Jordan. No one is good enough for romantic Nick, who admires gesture but abhors emotion; who wants the world to stand at attention but feels riotous at heart; who desperately wants to join the party that both enchants and repulses him.

And so we have a character of profound contradictions, and we have an authoritative narrator whose self-awareness is in doubt. But this is not a flaw in the novel; rather, it's what brings the novel to vibrant life. We can't say what woman—or man—will break Nick out of his shell, will meet with his approval. We don't know what sort of work he'll do or where he'll settle down. We don't know whether he'll ever recognize the aspects of his character he has unconsciously exposed to us. At the end of the novel, our understanding of Gatsby and of Nick is both multifaceted and incomplete. Both the fragments and the blank spaces are too numerous and consequential for us to assemble a simple whole. Gatsby and Nick have not been "enlightened," "corrected," or "solved." They have been contemplated; their mysteries have been deepened and enlarged.

SEVEN BOARDS OF SKILL

You know ... all of this could be rearranged to form quite a different story.

— JAN KJÆRSTAD

Oliver Wendell Holmes suggests that trying to make sense of a life is like trying to assemble a jigsaw puzzle that can't, ultimately, be put together.

But how does a narrative re-create the sense of assembling a puzzle, the desire to complete the story of a life, or part of a life, and at the same time convey the impossibility of assembling the whole?

In *The Seducer*, Norwegian novelist Jan Kjærstad's playful, anonymous first-person narrator tells the story of Jonas Wergeland, who is famous nationally as the creator of *Think Big*, a series of television documentaries about well-known Norwegians. Wergeland sees his task as telling the stories of these familiar public lives in unexpected ways, so as to expose a larger truth; and the anonymous narrator regularly questions his own ability to tell the story of Jonas Wergeland. He suggests he can tell his tale in almost any sequence, as the individual anecdotes are like spokes on a wheel leading to a hub; at the same time, he wonders whether it's possible to tell "the" story of a life. Jonas and a friend have the following conversation:

> "There are some things that occur in biology for which there is no simple explanation."
>
> "Like what?"
>
> "How a person is formed. How the pieces of a life fit together. Why a person can suddenly change."
>
> "I thought that was exactly what DNA was—quite literally the story of how the pieces of a life fit together."
>
> "Yeah, right, a life, in purely biological terms, but what is Life?" . . .
>
> "Amazing as it may seem, the most important experiences in my life are experiences I have heard about from other people."
>
> Axel waved his arms in the direction of the other people in the restaurant. . . . "In other words, other people's experiences have become my experiences . . . every human being could be said to be as much an accumulation of stories as of molecules. I am, in part, all the things I have read over the years."
>
> "So . . . you think a person can actually be changed by hearing a particular story?" . . .
>
> "It's not the sequence of the base-pairs, the genes, we ought to be mapping out, but the sequence of the stories that go to

A MUSE AND A MAZE

make up a life," said Axel. "And who knows? Arrange them differently and you might get another life altogether."

This suggests that a better analogy for the story of a life may be a tangram.

The classical tangram is a Chinese puzzle game based on a square cut into seven pieces: five right triangles, a square, and a parallelogram. Tangrams were brought to the United States in the early nineteenth century and were highly popular then and again, throughout Europe, during World War 1. The game requires players to re-create images by using all seven pieces without overlapping any of them. When presented as a puzzle, the images give no indication of how the individual pieces are deployed. While it's fairly obvious how some of the shapes can be re-created—

—others are more challenging:

Every writer knows that there are countless ways to tell any given story—that every story is defined by sequence and selection. The tangram reminds us that what we tell the reader first, and what we emphasize (a character's dialect, a dramatic incident from her past, her romantic interest in a colleague, her participation in public demonstrations for social justice), will go a long way toward defining her in the reader's eyes. Rearranging the same parts can create a significantly different effect.

The tangram also offers a different way to think of persuasive character change, including epiphanies, those moments of illumination or understanding that often serve as the climax of psychologically realistic fiction. If the character change or moment of insight seems too obvious or easy, it may be because the reader could see it all along. If the character change or insight seems unbelievable, it may be because the reader feels the character's final "form" can't be produced from the parts presented—it seems something has been added at the last minute (as if we used the seven pieces of the tangram, but also a circle). The self is always under construction. The multiplicity of selves is what allows change. If the change in character or insight is persuasive, it's because it is both surprising and plausible. We can see how the character at the outset became the character at the end, and the story enacts the transformation.

The tangram also helps us to see that no character, or person, is ever "finally" assembled. A typical jigsaw puzzle has one correct final shape. Tangram's "seven clever pieces" (alternately translated as "Seven Boards of Skill") can be arranged to create a great many possible shapes, as different as dog from cat, robot from acrobat.

Similarly, unresolved characterization shows the reader two or more of the shapes that can be made from the pieces available. While the narrative may show a preference for one, it does nothing to make the others invalid. Is Nick Carraway a man whose insight into and perspective on the people around him allows him some unique and provocative understanding? Absolutely. Is he a man whose motivations and responses are deeply confused in a way he seems unable to recognize or understand? It seems so; and he can be both.

In *The Seducer*, Jonas Wergeland faces a particular challenge when he creates a documentary about the real-life Nobel Prize–winning novelist Knut Hamsun:

> The writer showed him what a little way we have come in terms of understanding a man, or how the pieces of a life fit together. In studying Hamsun, Jonas discovered how dangerous it could be to hang onto some time-honored psychological theory, to saddle an individual with an identity, a persona, an essence: and equally dangerous to cherish the belief

that there has to be some sort of continuity, a thread running through life, as if without this comfort one were liable to become lost in a maze. Some notions prevented one from imagining that there could also be leaps, that there could be interruptions in a life, that it might not hang together at all, at any rate not in the way one thought. It was only when one held him transfixed, in a still shot, so to speak, that he became *either* a Nazi sympathizer *or* the great writer. But Hamsun was both at the same time, and something more, something you could never quite put your finger on.... It is paradoxical—but also very comforting—that an author, a wordsmith, should constitute a mystery that defies description.

BOUNDLESS ALTERNATIVES

From the very opening of *Lolita* we're confronted with multiple views of the main characters. We're told "Humbert Humbert" is a pseudonym for the book's narrator, and that while "Dolores" is the girl's actual name, "'Haze' only rhymes with the heroine's real surname." The second paragraph of what we might think of as the novel proper tells us that the title character is many-faceted: "She was Lo, plain Lo, in the morning, standing four feet ten in one sock. She was Lola in slacks. She was Dolly at school. She was Dolores on the dotted line. But in my arms she was always Lolita." The young woman called Dolores Haze is obscured from our view by Humbert's projection of Lolita the Ideal Nymphet. We catch glimpses of her, but the "real" Dolores Haze is conveyed as a series of fragments. She is sometimes the innocent child, sometimes the scheming adolescent. Even at the end, when we meet her as pregnant Dolly Schiller, we don't see the "true" Dolores so much as we see another one.

Lolita is a projection of Humbert's ideal love object, much as Gatsby is a projection of Nick's romantic self and Daisy is a projection of Gatsby's. To different degrees, and for very different reasons, Humbert and Nick are torn in their response to the objectified person who enchants them. Humbert is demented by sexual desire for the ideal nymphet, but at other times he calls Lolita/Dolores "a most exasperating brat" and "a disgustingly conventional little girl"; he recognizes that he is doing great damage to a child; he tells us he engages in acts of "adoration and despair" and that he feels "an oppressive, hideous constraint as if I were sitting with the small ghost of somebody I had just killed." His view of himself is equally kaleidoscopic; Humbert calls himself "courageous," "blind [and] impatient," a failed father, a monster, and a lover. He anticipates every criticism we have of him. He is at once one of the most despicable characters in fiction, one of the most erudite, and one of the funniest.

Humbert is highly self-analytical. Early on he tells us,

> I leaf again and again through these miserable memories.... When I try to analyze my own cravings, motives, actions and so forth, I surrender to a sort of retrospective imagination which feeds the analytic faculty with boundless alternatives and which causes each visualized route to fork and re-fork without end in the maddeningly complex prospect of my past.

While a thoughtful reader could read *The Great Gatsby* without immediately recognizing the depth of Nick Carraway's confusion, Nabokov immediately confronts us with a dynamic, complex, perplexing narrator. Humbert's extremes are so extreme that readers often don't know what to make of his contradictions, how to assemble the parts, and the easiest solution is to find him morally reprehensible. But Nabokov refuses to let the thoughtful reader stop there. Humbert the despicable may dominate because of the emotional impact of his deeds, but the novel's power is a result of the fact that we cannot overlook the other Humberts. And as persuasive as we might find Humbert's expression of regret in the final paragraphs, Nabokov makes it impossible for us to simply take them at face value, to accept Humbert's last words as a confession, or apology, and to see him as sympathetic after all.[21] In giving us so many different possible views of his main character, Nabokov illustrates the danger, the foolishness, of trying to reduce a human being to a single, simple image. To underscore the point, he gives Humbert a reflection to that effect:

21 He does this in part by having Humbert make a crude joke in the midst of his apparently sincere final statement to Lolita, now Dolly Schiller.

I have often noticed that we are inclined to endow our friends with the stability of type that literary characters acquire in the reader's mind. . . . Whatever evolution this or that popular character has gone through between the book covers, his fate is fixed . . . similarly, we expect our friends to follow this or that logical and conventional pattern we have fixed for them. Thus X will never compose the immortal music that would clash with the second-rate symphonies he has accustomed us to. Y will never commit murder. Under no circumstances can Z ever betray us. We have it all arranged in our minds, and the less often we see a particular person the more satisfying it is to check how obediently he conforms to our notion of him every time we hear of him. Any deviation in the fates we have ordained would strike us as not only anomalous but unethical. . . . I am saying all this in order to explain how bewildered I was by Farlow's hysterical letter.

To the extent that we look for a pattern in our friends and neighbors, assembling them, what fascinates us is the challenge; we're most interested in people when they do something "out of character"—something that forces us to reevaluate them or reconsider what we thought we knew. Similarly, as writers we might tend toward logical or conventional patterns in our characters—not stereotypes, but understandable people. Resolved characters. That's not surprising, because when we read, we look for ways to understand character. If we aren't persuaded, we might say, "I don't believe this character would do that"; if we are, we might say, "I know exactly what kind of woman this is." We look for behavioral and psychological consistency. While unresolved characters are made of more challenging patterns, they still need to make sense to us. We need to believe that Humbert Humbert is an accomplished academic fluent in several languages, a wit, *and* a despicable sexual deviant; we need to find Nick Carraway's understanding of Gatsby and the people around him persuasive even as we entertain doubts about his self-understanding.

If, as readers, we can't believe the range of thoughts and behaviors attributed to a character, if all we have are a few isolated pieces of a puzzle, or if we seem to have pieces from four different puzzles, the depiction of character has failed. It isn't enough for there to be contradictions and mysteries: some of the pieces we're given need to interlock, or sit snugly against one another, and the spaces we're left with need to be precisely shaped. Precision is not opposed to mystery; precision is necessary to *define* mystery. The tangram game is pointless if the player can re-create each image with any number of random pieces.

Memory, by Anish Kapoor

THE PUZZLE THAT HAS NO NAME

The inner nature of a human being is not as easily mapped out as all that.... It is, in essence, pretty much unfathomable.

— JAN KJÆRSTAD

The tangram is a useful analogy—but, like all analogies, it is inexact. While it allows that a number of chosen pieces can form many different wholes (a boy, a duck, a boat; or Thomas Jefferson the inventor, Thomas Jefferson the statesman, Thomas Jefferson the slave owner), it doesn't sufficiently illustrate the challenge of seeing those images simultaneously, and trying to understand what they—and the gaps between them—combine to form. The best model may need to be three-dimensional.

One possibility is Anish Kapoor's sculpture *Memory*. Imagine a gallery in a museum. The gallery has three openings. One, a doorway, is almost completely blocked by a large, curving metal object. Through a second we can see more of the steel oblong, which looks to some viewers like part of an old submarine.

The third opening looks, as we approach, like a black square on the wall.

As our eyes adjust, we realize we're looking into the completely dark interior of the object. To go from one opening to the next requires

A MUSE AND A MAZE

walking through other galleries. There is no opportunity to see the object in its entirety. Instead, we have three partial views. At any point we have to remember at least two of them; we can only picture the whole by imagining it, creating it in our minds. Nothing is missing. The room is brightly lit, the air is clear. But our view is fragmented, and we can only speculate about what we can't see. We might assume that the parts of the object out of sight are consistent with those that are visible, but for all we know, the rest of the sides are made out of rubber, or bottle caps. We make similar assumptions about the stranger across the aisle on the bus. This is how we see our neighbors; it's how we see the people nearest to us, and even ourselves. We base our sense of the whole on what we can perceive, which is necessarily partial. We can only see mirror images and photographs of the back of our head, the small of our back; and of course we're blind to other aspects of ourselves as well.

Most of us are struck by the mystery of an individual when someone close to us—a parent, a sibling, a spouse—dies. We inevitably think of things we wish we could ask that person we knew so well, that person we sat beside quietly in the doctor's office, that person whose secrets might not have seemed profound when, any day, we could have asked, "But why on earth did you—?"

Alison Bechdel's *Fun Home* is one example of a memoir as a quest to understand someone else, and the quest to know oneself. In the book she tells the story of her father's death, possibly an accident, possibly a suicide, which occurred not long after she told her parents she was gay. She also tells us that, in response to her coming out, her mother revealed

A page from Alison
Bechdel's *Fun Home:
A Family Tragicomic*

that Bechdel's father had a series of relationships with young men. An English teacher particularly fond of the work of F. Scott Fitzgerald, he devoted himself to restoring and decorating his home, more attentive to furniture than family. She writes, "He was an alchemist of appearance, a savant of surface, a Daedalus of décor," using his artifice "not to make things, but to make things appear to be what they were not." While her father's secrets and disclosures might seem particularly dramatic, every family has its secrets and disclosures; and while Bechdel's book is in part an attempt to articulate her understanding of her father, and of her relationship to him, it also argues for the impossibility of understanding, in the sense that there is no clear cause and effect, no single logical sequence to his life and death. Instead, there are possibilities to ponder.

Most of the details...have long since been transformed or rearranged to bring others of them forward. Some, in fact, are obviously counterfeit; they are no less important.... The myriad past, it enters us and disappears. Except that within it, somewhere, like diamonds, exist the fragments that refuse to be consumed. Sifting through, if one dares, and collecting them, one discovers the true design.

— JAMES SALTER

Graham Greene's *Journey Without Maps* isn't about a mysterious or partially known individual; it's a meditation on an actual journey. But Greene was accompanied by his young cousin, Barbara, and years later she wrote her own book about their trip. In *Too Late to Turn Back*, she tells us a great many things Graham didn't see fit to include, including the fact that, while he would have us believe he walked through the jungle, more often he was carried by natives. To read her book is to see their trip from quite a different perspective; and to read both books forces the reader to recognize that there's not just a third, unwritten book—the "true" or complete story—but the story as it would have been told by one of their native guides, the story as it would have been told by the various villagers they visited, and so on. We're reminded that our perspective of any event is, like our view of Anish Kapoor's *Memory*, partial, limited. Ryūnosuke Akutagawa's short story "In a Grove," on which Akira Kurosawa based his film *Rashōmon*, and Robert Coover's "The Babysitter" are two extreme examples of narratives that force the reader to recognize contradictory and equally persuasive views of the same events. As any policeman interviewing witnesses after a traffic accident can attest, narrative has its own tangram-like quality.

Several years ago the Norwegian government sponsored an international competition for site-specific art. The winning projects would be placed in various locations, many of them remote, in northern Norway (though by just about any standard, "remote" is a redundant modifier for northern Norway). The works are tremendously varied, and many, like the one above, are set in places where, if it weren't for a published guide to the artwork, almost no one would see them.

Head, by Markus Raetz

Head, by Markus Raetz, is set in Eggum, on the shore of Vestvågøy, one of the Lofoten Islands. There's a rocky beach, but the public road ends before you get to the sculpture, so to see it you need to park and get past a fence, then walk. Mounted on a pedestal, the sculpture appears to be a simple, even generic, bust—a head looking out to sea. It's made out of stone. It seems safe to say that a character set in stone is a resolved character.

But here's what you see if you stand "in front of" or "behind" the statue.

The identical figure, only upside down. Which is to say, entirely opposite. And as you circle the statue, it reveals something else.

What's initially intriguing is that, depending on where you stand, the head can appear to be either right-side-up or upside-down. But from other vantage points the sculpture doesn't

A MUSE AND A MAZE

clearly depict a head at all. We might see these as transitional views, but if we were to stand still, our perception, like that of one of those blind men beside the elephant, would be both limited and badly misleading. Who's to say which view is "correct"? We might favor the perspective that reveals a human head, but that's like favoring the image of Jay Gatsby the wealthy party host, or Lolita the ideal nymphet. If we take a single photograph of this character, he is clear, vivid, easily understandable. If we view him from all sides, he's mysterious, enchanting.

THE UNQUIET DARKNESS

Many fragments come to me, are discovered, reappear. I wander about the room picking up or remembering things which are narcotic, which induce me to dream.

— JAMES SALTER

James Salter's novel *A Sport and a Pastime*, set in the 1950s, focuses on a trio of characters very much like Nick, Gatsby, and Daisy. Salter's narrator, however, is more obviously questionable in his authority as he tells us about the affair of Philip Dean, his friend, with a young woman. The narrator is clearly inventing details, even scenes, as he imagines the couple's relationship. The novel begins in late summer: "September. It seems these luminous days will never end." The usual connotations of late summer turning to autumn, emphasized by the explicit recognition of an inevitable ending, make the novel's temporal setting a kind of twilight. The penultimate paragraph reads,

> But of course, in one sense, Dean never died—his existence is superior to such accidents. One must have heroes, which is to say, one must create them. And they become real through

our envy, our devotion. It is we who give them their majesty, their power, which we ourselves could never possess. And in turn, they give some back. But they are mortal, these heroes, just as we are. They do not last forever. They fade. They vanish. They are surpassed, forgotten—one hears of them no more.

Dean is fading; Dean is vanishing; the narrator is struggling to see him.

In *The Great Gatsby*, several of Nick Carraway's most significant reflections occur at twilight. Here's that passage from the party in Tom's New York apartment, with the references to light emphasized: "I wanted to get out and walk . . . *through the soft twilight*, but each time I tried to go I became entangled in some wild, strident argument . . . Yet high over the city our line of yellow windows must have contributed their share of human secrecy to the casual watcher *in the darkening streets*, and I was him too, looking up and wondering." After the confrontation in the Plaza Hotel, Tom and Nick and Jordan ride together in Tom's car. As they're leaving the city, before we know about the accident that claims the life of Tom's mistress, Nick tells us, "So we drove on toward death through the cooling twilight." Gatsby tells Nick the true story of his youth "toward dawn" of the day of Gatsby's death. Nick first sees Gatsby at twilight: "I saw that I was not alone—fifty feet away *a figure had emerged from the shadow* of my neighbor's mansion and was standing with his hands in his pockets. . . . *When I looked once more for Gatsby he had vanished, and I was alone again in the unquiet darkness.*" That closing line of the first chapter also describes Gatsby's disappearance from Nick's life at the end of the novel.

These references to twilight, dying light, and partial light are not just happy coincidence; together with the novel's numerous uses of the word "ghostly," they underscore the fact that Gatsby is dead, that Nick is recollecting him in melancholy tranquility. While death might seem to be the ultimate finality, it is in fact the capstone of mystery. We're left with fragmentary evidence of the deceased; we're left to contemplate all that we don't know about them. Dolores Haze is dead and Humbert is writing in anticipation of his own death in *Lolita*. If life is daylight, and death is darkness, recollected life is twilight; and to the extent that a first-person narrative depicts an act of recollection on the part of the narrator, its characters and events are necessarily seen in dim light, the narrator struggling to make out the essential.

Self-Portrait with Night 1,
by Charles Ritchie

After Gatsby's funeral, when Nick has packed his trunk and is ready to leave, he takes one last walk down to the beach. Here is the paragraph that leads to the novel's famous final lines:

> Most of the big shore places were closed now and there were hardly any lights except the shadowy, moving glow of a ferryboat across the Sound. And as the moon rose higher the inessential houses began to melt away until gradually I became aware of the old island here that flowered once for Dutch sailors' eyes—a fresh, green breast of the new world. Its vanished trees, the trees that had made way for Gatsby's house, had once pandered in whispers to the last and greatest of all human dreams; for a transitory enchanted moment man must have held his breath in the presence of this continent, compelled into an aesthetic contemplation he neither understood nor desired, face to face for the last time in history with something commensurate to his capacity for wonder.

There are hardly any lights; the inessential houses melt away; trees have vanished. Nick strains to perceive, strains to understand. As a result, we are allowed what Graham Greene said he set out to find: a glimpse, beyond surface detail, into the darkness of the human heart.

THE TREASURE HUNTER'S DILEMMA

Long after I had grown up and was practicing the calling of writer, I frequently tried to disappear behind my creations. … I came to aspire to replace the crude invisibility of the magic cloak with the invisibility of the wise man who, perceiving all, remains always unperceived.

— HERMAN HESSE

22 One of the most famous
footnotes in show business is
that Houdini died as the result
of an unexpected punch to the
abdomen delivered by a "fan"
backstage, a sort of adulatory
test of strength. In fact he
succumbed to the effects of
a ruptured appendix which may
or may not have been caused
by the attack. In either case, he
proved mortal.

23 Houdini and Conan Doyle were
friends for some time, as Conan
Doyle believed there was no
doubt that spirits can contact
us from the afterlife. The two
had a falling-out due to Conan
Doyle's insistence that Houdini
was an actual medium, able to
convey messages from spirits,
while Houdini insisted he was
an illusionist. Conan Doyle told
his side of the story in *The Edge
of the Unknown*, the last book
he published before he died
(of a heart attack). Houdini
told his in *A Magician Among
the Spirits*.

Harry Houdini gained tremendous fame and no small fortune by extricating himself from apparently precarious and life-threatening situations. Houdini allowed himself to be hung upside down high above a Manhattan street in a straitjacket; to be handcuffed and locked in a tank of water; to be shackled and tied up in a sack, the sack then placed in a solid trunk, the trunk chained shut and tossed in a freezing river. And he escaped. Just as Sherlock Holmes offered readers hope that the rational mind could overcome villainy, Houdini's fundamental appeal was based on the belief that cleverness, combined with courage and strength, allowed him, and so might allow his viewers, to defeat death.[22]

Secondarily, Houdini is remembered as a man so torn by his mother's death that he devoted himself to exposing fraudulent "seers" and their séances, in the hope that he could find one who could reunite him with her.[23]

But almost no one remembers Houdini as a magician—which is what he most wanted to be.

Born in Budapest, Erik Weisz wanted to be a magician so badly that he adopted the name of the Parisian magician Jean Robert-Houdin, author of a fabulous and, in the mid- to late nineteenth century, famous memoir. Young Erik practiced Robert-Houdin's tricks, but when those led him only to carnival midways and burlesque shows, he began borrowing, from other performers, other kinds of tricks, including escapes. According to Jim Steinmeyer, magic historian, designer of illusions large and small, and author of *Hiding the Elephant*: "There wasn't anything magical about it. . . . Houdini seldom took real chances with his escapes. . . . [They] were thrilling examples of showmanship and . . . vaudeville. Houdini never failed in an escape. . . . His specialty was convincing each person that they had witnessed a near catastrophe."

Orson Welles, who, as a boy, saw Houdini during his last tour, in 1926, called the magic "awful stuff." Despite his hyperbolic claims to the contrary, there is no evidence that Houdini invented or designed a single illusion—he simply imitated those of other magicians or, just as often, bought them. All magicians borrow and steal from one another, but the best make the illusions their own. Steinmeyer argues that a low point in the career of Houdini the magician came in 1918, at the height of his fame, in New York's Hippodrome, when Houdini made a live elephant

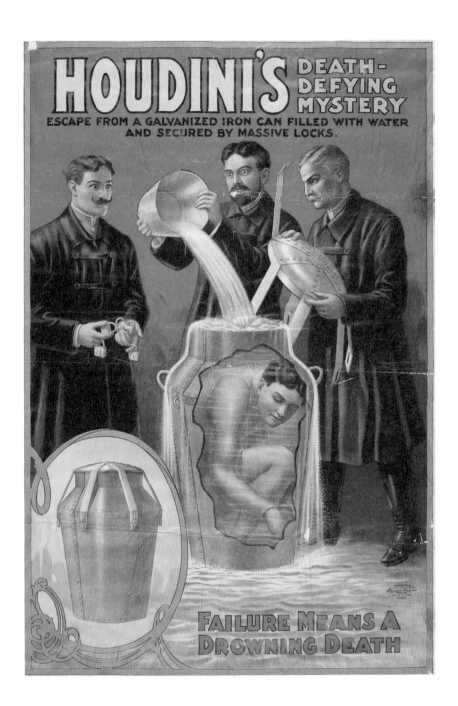

disappear on stage—and the trick was a flop. Audience response was so halfhearted, the presentation so unimpressive, that he dropped it from his act.

One fellow magician said, "As an illusionist, [Houdini] never left the commonplace. [But] his escapes were incomparable. I frequently wondered at the indifference of the one and the perfection of the other and finally was forced to the conclusion that his want of originality was the answer." That "want of originality"—both a lack of originality and a desire for it—made Erik Weisz into world-famous Harry Houdini. He was his most captivating, his most exciting, his most mythical, when he—not a deck of cards, not an elephant—was squarely at the center of attention.

I don't think of myself as Bob Dylan.
It's like Rimbaud said, "I is another."

— Bob Dylan

THE (WO)MAN BEHIND THE CURTAIN

Fiction is a kind of magic, in that it leads the audience to suspend disbelief and, in some cases, be transported to a state of wonder. A story or novel is also like a magic trick in the way that information (characters and events in one, cards and balls and attractive young women in glittering costumes in the other) is both offered and concealed to create dramatic effects. Magic is an entertaining illustration of information design—or, as Edward Tufte puts it, *dis*information design, as the magician's aim is to persuade the audience to see something apparently wondrous (a woman is sawn in half then restored, a card chosen at random turns up in the center of a baked cake) when in fact something much more mundane (a blade retracted, a "choice" was forced) has occurred.

A magician is a performer; and one of his first challenges is to create and embody a particular magician character. He might be a bold baritone, she might be a boisterous blonde, he might perform without speaking, she might maintain comic banter, he might present himself as a bumbler, she might seem aloof. Whatever the details, that character is every magician's first illusion.

As writers, we may or may not think of ourselves as wanting to be the focus of attention, but in asking people to stop and listen, to sit down and read what we have to say, we are dimming the houselights, taking center stage. Some forms of writing—kitchen appliance instruction manuals, for instance—mean to be anonymous, authorless. That illusion is part of their authority. Only if something seems unclear or wrong do we wonder, "Who wrote this?" Certain fiction written in the third person aims for a similar effect: the focus is meant to be entirely on the characters and events, not on the godlike presence telling us about them. But a great deal of third-person fiction has a narrator readers might think of as a character called the Author (as in the work of Henry Fielding, Jane Austen, Charles Dickens, George Eliot, Leo Tolstoy, Flannery O'Connor, John Barth, Lorrie Moore, and David Foster Wallace), and of course all first-person fiction has an identifiable narrator. No matter whether our narrator feigns objectivity or offers an opinion in every sentence, stands in the wings or hogs the spotlight, she exerts tremendous influence over what the reader sees and what he thinks of it.

[My book will be] immensely flavored with me.... [It will be] about me, [with my experiences] transmuted and recreated in writing.

— THOMAS WOLFE, on *Look Homeward, Angel*

We write to share our experiences and/or the way we see things and/or what we imagine. But the creation and control of a narrator is particularly challenging when that narrator is most like us—when most of her experiences, her attitudes and opinions, are ours. We're interested in what we've done, and what we think; we agree with ourselves. To write for readers is to make that experience and those ideas interesting to others, to make our perspective persuasive—and, ideally, to learn something about our own predilections and blind spots.

We might resist thinking of stories and poems as illusions, since the word "illusion" has a negative connotation and is often used synonymously with "fake," or something intentionally deceptive created with ill intent. But as writers we create illusions in the form of alternate realities, realities we very much want readers to believe in, temporarily. Even a depiction of an actual place is a kind of alternate reality. The American West doesn't look the same in Cormac McCarthy's fiction as it does in Larry McMurtry's, Pete Dexter's, Wallace Stegner's, Willa Cather's, or James Michener's—or, for that matter, as it does in nonfiction by John Wesley Powell, Joseph Wood Krutch, and John C. Van Dyke. Instructions to magic tricks often refer to "the effect." "The effect" is what the audience thinks it sees. As writers, we are constantly working to create carefully considered effects.

Privately, we might be outgoing or shy, talkative or quiet, assertive actors or passive observers. But our alter egos, our narrators, are storytellers. Whatever grammatical point of view we choose, the narrator we create is, like a magician, asking for the audience's attention, asserting control. The narrator promises to tell the reader something worth reading. The nature of that story or poem, its tone and content, is up to us; but key to the success of the work is our creation of the narrator, the speaker, the voice that can tell it most effectively.

While this might seem obvious, a remarkable number of developing writers are reluctant to assume the authority of the storyteller, particularly when writing in the third person. This is one of the reasons that the limited third person, or a narrative adhering closely to one character's thoughts and feelings, is much more common among beginning writers than the omniscient third person.[24] And while many more writers are comfortable asserting the voice of a first-person narrator, a variety of problems arise when that narrator is someone very much like the author.[25]

24 Some writers fear omniscient narrators might lessen the reader's intimate connection to her characters; others worry that readers might disagree with a narrator who expresses opinions. But the narrator's attitude toward his or her story animates most great fiction. Was it really the best of times and the worst of times? Do all ships at a distance really have every man's wish on board? Is it really a universal truth that a single man with a fortune must be in want of a wife? Maybe not, but we're delighted to be in the company of an entertaining speaker with strong opinions.

25 Frederick Reiken's excellent essay on this pitfall of first-person fiction, "The Author-Narrator-Character (ANC) Merge," is available online and in the anthology *A Kite in the Wind*.

The poem, no matter how charged its content, will not survive on content but on voice. By voice I mean the style of thought, for which a style of speech—the clever grafts and borrowings, the habitual gestures scattered like clues in the lines—never convincingly substitutes.

— LOUISE GLÜCK

A MUSE AND A MAZE

In the 1939 Metro-Goldwyn-Mayer film adaptation of L. Frank Baum's 1900 novel, when Dorothy and her friends finally reach the Emerald City, they quiver in fear and awe at being in the presence of "the great and powerful" Wizard of Oz. But the wizard's authority rests largely on reputation and rhetoric, and Toto, like most dogs, is not impressed by such things. Taking a curtain in his teeth, Toto pulls it aside to reveal an ordinary man speaking into a microphone, tugging frantically at various

The wizard exposed

levels and knobs in order to create towers of flame and other indications of "greatness." Exposed, he makes one last desperate attempt to maintain the fiction: "Pay no attention to that man behind the curtain," he tells them.

But the jig is up. The Scarecrow says, "You humbug!" The stammering would-be wizard (whose name, revealed in the novel, is Oscar Zoroaster Phadrig Isaac Norman Henkel Emmanuel Ambroise Diggs, or

O.Z.P.I.N.H.E.A.D.) ashamedly agrees, and Dorothy adds, "You're a very bad man." A bad man and, without his mechanical effects, not much of a wizard.

Failed fiction can look a lot like failed wizardry: a combination of pyrotechnics, frantic motion, and unpersuasive claims. But successful fiction also has something in common with wizardry, as it issues from someone with a persuasive and enchanting combination of knowledge, wisdom, insight, attitude, and experience—and maybe even a few nifty tricks up her sleeve. What's interesting about poor Oscar Diggs is that, once he's forced to do without all his bluster and amplification, he's reasonable, even mildly likeable. He points out that the Scarecrow has already demonstrated his intelligence, the Lion has already demonstrated his courage, and the Tin Man has demonstrated his good heart. While he's a bit of a bumbler (he wound up in Oz when his hot air balloon was blown off course from Omaha), Oscar is much better off being Oscar than he is pretending to be a wizard.

In fiction, there is always a man (or woman) behind the curtain. We might think of him as the author, the actual human being who sits at the keyboard or desk. The narrator he creates might sound a lot like him, but even if it does, the narrator is more polished, more articulate, more consistently aware of what he's saying (and not saying) and why. And of course the narrator he creates might be dramatically different from him. Baum was, by all accounts, a bashful young man.[26]

26 And he didn't go far to assemble the materials for his fantasy world; Dorothy was the name of his wife's beloved and recently deceased niece, and "Oz," as every fan of the books or film knows, came from the label on the bottom drawer of his filing cabinet: "O–Z."

MIRRORS AND LENSES: LOOKING IN AND LOOKING OUT

For centuries, mirrors had been used to reflect *something.* . . . Far less logical was that a mirror could reflect *nothing.* . . . In other words, something could be hidden by the use of a reflection. It was, very simply, an optical formula for invisibility.

—JIM STEINMEYER, on a patent for an illusion filed by Joseph Maurice

Because Houdini's disappearing elephant failed to impress audiences, and because he dropped the trick from his act, no one knows exactly how he did it. Jim Steinmeyer suspects the illusion was a variant of one that debuted in April 1865 under the title "Proteus, or We Are Here but Not Here." It went something like this: The magician stood onstage in front of a wheeled structure roughly the size and shape of a phone booth. The front doors were opened to reveal that it was empty. The magician rapped on the sides, back, top, and bottom of the booth, demonstrating that they were solid. The magician's assistant stepped into the box. The magician closed the doors, waved his wand, opened the doors, and shazam—the assistant was nowhere to be seen.

A common complaint about contemporary fiction in the United States is that it is overly concerned with the "domestic," with the daily lives of ordinary individuals. The people who make that complaint often speak nostalgically of novels like *Don Quixote* and *War and Peace*; they urge writers to embrace the epic, or to think politically, to address large-scale societal concerns. But of course there never were many books like *Don Quixote* and *War and Peace*, and there is no shortage of awful novels dedicated to various political visions. Chekhov, a great short-story writer, avoided politics, focusing instead on individuals. Some of the most celebrated American writers, including Herman Melville, Mark Twain, Stephen Crane, Ernest Hemingway, Thomas Wolfe, Katherine Anne Porter, and James Baldwin, wrote directly from their own experiences, and some other cherished novelists, such as Barbara Pym, dedicated themselves to what might be considered "domestic" matters.

The complaint that a great deal of contemporary fiction seems unlikely to stand the test of time can't be argued, since most attempts at art don't stand the test of time. But writing about politics and social concerns is not (necessarily) the answer. *Mona Lisa*, or *La Gioconda*, was for many years thought to be a good but not particularly remarkable painting. For the last century or so it has been one of the most popular and highly valued paintings in the world—and it's simply a portrait of an anonymous woman. It isn't the mystery of her identity that has earned the painting a prominent place in our culture, and it certainly isn't the landscape in the background, though that's of some interest. No, what captivates viewers is the subject's famously enigmatic expression: the hint of a smile, the look in her eyes. The image is both precisely detailed and mysterious, open to the viewer's interpretation. That isn't to say great art can't be about political or social issues; of course it can. But content isn't the defining element of great art. Vision is.

So many people can now write competent stories that the short story as a medium is in danger of dying of competence. We want competence, but competence by itself is deadly. What is needed is the vision to go with it.

— FLANNERY O'CONNOR

Artistic vision is a label for a difficult-to-define combination of close attention, perception, understanding, intuition, and ambition, and none of that counts for much unless it is combined with remarkable execution, or the communication of that vision. Vision may not be teachable, but it can be cultivated. As the amateur astronomer who discovered Uranus, William Herschel, said, "Seeing is an art which must be learnt." Most of the effective tools of communicating through poetry and fiction can be taught. Vision alone isn't enough, and demonstrating it once is no guarantee of demonstrating it again. Chekhov, Twain, Porter, Fitzgerald, Faulkner, and Hemingway all wrote stories that are forgettable, and would be forgotten if not for the better work they also created.

If you learn to organize your desires and demands and shoot them into something that is more than just about being you, you start to communicate.... I will steal directly from life, [but] I don't want to tell you all about me. I want to tell you about *you*.

— *Bruce Springsteen*

So: writing from one's own experience does not, in itself, make it likely that a work will be good or bad. Writing about oneself under the assumption that others will necessarily be interested or moved, however, will nearly always doom a piece. While it's perfectly understandable that we find our own lives fascinating, each reader has his or her own life that is, for him or her, much more important than ours. The greatest fiction connects the concerns of the author with the concerns of the reader.

That connection doesn't have to be explicit. As Walt Whitman reminded the world, universal experience can be expressed through the individual:

> I celebrate myself,
> And what I assume you shall assume,
> For every atom belonging to me as good belongs to you.

The way we see the world is the lens that defines us.

Writers typically begin at one of two extremes. Either we write work that is far from autobiographical, about wholly invented creatures in far-away places—or we write stories and poems that are transparently auto-biographical. Writers at either extreme benefit from exploring different relationships between their experience and their work. Typically, writers in that first group are, eventually, encouraged to make more direct use of their experience (which can inform even the most fantastic fiction). Even fantasy and horror novels benefit from characters with identifiable human emotions, and the emotions we draw from most powerfully are our own. Typically, writers in the second group are encouraged to "gain some distance" from their experience. To write about one's own experience without considering why and how it might interest a reader is to write from a sense of selfishness, or self-absorption, which often hampers communication. Even in the case of a celebrity autobiography, which the reader presumably picks up to learn about the author, the writing is most effective when it offers points of connection and understanding.

CHOOSING A PLACE TO STAND

A writer I know once succumbed to the lure of supposedly easy money by agreeing to help a man "polish" his memoir, which featured that man's rediscovery of a gold mine in the Southwest. The mine, which predated the famous California gold rush, had been discussed and described in any number of popular books and articles and had been the subject of countless searches for over a century, and it was the subject of the usual tall tales and grisly stories of people who had "gotten too close," only to meet some suspicious end. Given that he had proven at least some of the old stories to be true and the doubters wrong, the man's tale had obvious appeal. ("If I can't tell a good story about finding lost treasure, I should quit writing," my friend regrets having said.) By the time my friend and the memoirist crossed paths, the events recounted in the (badly typed) manuscript were long over. To fill in holes, then, the writer had to interview the treasure hunter.

A number of problems became evident, but the one that ultimately undermined the book was this: the treasure hunter couldn't decide how he wanted to be depicted. Some days he wanted to be portrayed like a real-life Indiana Jones, a brave individual boldly taking action when people all around him were saying there was nothing to find, or it couldn't be found, or whatever was found wouldn't repay the risk and effort to find it. Other days, he wanted to be seen as the victim of shortsighted archaeologists, an evil corporate landowner, and some inconvenient laws. In a typical week, the treasure hunter would tell my friend a story over the phone, my friend would write it up and email the draft to a helpful woman who served as liaison (the treasure hunter believed certain unnamed agents of the government were reading his email and would take drastic action to suppress his story), the treasure hunter would read it over, and he'd want to change nearly every detail.

To be fair, while his ambivalence made the work exasperating, both of the treasure hunter's views of himself could be justified. On one hand, he had done something remarkable, difficult, and expensive, something countless people had tried and failed to do for nearly 150 years. On the other hand, archaeologists, landowners, and governments have their own interest in historically significant and potentially financially lucrative discoveries, and those interests are often at odds with those of someone whose primary objectives are to find something, bring it to light, and make a lot of money himself.

The treasure hunter could be an engaging and persuasive storyteller, which is how he was able to raise the funds necessary for his extended search in isolated country, to persuade a local college to create a touring exhibit of artifacts he found at the site, and to convince my friend to work with him. But his mercurial relationship to his story was a serious problem; it impacted virtually every sentence, and of course it influenced the tone of the book. Who exactly was he trying to depict? To create what ultimate effect?[27] The problem was never fully resolved. (Never: a few years after the book came out, the treasure hunter found another co-author and sold his story to another publisher.)

27 I am trying to be a good friend here, so I have suppressed identifying details, but take every reviewer's word for it: the book is not good.

One of the last things the book's editor asked for was a new opening chapter. The publisher's sales staff thought the book would find a wider audience if the treasure hunter was still active, in the midst of some new adventure. He wasn't—he spent most of his time trying to persuade the national morning talk shows that he'd be the ideal guest—but the editor suggested it might be enough to "consider" a new adventure. So my friend, who had spent time in Arizona, did some quick reading on the famous Lost Dutchman mine and wrote a quick prologue describing the treasure hunter bushwhacking deep into the Superstition Mountains, narrowly avoiding Gila monsters (which aren't actually dangerous, but they've got that great name), squatting in the shade of a towering saguaro to check his yellowed map, pausing to wipe his brow only to spy a scorpion nestled in the folds of his bandanna—you get the idea. The punch line? The treasure hunter said the prologue, a work of fiction, was his favorite part of the autobiography.

> Do I contradict myself?
> Very well then I contradict myself,
> (I am large, I contain multitudes.)
> — WALT WHITMAN

The treasure hunter's dilemma is one we all face. Of all the possible stories we could tell about our experience, of all the approaches we could take, which one should we choose? How do we want to be seen, or understood? Why?

Give me a lever and a place to stand and I will move the earth.

— ARCHIMEDES

Here's how the Proteus trick is done:

The magician's assistant steps into the phone booth–sized box and stands with her back against the back of the booth. When the doors close, she pulls toward herself two panels, one on each side. The panels have mirrors mounted on the side she can't see—the side facing the audience. The mirrors meet at a perfect 45-degree angle, and the front edges have been treated so that there is no visible seam. Each mirror now reflects a side of the booth.

Since the sides and back of the booth are identical (often simply black), when the doors are opened, the audience thinks it sees exactly what it saw before—the interior of a black box. The "disappeared" assistant is standing directly in front of them, behind the two panels—but because the mirrors are carefully angled, the box is carefully sized, and the theater's lighting has been strategically placed, no member of the audience can see any unintended reflection.

As with virtually any illusion, to know how it is done is to be profoundly underwhelmed. Everything—which is to say, the magic—is in the presentation.

Here's the challenging bit:

Most viewers immediately assume that the booth has a false back. In order to persuade them that the booth is both solid and empty, the magician once again needs to rap on the sides of the box or to roll the entire box aside. But if his hand, wand, or body were to be reflected in either of the mirrors, the illusion would be ruined. And so the magician has to learn precisely where to stand, and how to move.

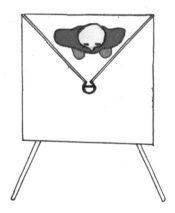

The "safe zone," determined by the size of the cabinet and the angle of the mirrors, is the area the magician can stand in or pass his hand or

The Proteus cabinet, and the view from above if the cabinet top were removed.

A MUSE AND A MAZE

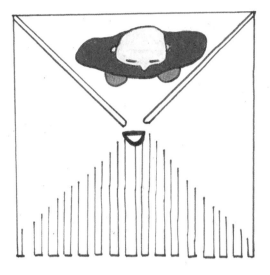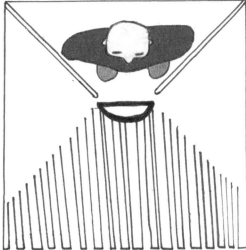

wand through without ruining the effect. The success of the presentation, the art to the illusion, lies in the magician's moving gracefully, apparently unselfconsciously, even though he is in fact doing everything possible to work the boundaries, to stop just short of disastrous exposure.

Many variations of this illusion were created, and they're still performed today. A common one is a box that appears to be empty, but from which the magician pulls all sorts of apparently large objects. One variant involves a three-legged coffee table, where the mirrors run between the legs. The table has a trap door, and the "art" is in the ability of the assistant to drop down through the door and contort herself into the space between the table legs quickly and silently.

It took quite a while for magicians to discover how to use different angles for mirrors, but eventually solutions were found, so that even audiences who thought they were above being tricked by mirrors *were*, again and again. Which is to say, once audiences became aware of how an illusion was created, the "magic," or sense of wonder, was gone, forcing magicians to find new methods to produce the same essential effects. Archimedes was talking about physics: with a long enough (and sturdy enough) lever, and a well-chosen fulcrum, or pivot point, an ordinary person can move a remarkably heavy object. A writer chooses the best place to stand based in part on proximity to the material and on his desired relationship with the reader. The most remote stance might be seeming objectivity—the narrator is offstage, or in the wings. The most intimate stance might be that of the poet or fiction writer who openly acknowledges drawing from life and who blurs the boundary between fact and invention, like Houdini—or is that Erik Weisz?—himself.

> Don't talk to me of your Archimedes' lever. He was an absentminded person with a mathematical imagination. Mathematics commands all my respect, but I have no use for engines. Give me the right word and the right accent and I will move the world.
>
> — *Joseph Conrad*

There are many ways to create psychic and artistic distance between ourselves and our experience in order to see it more clearly, to understand it more fully, and so reproduce aspects of our experience in ways that serve the work we mean to create. They include changing the character who represents us in some significant way (gender, family or marital status, or profession); moving the events in time (from the past to the present day, or from the present to the character's past); changing the setting (from the country to the city, from Texas to Chicago, from France to Kansas); making what was a crucial event for us a secondary event for our character, so shifting the emphasis; changing crucial plot details (if our father died, let him recover; if the story draws from our divorce, make one member of the couple ill, instead, and see if we can still gain access to the emotion prompting the story); changing point of view (not only from first person to third, but changing the point-of-view character entirely); and imposing technical constraints on the work (the story needs to have three scenes, each paragraph needs to have five sentences, authority needs to rotate among three characters, etc.) so as to elicit attention to the work as a creation apart from its motivating content.

The goal of these strategies and others like them is to help us see the core material, the event or feeling we want not only to re-create in writing but to explore, without being beholden to the details of what actually happened. Forcing ourselves to invent can help us see what feels essential and what doesn't. Perhaps the greatest difficulty in writing about our

A MUSE AND A MAZE

experience is gaining distance from our own emotional response—then and now—to the people and events involved. Ideally, we aren't simply documenting our experience but investigating it. In some cases, that might be best achieved not by making the character less like ourselves but by staring at ourselves intently, as if we were foreign, like a scientist looking through a microscope at his own blood. Why did we act so shamefully? Why were we ashamed? Who taught us what to be ashamed of? Focusing on the aspects of the story we least understand, or are least inclined to question, is most likely to lead to new perceptions.

WINDOWS AS MIRRORS: LOOKING OUT, LOOKING IN

The word *reflection* can be defined as both mirroring and meditation; I see self-portraits as encompassing both.... I prefer a window's reflections to a mirror's. A window's transparency provides an underlying vista and diffuses the graphic power of a reflected figure. The hard opacity of a mirror tends to substantiate the very presence I want to subvert. I aim to assimilate my presence into a continuum.

— CHARLES RITCHIE

Obvious uses of the self in art are autobiography and the self-portrait. Several years ago the Musée du Luxembourg, in Paris, assembled an exhibition called *Moi! Self-Portraits of the Twentieth Century*. The show included 150 artists, among them Picasso, Matisse, and Degas. "The self-portrait is the most intense unmasking of the artist's identity," the curator said, adding that the exhibition revealed 150 different responses to the question "Who am I?" But the exhibit might have included six self-portraits each by 25 artists and still gotten 150 different responses to the question "Who am I?" There is no one answer to that question for any of us; each self-portrait selects from all of the artist's possible selves.

The irregular blank space on the left of *Erased Self-Portrait* expresses Charles Ritchie's frustration, not with being unable to draw the figure, but with not being able to find an acceptable balance between the depiction of himself and the rest of the composition. The writer who struggles to integrate a character based on herself or her experiences might feel something equivalent. Her image, emotions, and experiences haven't yet been transformed into part of a story or poem that can communicate effectively to readers.

Erased Self-Portrait is evidence of my difficulties with the mirrored subject. My bust was originally situated at left, in the arched mirror, but was finally scrubbed out in frustration, leaving the irregular white patch. The quality of my depiction was unacceptable, and the dominance of my visage was exasperating.

— *Charles Ritchie*

A subgenre of self-portraits illustrates one extreme approach to creating art based on the self: leaving the self out of it. While everything we touch carries our fingerprints, this approach works to create distance by eliminating any explicit depiction of the artist. This option may be most attractive if we find depiction of personal experience too "charged," or difficult to gain separation from, or if we

Erased Self-Portrait,
by Charles Ritchie

simply choose to focus outward. Artists as diverse as Vilhelm Hammershoi, Van Gogh, and Robert Rauschenberg created self-portraits using objects. Van Gogh's is one of the most famous.

Van Gogh's Chair was painted in 1888, after the artist's falling-out with Paul Gauguin. The two argued over aesthetics—Gauguin saw Van Gogh as an old-fashioned romantic—and Van Gogh responded by making paintings of his chair and Gauguin's. Gauguin's, depicted at night, is red, baroque, holding a burning candle and books, sitting on a flowery carpet, in front of a green wall with a blazing lamp. Van Gogh's chair is simple, even crude, a box of onions behind it and his pipe on the seat. No human figure appears. What Van Gogh presents instead is an image carefully designed to create a psychological self-portrait, a depiction of the self via his familiar, chosen surroundings.

Van Gogh, who collected illustrations from magazines and newspapers, was inspired by a "portrait" of one of the world's most famous

Empty rooms, bereft of a familiar presence, mournfully whisper what your room and what mine must one day be.

— *Charles Dickens*, Bleak House

novelists. According to the *Guardian*, "In 1870 the Victorian magazine the *Graphic* published a valediction for an absent fixture of Christmas past: Charles Dickens had died that year, and Luke Fildes' illustration 'The Empty Chair, Gad's Hill —Ninth of June 1870' depicts Dickens's chair at his desk, pulled back, but empty, no one there to write that year's Christmas story."

In *The Empty Chair*, Dickens's absence signifies death. A month after painting his chair and Gauguin's, Van Gogh threatened Gauguin with a razor, then cut off his own ear. A year and a half after that, he killed himself. If you've looked at *Van Gogh's Chair* before and seen it as warm or comforting, it may change your sense of it to know that Van Gogh smoked a pipe because Dickens advised it as a cure for melancholy. In the painting, his pipe lies abandoned.

In these portraits, omitting the figures required the artist to express character in other ways: through the choice of what *is* depicted, and how; through color; and through composition.

I think it is impossible for [Hemingway] to write of any event at which he has not been present; his is, then, a reportorial talent, just as Sinclair Lewis's is. But, or so I think, Lewis remains a reporter and Hemingway stands a genius because Hemingway has an unerring sense of selection.... The simple thing he does looks so easy to do. But look at the boys who try to do it.

— DOROTHY PARKER

In stories like "Hills Like White Elephants" and "A Clean, Well-Lighted Place," Hemingway's narrators can seem distant, removed; the stories themselves seem far from mere documents of personal experience or observation. Even in the stories about Nick Adams, who is generally considered a stand-in for the author, the narrator is capable of expressing things beyond Nick's understanding. Hemingway often focuses intently on objects and setting to reveal what is felt but never explicitly expressed. One of the most dramatic examples is his early story "Big Two-Hearted River," which evokes Nick's devastation after the war almost entirely through description of the landscape. While working on the story, Hemingway wrote to Gertrude Stein, "I am doing the country like Cézanne." That "unerring sense of selection" is the prose equivalent to the arrangement of objects and the choices of color and composition in visual art. Even though his stories and novels were based on his experience, Hemingway created the equivalent of mirrors carefully arranged to give readers a precisely controlled view, a unique angle of perception.

From behind the screen where I hid I advance personally, solely to you.

Camerado! This is no book;
Who touches this, touches a man....
I spring from the pages into your arms.

— *Walt Whitman*

Charles Ritchie's choice of subject—what he can see from inside his house, looking out, in near darkness—led to a conflict. He works with one or more lights illuminating his work space. Those lights are reflected in the windows he looks through, and among the things they illuminate is him: the artist at work. While he embraced the complex play of reflected light on glass, for years he had eliminated various visual distractions—including his own image. Eventually, in order to be more true to what he saw, he decided to stop eliminating himself from the world he observed. What he saw reflected was not a neat image, as we might see in a typical portrait, but a dim, partially obscured, ghostly image, sometimes all but imperceptible behind other objects or reflections. In *Self-Portrait with Paper Whites* (left), his figure is fragmented by the window mullions and white blossoms. In *Kitchen Windows with Reflections* (facing), only half of his upper body and head are visible, in deep shadow.

Every creation is a reflection, however indirect, of its creator. In revealing our obsessions we reveal what concerns us. By choosing to work in a particular way, by choosing particular materials and subjects, we enter into conversation with art and artists of the past as well as with our contemporaries.

We are not in complete control of the way our work reflects us, any more than we are in complete control of the way the pitch of our voice reflects our timidity or assertiveness, or the way our perspiration reflects our nervousness. Some of us just perspire a lot. But our interest here is in the struggle to gain control, to be aware, to assert an artistic point of view—to make conscious and determined choices. Just as we can improve our posture, or teach ourselves to make eye contact with strangers, by being more conscious of how we present ourselves in prose we can achieve greater control over the effects we create.

A magician is a particular type of actor, his every movement and act

of speech intended to create a tone or to (mis)direct our attention. An actor shaves himself one way at home, in his bathroom, with no one else around—and entirely differently on stage, in a role, with an audience watching. At home, his goal is to remove the stubble from his face; on stage, where the razor may not have a blade, his goal is to project a character at a particular moment in a larger narrative and to create one or more particular effects. His movements are designed to communicate with the audience.

Like a magician practicing for hours in front of a mirror, we need to learn to see our work and the effects we mean to create from the audience's point of view.

THROW IN A LITTLE FANCY

Herman Melville's first novel, and his most popular book during his lifetime, was an exotic, romantic travelogue. *Typee: A Peep at Polynesian Life* tells the story of a sailor who finds himself captive on an island inhabited by cannibals, and who soon falls in love with a cannibal maiden. Unlikely as it may seem, the novel is based on actual events. In 1842 Melville deserted the *Acushnet* and spent three weeks on Nuku Hiva in the Marquesas Islands, where he saw the Tai Pi Valley and quite likely met the model for his novel's feast for the eyes, Fayaway. Over the course of *Omoo*, *Mardi*, and then *Moby-Dick; or, The Whale*—the book now most commonly considered his masterpiece, but a financial and critical failure when it was published—Melville moved further from his own experience, unless we include his reading among his experiences. *Moby-Dick* was inspired by the story "Mocha Dick; or, The White Whale of the Pacific," about an actual notorious sperm whale, published in *The Knickerbocker* magazine in 1839. Melville was fully aware of the challenge of transforming his time at sea and the first-hand accounts of others into fiction. In 1850, as he was composing *Moby-Dick*, he wrote Richard Dana, author of *Two Years Before the Mast*, "It will be a strange sort of a book, tho', I fear; blubber is blubber you know; tho' you may get oil out of it, the poetry runs as hard as sap from a frozen maple tree; —& to cook the thing up, one must needs throw in a little fancy. . . . Yet I mean to give the truth of the thing, spite of this."

"One must needs throw in a little fancy. . . . Yet I mean to give the truth of the thing." We understand the sort of truth he's talking about. We also understand the confounding banality of experience: blubber is blubber.

In a long letter to Nathaniel Hawthorne, Melville wrote, "In reading some of Goethe's sayings . . . I came across this, 'Live in the all.' That is to say, your separate identity is but a wretched one,—good; but get out of yourself, spread and expand yourself. . . . What nonsense! . . . [but] there is some truth in it. You must often have felt it, lying on the grass on a warm summer's day. Your legs seem to send out shoots into the earth." This was in 1851, just four years before Whitman published *Leaves of Grass*. The notion of reaching toward universal experience, so universal truth, through individual experience and awareness, was in the air. And, like Whitman, Melville wanted to include everything: what he had seen, what he had done, what he had read, and what he had imagined. This ambition led to an unusual book—a combination of fact and fiction, varying in mode from traditional scenes to short essays to lists to digressive expository excursions—not far removed from supposedly in-novative books of our own time. In a contemporary review of the novel, Evert A. Duyckinck simultaneously recognized Melville's ambition and found the execution wanting:

> There are evidently two if not three books in *Moby-Dick* rolled into one. Book No. 1 we could describe as a thorough exhaustive account admirably given of the great Sperm Whale.... Book No. 2 is the romance of Captain Ahab & Co... very serious people... concerned a great deal about the problem of the universe.... After pursuing [Moby-Dick] in this melancholic company over a few hundred squares of latitude and longitude, we begin to have some faint idea of the association of whaling and lamentation, and why blub-ber is popularly synonymous with tears.... Book III... is half essay, half rhapsody.... These are strong powers with which Mr. Melville wrestles in this book. It would be a great glory to subdue them to the highest uses of fiction.

Duyckinck thought he was describing the shortcomings of the novel; later readers decided that these are its virtues. Whatever you think of *Moby-Dick*, it's hard to imagine a book more tightly bound with its cre-ator. It amply demonstrates not only his experience but also his interests, his passions, and his habit of mind—which was sprawling, philosophical, and less interested in certain kinds of detail (Melville was notoriously careless about proofreading) than in the grand vision that drew together apparently disparate parts. In the progression from *Typee* to *Moby-Dick* we see Melville standing back from his exploits, doing more than pol-ishing them into adventure tales, and relying less on recording things that he actually did, or nearly did; at the same time, we see him investing himself more fully, actually incorporating *more* of his total experience in the work—if, again, we include his reading and thinking as his life expe-rience. That is the development we see in any number of writers who, as they mature, rely less on recounting and being faithful to specific events and grow to see experience as raw material, the way a visual artist sees paint, a sculptor sees marble, or a magician sees a deck of cards.

A quarter-century after the publication of *Typee*, another American writer chronicled a different voyage—this one across the western half of the country—in the comic travelogue *Roughing It*. "Mark Twain" was, everyone knows, the pseudonym of a man named Samuel Clemens—a pseudonym taken from riverboat navigation. While Erik Weisz (born just two years after *Roughing It* was published) wanted to be a magician, Sam Clemens wanted to be a riverboat pilot. Happily for us, while working on the Mississippi he fell into company where the ability to tell an engaging story was hard currency: the more outrageous the story, the better. His early work is highly autobiographical, often detailing trips he made, but with the actual events seen through a distorting lens, a funhouse mirror designed to exaggerate and poke fun at everyone, including himself. Assuming the role of a comic journalist, he had found a place to stand.

But as is true of most comedians, a demon drove his humor, in his case a sadness turning to cynicism that threatened to ostracize audiences, editors, and advertisers. In 1866, at the age of thirty-one, just a few months after publishing what is now his most famous short story, "The Celebrated Jumping Frog of Calaveras County"—before he had written *Roughing It*, *The Adventures of Tom Sawyer*, and *Adventures of Huckleberry Finn*—Samuel Clemens put a gun to his head.

Justin Kaplan, author of *Mr. Clemens and Mark Twain*, writes that

> he was always his own biographer, and the books he wrote about [his first thirty] years are incomparably the best possible accounts, even if they may not always be the truest. . . . But the central drama of his mature literary life was his discovery of the usable past. He began to make this discovery in his early and middle thirties—a classic watershed age for self-redefinition—as he explored the literary and psychological options of a new, created identity called Mark Twain. . . . This usable past, imaginatively transformed into literature, was to occupy him for the rest of his life.

In other words, Mark Twain's development was a lifetime project focused largely on learning to shape his experience toward a variety of effects. Past experience was his raw material, and the full development of the persona who became his narrator, Mark Twain, was the result of exploring "literary and psychological options."

Like Melville, Twain made different uses of his material. As a hyperbolic travelogue full of strong opinions about everything the author encountered, *Roughing It* can be seen as a precursor to Tom Wolfe's *Electric Kool-Aid Acid Test* and Hunter S. Thompson's *Fear and Loathing in Las Vegas*. *The Adventures of Tom Sawyer*, a romanticized version of his youth in Hannibal, Missouri, is a more conservative crowd pleaser, a novel woven from anecdotes about actual people and places. *Adventures of Huckleberry Finn* takes a dramatically different perspective on the setting and people in the world of *Tom Sawyer*—the "usable material" of Sam Clemens's past—with an emphasis on slavery, morality, and the individual's relation to society. Those were significant issues for the author as an adult, as he felt increasingly alienated from the hometown and even the river of his youth. Instead of striving for a single emotional effect—comedy, or nostalgia tinged with comedy—in *Huckleberry Finn* Twain reached for a broad tonal range. By considering his childhood years in light of the Civil War, and by including both the ugliness and the beauty of the Mississippi and the people living near it, he created his finest novel. Certainly his choice of point of view is instrumental to the book's success, but that's "point of view" in the largest sense—not just the grammatical shift from the third-person narration of *Tom Sawyer* to the groundbreaking first-person vernacular of Huck, but the shift from a safe, static relationship to his past to a much more dynamic and potentially dangerous one. Initial responses to *Huck Finn* were mixed: the book was seen as unfunny, a failed sequel unfit for boys; and it continues to be banned and censored because Twain dared to use a word common not only in the world he described but also in ours.

On the surface, young Sam Clemens was less like rebellious, independent Huck Finn, more like mischievous Tom Sawyer. Creating Huck, then fully imagining the world as seen through the eyes of the son of the town drunk, encouraged his creator to view the world differently. The adult Sam Clemens grew to be more like Huck, the outsider, since he was observing, more than fully participating in, his hometown of Hannibal

(St. Petersburg, in the books). What he saw made him want to inspire more than laughter in his readers.

The movement from comic travelogue to boyhood adventure tale to more introspective novel was by no means natural or easy. Clemens worked on *Huckleberry Finn* fitfully, setting it aside for several years. The book had been conceived as a sequel to *Tom Sawyer*, but Clemens began to resist that novel's voice and perspective. In the same way that he created the character Mark Twain—the acerbic, white-suit-wearing, publicly performing Great Man—he had created a world for *Tom Sawyer* that made it a boys' book: a book *for* boys (and nostalgic adults) as much as it was about boys. Just as Erik Weisz / Harry Houdini moved from traditional magic tricks to dramatic "escapes"—from illusions focused on anonymous assistants and elephants to illusions focused directly on the Houdini character he was creating—Clemens/Twain reevaluated both how he wanted to sound on the page and what that voice would allow him to say. Clemens's brother was killed in a steamboat accident; Sam himself served briefly in a band of Confederate guerrillas before withdrawing and reconsidering his allegiances. By the time he was working on *Huckleberry Finn*, the steamboats of his youth had all but disappeared, and any number of towns he knew had been destroyed by the war. The voice he had created for *Tom Sawyer* didn't allow him to access the complexity and darkness of the world that now interested him.

Well, my book is written—let it go. But if it were only to write over again there wouldn't be so many things left out. They burn in me; and they keep multiplying; but now they can't ever be said. And besides, they would require a library—and a pen warmed-up in hell.

— *Mark Twain,* letter to William Dean Howells, September 22, 1889

When his progress on *Huckleberry Finn* stalled, Twain turned to another project: he developed a series of autobiographical sketches he had written for the *Atlantic Monthly* under the heading "Old Times" into *Life on the Mississippi*. Like *Moby-Dick*, *Life on the Mississippi* is a compelling but curious combination of fiction and nonfiction, anecdote and philosophizing. Twain combines essentially true sketches and stories with comic exaggerations à la *Roughing It*; he follows a serious and angry brief essay on the marketing of burial services with a satirical bit of fiction on the same topic; and he quotes and paraphrases a wide variety of source material. He ranges from yarn-spinner to sage, lying outrageously on one page and writing sincerely, movingly, on another.

A MUSE AND A MAZE

Jonathan Raban writes,

> The young humorist Mark Twain was an entirely different
> kind of animal from the young pilot Samuel Clemens; and
> Mark Twain would commit himself to so befogging and my-
> thologizing the past of Samuel Clemens that it would turn
> into the best and most glorious of the writer's inventions. The
> "Old Times" pieces were fiction—a fiction made credible, in
> every sentence, with autobiographical fact.... They created
> a golden age of innocence and harmony.... [But] it was a fic-
> tion that could not be indefinitely sustained.... [He] created,
> in manuscript, the clear and powerful voice of Huckleberry
> Finn: a voice without literary precedent. *Life on the Mississippi*
> counts the cost of that creation. It shows Twain in the act of
> wrestling with the demons of language—battling, in parody
> and pastiche, toward a new way of rendering the world in
> writing. Style after style is tried and found wanting.

We may be inclined to think of great pieces of writing as perfect from
beginning to end, weaving a consistent and long-lasting spell. While
there may be poems and even stories that seem unimprovable, word for
word, perfection is harder to sustain for the duration of a novel. Many
readers (including Hemingway) feel the final section of *Huckleberry Finn*
is badly flawed. But one can easily imagine that, if he had written it earlier in his career, Mark Twain would have been satisfied to make *Huck* a
comic novel; and if he had written it late in his life, he might have made
it more didactic, similar to his late stories. *Huckleberry Finn* and *Life on
the Mississippi* capture his writing at a particular state of crisis, between
times when he felt confident about what he wanted to do and how to do
it. That struggle animates both books.

While Mark Twain is one of the most famous cases of an American
writer adopting a persona, we all do it: the voice we present in our writing, no matter how sincere, no matter how well-intentioned, in fiction,
nonfiction, or poetry, is a guise—one we're constantly working to create
and refine and adapt to the project at hand.

A review of a collection of John Updike's early stories noted that it is surprisingly easy to read them from beginning to end because they essentially tell the story of a life, a life of a man in many ways quite similar to John Updike. Updike himself wrote a great deal about his use of life experience.

> The small town was Ipswich, Massachusetts, a coastal mill town with a variegated population and a distinguished Puritan past. It seemed a town full of stories. . . . We shopped at the Atlantic & Pacific supermarket, so I cooked up a story called "A&P." I drove my daughter to her music lesson, and out came "The Music School." A car accident occurred at our corner, and thus "The Corner." I fell into the local version of the sexual revolution, and out came a bundle of variations on the story of Tristan and Iseult. My wife, as a fictional character, got ever more talkative and alluring as our marriage became ever more fraught with resentments and tensions. I was hip-deep in neighbors and friends, children and pets; I gossiped, I drank, I played golf, I attended church. This was life, and I shaped and polished off odd fragments of it to send away in brown manila envelopes.

Updike is sometimes criticized for the very casualness implied there: "I drank, I played golf . . . I shaped and polished odd fragments of [my life]." A remarkably prolific writer, he devoted his days to writing novels, stories, poems, reviews, essays, and more. It's no surprise that the work isn't consistently intense or evocative, and that some of the stories read like "polished fragments." In another essay he's a bit more forthcoming about recognizing and confronting challenges to this approach:

> I wrote a ten-page non-fictional memoir, called "The Real Story" [about being taken] to the local factory where footballs were made. . . . I wished to enter into this toilsome noisy creation of something real, solid, kickable, tossable. But the story

came out too reminiscent, for me, of an earlier story.... My voice and invention faltered once the bliss of grafting muscles and a jingly-jangly, bar-snappy wife onto my alter ego were past. So I gathered my courage and dismissed the flimsy celebrity-persona and plunged nakedly into the lives of these factory workers.

Transforming experience into fiction involves "grafting" parts onto an "alter ego"—and realizing when to dispense with that alter ego. Which is to say, we need to recognize when to dismiss a representation of the self and to "plunge nakedly" into invention of character and voice.

EXPLORE, INVESTIGATE, ARTICULATE

David Shields began his career as a fiction writer whose work drew on autobiography. His later work, which still draws heavily on his own experiences and observations, is most often classified as nonfiction, but he has little interest in the distinction. Many of his books contain what appear to be candid revelations—about his health and his father's, about his fantasies as he makes love with his wife—as well as what appear to be invented or reconfigured events. Factual truth is not the point. In an interview in the *Writer's Chronicle*, Shields said,

> At its best, the work is what Yeats called "a mirror turn lamp." That is to say, you explore yourself as deeply as you possibly can, and by getting to the deepest parts of yourself, you're actually getting to what makes all of us human, which is trouble ... At its worst, you are just reciting the facts of your life, or are flattering yourself or celebrating yourself or promoting yourself or even just simply lambasting yourself. It's a very difficult balance.... I'm interested in ... going as deeply into myself as I possibly can, and via that excavation, getting to very difficult things about myself, and thereby creating, I hope, as rigorous a portrait as possible of one person's existence on the

planet ... what excites me is the depth of the emotional and intellectual investigation.

Strange as it might seem, several of his books—which are not so much plotted as thematically arranged—have something in common with *Moby-Dick* and *Life on the Mississippi*, as they combine observation, quotation, paraphrase, and fiction, and what they capture, as much as their stated subjects, is the writer's passionate engagement with his material, in whatever form it takes. Unlike Melville, and even more than Twain, Shields stands close to center stage—increasingly, his books are about his attitudes, his opinions, his actions, the writing he likes, and the writing he dislikes—and he clearly enjoys playing the role of provocateur. But he isn't simply being "honest" or "revealing"; he is still taking a stance, striking a pose, "creating ... a portrait."

MEET THE DEMANDS OF THE THING BEING MADE

In case you're wondering about that elephant:

Houdini's assistants rolled a very large rectangular cabinet—possibly eight feet high, eight feet wide, and fourteen feet long—onstage. Doors were opened on one end. A trainer led the elephant into the cabinet, the doors were closed, and the assistants turned the cabinet so that the opposite end was facing the audience. The front doors were opened, then the rear doors, allowing spectators—or at least the ones in the middle of the auditorium—to see through to the back of the stage.

According to Jim Steinmeyer, Houdini had a diagonal wall built inside the rectangular cabinet. The wall ran from the front corner to the center of the back of the cabinet, and one side was covered by a mirror that reflected the black interior. When the illusion began, with the cabinet turned sideways, the elephant was simply led straight into the space between the outer wall and the interior diagonal wall.

Ta-da: the elephant was nowhere to be seen.

Unless you get great pleasure from what you're doing, performing a magic trick can feel like taking actual candy from an actual baby. A great many prop-dependent tricks require no special talent except for the one

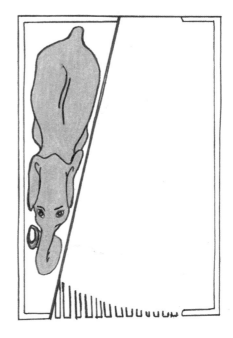

Houdini's elephant cabinet, viewed from above

Houdini didn't have: the talent to play the role of magician. Or, to put it another way, the talent to make believers believe. Because the great majority of people who pay to see a magic show *want* to be deceived, or enchanted: they want to see something magical, just as the reader who picks up a novel or story wants to be transported. We may never know why, but it could be that the role simply didn't fit. Hungarian-born, Wisconsin-raised Erik Weisz started out, after all, trying to imitate a famous Frenchman. So while it's true that Weisz was his most captivating, his most exciting, his most mythical, when he was squarely at the center of attention, Harry Houdini was a disguised self, an artistic creation—sometimes dressed in the traditional white shirt and black suit that never seemed to fit him, but often, more characteristically, stripped to the waist, displaying his impressive physique, as if he had nothing to hide. *As if.*

Poorly presented, magic tricks can seem like just that: trickery. The performer presents the audience with a puzzle to solve (How did that happen? or What really happened?), but the audience knows that it has been denied crucial information. Viewers aren't really being invited to solve the puzzle. The resulting tension can lead to anger, heckling, even violent attempts to storm the stage or dismantle props. The magician needs to create an air of belief, of possibility. His goal is to transform the puzzle into seeming mystery—to persuade the audience to marvel at the effect rather than to focus on how it was achieved. Magic, like fiction, plays on our childlike desire to believe in other worlds, transcendent possibilities, if only for a little while. Houdini was able to do that as an escape artist, in the guise of an enormously successful persona that didn't happen to be the magician persona he initially aimed to create. Many of us begin writing by imitating, consciously or not, writers we admire; eventually we might "find our voice," as the cliché goes—but only if we work to find it. And we might discover, while we're hunting, that a persona chooses us, that a particular stance serves our work best.

Why is it so important to create that persona, to carefully consider which of our many possible and invented selves we use to tell a particular story? Because while a piece of writing can access the universal only through the individual, there is danger at either extreme. Attempts to reach the universal directly yield blandness, cliché, or a generality true, finally, to no one's experience. At the other extreme is the self-indulgent, the narcissistic, the selfishly private. "The writer has to judge himself with a stranger's eye and a stranger's severity," Flannery O'Connor wrote. "No art is sunk in the self, but rather, in art the self becomes self-forgetful in order to meet the demands of the thing being seen and the thing being made." Poet Ellen Bryant Voigt echoes her: "There is a way, I think, in which the careful making of poems can distance or externalize the self—the gaze remains steadily outward, and the self becomes another small part of the world. The point is not to prohibit the personal, but to examine it with utter ruthlessness."

The model magician was Robert-Houdin because, more than anything else, magicians had been captivated by his astounding memoirs ... that painted the portrait of a magician as an artist.

— *Jim Steinmeyer*

The creators of that exhibit of self-portraits in France chose for its posters and advertisements not a work by one of their own countrymen but one by an American: Norman Rockwell's *Triple Self-Portrait*.

At first glance, Rockwell's image is simply a self-portrait one step removed, showing the artist at work. Almost immediately, though, we see another level of artifice: the image of the artist reflected in the mirror borders on comic in a way that Rockwell made famous. If we're uncertain whether we're laughing *at* or *with* the painter, we're tipped off by the painting within the painting. The presumed self-portrait, or supposedly accurate transcription of what the artist sees, bears only partial resemblance to what the painter sees in the mirror. The image on the canvas is

Triple Self-Portrait,
Norman Rockwell

something like noble. Gone are the glasses; the sagging pipe is raised, as are the eyebrows; and the painting appears to be in black and white, further emphasizing its removal from reality. Tipping the scale is the prop helmet at the top of the easel, further mocking the image of Greatness. Attached to the canvas are reproductions of self-portraits by painters Rockwell especially admired: Dürer, Rembrandt, Picasso, and Van Gogh.

The curator of the French exhibition of self-portraits claimed the paintings answered the question "Who am I?" Yet Rockwell seems not to be answering that question so much as asking it: "Who am I, to be making this self-portrait? Who am I to assert myself into such lofty company?" The portrait conveys a sense of humility, even self-mockery. The image is surprisingly complex—the artist painting himself looking into a mirror and painting himself, with every "self" distinct—and at the same time harmonious with the tone of Rockwell's most famous work, and his public persona. In representing himself three times, he gives us the comic figure (in the mirror), the Great Man (on the canvas), and then something we might be tempted to call the actual man, the painter at work. But the very fact that the three characters are different tells us that the implied fourth—the actual Norman Rockwell, who designed and executed the image—is not any one of these, exactly, but some combination of them, and of other characteristics we can't see. Norman Rockwell is the man who can stand back from himself well enough to see—and depict—these three different selves.

Like Erik Weisz playing Harry Houdini, Samuel Clemens playing Mark Twain, and David Shields playing David Shields, in his triple self-portrait Rockwell is on center stage yet out of sight. The curator who thought self-portraits are "the most intense unmasking of the artist's identity" missed the point. In their self-portraits, artists aren't exposed like poor stammering O. Z. Pinhead, the defrocked wizard. They are no more exposed than Houdini in that famous photograph reproduced at the start of this chapter. While the escape artist may be shackled and nearly naked, Houdini is neither vulnerable nor captive: he's in complete control. This was, after all, a publicity photograph. Rockwell, too, presented his audience with carefully calibrated images of himself. The casual viewer of his self-portrait might merely be amused or charmed. A more thoughtful viewer might recognize that Rockwell is, like Whitman, reminding us that we each contain multitudes. As writers, though, we recognize the true magic of the effect: while the artist appears to be captured on the page in front of us, in fact he is presenting exactly what he wants us to see, having found precisely where to stand in relation to his work.

THE LINE, THE PYRAMID, AND THE LABYRINTH

Line experiences many fates.

— WASSILY KANDINSKY

THE HEAD OF THE LINE

Some of our earliest experiences are related to lines. We trace lines, are told to color within the lines, and, in school, line up (the role of "line leader" being the first—and, in a few cases, the greatest—public honor some of us receive). An early game, for many children, is a simple sprint along a path ("Race you to the corner!"), where deviation from the line is poor sportsmanship ("You cheated!"). Board games from Candyland to Life require the players to make progress along a clearly marked path. But those journeys are a bit trickier; and as we develop, as our patience increases, movement along the line from beginning to end becomes

28 A secular version of an Indian game, Ladders to Salvation, in which the ladders rewarded virtue (faith, generosity, knowledge, etc.) and the slides downward punished vice (vanity, lying, debt, lust, and so on). In England the game became Snakes and Ladders. In his novel *Midnight's Children*, Salman Rushdie writes, "All games have morals; and the game of Snakes and Ladders captures, as no other activity can hope to do, the eternal truth that for every ladder you hope to climb, a snake is waiting just around the corner, and for every snake a ladder will compensate. But it's more than that; no mere carrot-and-stick affair; because implicit in the game is the unchanging twoness of things, the duality of up against down, good against evil; the solid rationality of ladders balances the occult sinuosities of the serpent; in the opposition of staircase and cobra we can see, metaphorically, all conceivable oppositions, Alpha against Omega, father against mother."

more complicated. In Chutes and Ladders,[28] a player's straightforward journey is influenced by ladders accelerating progress and chutes retarding it. In Trivial Pursuit, specific questions have to be answered before a player's or team's token can go forward.

We see the same phenomenon in sports. In theory, baseball involves completing circuits along a predetermined path more often than the members of the opposing team; but first there's the business of a ball to hit, and avoiding being put out. Golf involves hitting a ball from tee to green eighteen times—but high grass, sand, and water are there to impede progress. Football, on paper, is a walk in the park: all you need to do is carry a ball across a goal line. But there are those eleven hostile people who insist on getting in the way.... These games and sports, and others like them, occupy us not despite their obstacles, but because of them.

TIME/LINE

Lyric and narrative poetry are often distinguished by their relationship to time. A lyric poem can describe a moment, or even seem to hover outside of time, while a narrative, in relating one or more events, necessarily moves in time. I once heard a poet suggest that narrative's reliance on time meant that it is, by definition, linear. The implication was that while the lyric operates freely in any number of lovely ways, narrative is shackled to time like an old-school prisoner. The lyric is the music of heavenly spheres, while narrative is a steady progression of bowling balls tumbling from the closet: ca-thunk, ca-thunk, ca-thunk.

Many people, including the German aesthetician Gotthold Lessing, have asserted that the province of both poetry and prose, written forms, is time, while the province of visual art is space. But while time is certainly an element of narrative—any two events are related by sequence, causality, or both—narrative has no set or particular relationship to time. E. M. Forster helpfully defined story as a sequence of events, or a "chopped-off length of the tapeworm of time" (as opposed to plot, a series of events related by cause and effect), but that length can be (and is) re-chopped and rearranged in any number of ways. Narratives leap through time, go backward in time, and even, like a lyric poem, stand still in time. Charles Baxter's *First Light* moves back through the years, ending with the birth of one of the characters we've known as an adult; Joseph Heller's *Catch-22* seems to swirl in a vortex of time before spinning forward, to the main character's eventual decision to light out for Sweden, but also backward, to the shocking death he witnessed. Tobias Wolff's much-anthologized "Bullet in the Brain" begins with a scene in a bank in which the main character is shot in the head, then freezes time to tell us all that the dying man does and doesn't think. The story does not return to the present; time does not resume its movement forward.

This is simply to say that time in fiction is as elastic as it is in life. The three hours or so over which a professional football game is played pass in different ways for the head referee; the starting quarterback; the third-string quarterback on the sideline; the playback operator sitting in a truck in the parking lot; the studio commentator preparing halftime and postgame comments; the shivering cheerleader, her back to the action, smile frozen to her face; the passionate fan; her tolerant husband; the stadium concession worker cooking bratwurst; the small boy in the upper deck who can't see over the people in front of him and desperately needs to go to the bathroom, etc., etc. Even for the fan watching the final quarter on television, time moves in many different ways. There is the passage of fifteen minutes on the game clock, which will take place over something closer to forty-five minutes on the kitchen clock. Assuming he cares about the outcome, the part of those forty-five minutes spent actually watching the football field will pass differently than the time when the game is "interrupted" by commercials (though nonfans in the house might find the commercials a great relief). If his

A Ladders to Salvation game board

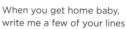

When you get home baby, write me a few of your lines

When you get home baby, write me a few of your lines

It would be consolation

To ease my worried mind.

— *Fred McDowell*

team is holding on to a slim lead, the time on the game clock is likely to seem to move with excruciating deliberation; if his team is behind, the seconds fly past like pennies on a gas pump. Between plays, he'll see carefully chosen clips from earlier in the game, even from previous games. Since the precious few moments of actual activity on the field have a heightened dramatic charge, significant moments will be replayed, often more than once, in slow motion, so that something that happened in a fraction of a second—a ball slipping from a player's hand just inches from the goal line—will be elongated in a kind of glorious ecstasy, or agony.

Were you thinking that those were the words, those upright lines?

those curves, angles, dots?

— *Walt Whitman*

Developing a structure is seldom that simple. Almost always there is considerable tension between chronology and theme.

— JOHN McPHEE

To say that the province of fiction is time, then, does not tell us much. While narrative may involve events, and while events take place in time, and while time itself might seem to move in one direction at a constant speed (though that is rarely the way we experience it), there is nothing particularly linear about narrative—or, more accurately, the narrative line is no simple thing. It is certainly not the sort of line most of us learned about in geometry class, without width or depth, straight and infinite.

In discussing fiction, we might refer to a particular story's or novel's linearity, but this is not usually praise. Readers don't tend to say "I love how linear this is." Instead, the term—often invoked but rarely defined— is used as a kind of vague criticism. "This story just seems so linear" means the story is direct, predictable, relentless, obvious, tedious, and/ or dull; it means the story lacks reversal, misdirection, tension, suspense, or surprise.

Most of us are of at least two minds regarding linearity. We use the terms "line of thought," "line of argument," and "linear thinking" both as high praise and as harsh criticism. How clear is her thinking? She articulates her line of thought with tremendous precision. What's his problem? Linear thinking—he's entirely incapable of thinking outside the box. Toeing the line can be a sign of virtue or repression; walking a fine line, dangerous. Some lines are pickups, some are putdowns. It's considered admirable to have a line of work, less admirable to give someone a line. More and more of us either need or want to be online throughout the day, though being forced offline can be a relief. Defending the front line is a good thing; adhering to the party line, maybe not so much.

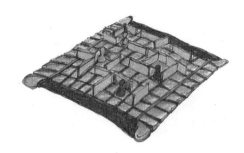

In the game Quoridor, each player attempts to construct a safe line of passage for her piece while impeding the progress of her opponent(s).

Prehistoric people seem to have recognized the significance of certain lines: think of the careful placement of openings in walls to align with the sun's rays on the solstice, the arrangement of monumental blocks of rock at Stonehenge. Geometric shapes and patterns cut into the earth (even, we've recently learned, in the apparently not-always-forested Amazon rainforests) may or may not have served as runways for alien spaceships, but they certainly indicate an early interest in man-made shapes. Long before tractors made them easier to create, farmers understood that orderly rows of crops increased efficiency of labor, fertilizer, and water; they also understood that some crops should be planted in lines parallel to the contours of the earth.

Linear thinking is often related to analysis and argumentation, something respected and promoted by Pythagoras, Euclid, and mathematicians, logicians, philosophers, and scientists who followed them. Linearity was also crucial to the Industrial Revolution—think conveyor belts,

Sing to me of the man, Muse, the man of twists and turns

Driven time and time again off course . . .

— Homer

assembly lines, and your car's alignment. Linearity, then, can be a virtue; but in fiction, as in games, our imagination is most energetically engaged when straightforward progress is challenged.

Discussions of fiction often involve wanton abuse of the terms of Euclidean geometry. In a single conversation, one person might refer to a story's narrative line, another to its narrative arc, and still another to Freytag's triangle, and everyone will proceed as if these three things—a line, an arc, and a triangle—were interchangeable.

Gustav Freytag's 1863 text *The Technique of the Drama* contains exactly one illustration. It appears in his chapter titled "The Construction of the Drama," which he begins by telling his readers, "Through the two halves of the action which come closely together at one point, the drama possesses—if one may symbolize its arrangement by lines—a pyramidal structure." What is often referred to as "Freytag's triangle" in writing handbooks is not called a triangle in *his* book, for the very sound reason that it is not a triangle.

A triangle, as most third graders know, has three sides. Freytag was not describing drama as something with three sides. He was instead elaborating on Aristotle, in order to apply his ideas to Shakespeare, among other playwrights. In the *Poetics*, Aristotle says, "Every tragedy consists of a complication and a resolution.... By *complication* I mean everything from the beginning up to and including the section which immediately precedes the change to good fortune or bad fortune; by *resolution* I mean everything from the beginning of the change of fortune to the end."[29]

Freytag has more to say on the matter but makes his way to this: "[The] two chief parts of the drama are firmly united by a point of the action which lies directly in the middle. This middle, the climax of the play, is the most important place of the structure: the action rises to this; the action falls away from this." Several pages later, introducing his diagram, he calls the starting point of the pyramid the introduction, the top point the climax, and the ending point the catastrophe. Three points, two sides, clear enough.

But in the very next sentence the pyramid begins to shudder: "Between these three parts lie [the parts of] the *rise* and the *fall*. Each of these five parts may consist of a single scene, or a succession of connected scenes, but the climax is usually composed of one chief scene. These parts of the drama, (a) *introduction*, (b) *rise*, (c) *climax*, (d) *return or fall*, (e)

[29] In translation, via the fragments of someone's notes that survived.

catastrophe, have each what is peculiar in purpose and in construction."

The situation gets worse, but let's pause here. Gustav Freytag was a scholar, poet, novelist, critic, playwright, editor, and soldier. His best-known creative work seems to have been a novel translated into English as *Debit and Credit*, "the purpose of which" was, according to the introduction to the translation of *The Technique of the Drama*, "to show the value and dignity of a life of labor." And here, as he tries to explain dramatic structure with an overly simple illustration, we see evidence of hard labor. To Freytag's credit, he recognized that things were much more complicated than his pyramid makes it seem. There are not three important points, but five (so far). The five can each consist of a single scene or more; but usually the climax is a single scene. His qualifications are like minor tremors. He continues:

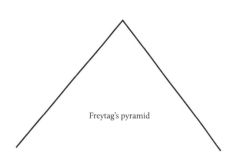

Freytag's pyramid

> Between them stand three important scenic effects, through which the parts are separated as well as bound together. Of these three dramatic moments, or crises, one, which indicates the beginning of the stirring action, stands between the introduction and the rise; the second, the beginning of the counter-action, between the climax and the return; the third, which must rise once more before the catastrophe, between the return and the catastrophe. They are called here the exciting moment or force, the tragic moment or force, and the moment or force of the last suspense. . . . In the following sections, therefore, the eight component parts of the drama will be discussed in their natural order.

We can almost hear the sweat dripping off the poor man's brow. Any writer who has seen a metaphor collapse can sympathize; but of course the proper course of action is to start over and try to get it right. Not Freytag. Having imagined a simple illustration, he seems to have had no interest in creating a more detailed one, one that would account for his eight important points (some of which, he explains, are optional). The copy of *The Technique* I consulted—like, one imagines, every copy of the book read by anyone sympathetic to the author's struggles—is filled with notes, an indication of where the missing points might belong on the diagram, and black bumps indicating interruptions of the path up to the climax and the path down to the appropriately labeled *catastrophe*. In the years since Freytag wrote, other writers have depicted "his" pyramid in a variety of ways, with any number of slopes and angles, to illustrate those three—or five, or eight—parts, and their relative duration. All of which is to say that Freytag's pyramid was never a precise illustration of how narratives are constructed.

More to our purpose: Freytag wasn't trying to tell anyone how to write a short story or novel. He was analyzing plays, with particular emphasis on the Greeks and Shakespeare, and how those earlier plays informed German practice.

Geometry means *earth measure*. Why on earth should we expect a nineteenth-century German's nontriangular illustration of Greek drama to describe twenty-first-century stories?

THE WRITER AS WAYFARER

In discussions of work in progress, and in evaluating our own drafts, we are sometimes inclined to overemphasize the movement from beginning to end, what we often call story or plot, actions or events. This is not to say story, plot, actions, and events are unimportant. William Goldman (Hollywood legend, author of *Butch Cassidy and the Sundance Kid* and *The Princess Bride*, among many other screenplays and novels) says that a screenplay needs to have a spine, and every scene must be attached to that spine, and that's useful advice, particularly for a certain type of tightly knit fiction. Before him, Aristotle said, "A whole is what has a beginning and middle and end," and

> plot . . . should imitate a single, unified action—and one that
> is also a whole. So the structure of the various sections of the

events must be such that the transposition or removal of any one section dislocates and changes the whole. If the presence or absence of something has no discernible effect, it is not part of the whole.

But overemphasizing that single line of continuity running from beginning to end can be a mistake. Even Aristotle recognized the value of reversal, astonishment, and the irrational.

Certainly, plot is a useful and often engaging element of fiction, just as paraphraseable content and even narrative can be among the memorable aspects of a poem. "The Charge of the Light Brigade" would not be much without the charge of the light brigade, Walt Whitman's "Noiseless, Patient Spider" needs its web-spinning spider, and without that horse and the snowy evening we'd care less about why Robert Frost was in a funk. Beginning, middle, and ending are important; but the thing we most prize in a story or novel or poem is rarely that simple journey from start to finish.

The line that describes the beautiful is elliptical. It has simplicity and constant change. It cannot be described by a compass, and it changes direction at every one of its points.

— RUDOLF ARNHEIM

The Orochon people of the Russian Far East have long depended on hunting reindeer. According to anthropologist Tim Ingold, "As they go on their way, [Orochon] hunters are ever attentive to the landscape that unfolds along the path, and to its living animal inhabitants. Here and there, animals may be killed. But every kill is left where it lies, to be retrieved later, while the path itself meanders on.... When, however, the hunter subsequently goes back to collect his kill, he drives his sledge directly to the site where the carcass has been cached." The path taken on the hunt, referred to as the saddle path, meanders, and has no predetermined destination; the return path, or sledge path, is, in contrast, the most direct path between the carcasses and the destination. The path out, Ingold says, is a line of wayfaring; the path back is a line of transport.

As readers, we patiently follow a narrative, both the sequence of events and the string of sentences. Uncertain of where we're heading, we are alternately absorbed in the moment; linking what we're reading to what we've already read; and imagining what's coming, or could be coming. We recalibrate with each turn in our reading that seems significant, each development that gives us a different sense of the whole. Opening a new book is like entering a stranger's house. We inhabit the work; we're actively engaged in it; we're discovering it. Similarly, as writers, in the process of drafting, we may have a general goal—something that feels complete, or the exploration of some moment or event or character—but our pursuit of that goal usually involves a good deal of meandering. We are in search of something at least as elusive as reindeer.

When we reread, we tend to see each part of a story in terms of how it contributes to the whole; we're more acutely aware of how the story accumulates, or makes sense. We're more aware of a destination. Even when the work eludes us, or our rereading yields new discoveries, every reading after the first is influenced by our knowledge of what will and won't happen. We know a good deal about where the path goes and where it ends.

As writers, when we revise, especially if readers of a draft have expressed confusion or uncertainty about aspects of our story or poem, or if we worry that we've made the reader's job too difficult, we might feel obliged to provide transport, to convey the reader efficiently from one point to the next. But while clarity can be a virtue, directness, reduction, and simplification don't always serve the work, our own interests, or our readers' deepest interests. If it seems perverse not to provide a reader with efficient transport, it might help to remember that, as early as the days of playing Chutes and Ladders, most people have gotten some pleasure from the tension caused by delays and obstruction, interruption of direct progress along a line.

The serpentine line, or the line of grace, by its waving and winding its different ways, leads the eye in a pleasing manner along the continuity of its variety.

— *William Hogarth*

A MUSE AND A MAZE

Guidelines for highly functional public pathways, best practices concerning width and slope and surface materials, are meant to promote

safe and efficient movement from one point to another. But when a path is meant to create interest, or to provide a place for contemplation or relaxation, the rules change. Garden paths, for instance, are often intentionally narrow, to encourage the visitor to slow down; they curve and meander, ideally with part of the path hidden from sight, to create a sense of mystery and discovery. Even when a path needs to be straight, edges are obscured to soften the walkway, and surface materials are employed to stop us short, physically or visually.

In the short segment of a path shown here, many things are being done to interrupt that straight line of "progress." The orientation of the pavers in the foreground immediately makes us hesitate—while there's no particular need to use them, our impulse is to step onto each of the turned squares. The space between and around the paving stones makes the path seem narrower, so makes us deliberate. The two slabs of stone that serve as the left side of the bridge seem perfectly solid, but there's something unnerving about the fact that they stop short of the far bank. Again, there's nothing especially precarious about this arrangement, but it's unusual, and our brain tells us to hesitate, to assess. We see we'll need to move to the right, and the two slabs on that side seem, oddly, to be balancing on just one support. We either worry about what we can't see, or, based on the

St. Jerome
in the
Wilderness
(detail), by
Albrecht
Dürer

Not a line nor dot of Dürer's can be displaced without harm.... All add to the effect, and either express something, or illumine something, or relieve something.... [In] modern tree drawings ... though good and forcible general effect is produced, the lines are thrown in by thousands without special intention, and might just as well go one way as another, so only that there be enough of them to produce all together a well-shaped effect of intricacy: and you will find that a little careless scratching about with your pen will bring you very near the same result without an effort; but that no scratching of pen, nor any fortunate chance, nor anything but downright skill and thought, will imitate so much as one leaf of Dürer's. Yet there is considerable intricacy and glittering confusion in the interstices of those vine leaves of his, as well as of the grass.

— *John Ruskin*

evidence of the slabs' apparent stability, we trust that there are other supports out of sight. Then, after crossing, we confront a gate—ajar, inviting, but another barrier, a place to pause. For that matter, even before we move forward, the visual arrangement of materials encourages us to stop, to take in what's ahead. One straight stretch of concrete would make it easier for us—even compel us—to hurry along. But getting to the end of this path is not the point. Everything about it tells us to slow down, to look around, to be engaged in a moment and a place. Similarly, even as fiction (or a book about fiction writing) promises to lead us somewhere, it encourages us to dwell in the moment, to inhabit our reading.

In *Lines: A Brief History*, Tim Ingold separates lines into two general categories: threads and traces. A thread, he says, is "a filament . . . which may be entangled with other threads or suspended between points": string, yarn, a spider's webbing. Traces, in contrast, are "enduring marks left in or on a solid surface" by addition or reduction: ink on paper, symbols chiseled out of stone. Ingold points out that "*linea* . . . originally meant a thread made from flax . . . woven into cloth we now call *linen*." The verb "to weave" in Latin was *texere*, the source of both "textile" and "text." In writing, then, we use traces, or marks on a surface, to weave threads in a text.

Weaving creates texture and draws things together. A large-scale example: in his *Canterbury Tales*, Chaucer weaves disparate tales, tellers, and storytelling styles together to create a work larger and richer than any one of the stories. Some might argue that the work maintains its place in our imaginations not despite the fact that it went unfinished but, in part, because it is unfinished—the loose threads invite us to imagine more. This is part of the appeal of fragments and ruins, but not all fragments are equally captivating. Chaucer's plan for the work—the framework he created—and the richness and variety of the pieces he did complete are what inspire us to imagine the whole, and what have inspired others (in literary fiction, graphic novels, and even a book of puzzles) to imitate it.

Within the completed tales we can see Chaucer's awareness of the usefulness of drawing our attention to the weave. In the Knight's Tale, for instance, after going on about Palamon, he has the knight tell us,

> Now will I cease (speaking) of Palamon for a little while,
> And leave him to dwell in his prison still,
> And of Arcite forth I will tell you.

and

> They began to smite like wild boars,
> That froth at the mouth white as foam for mad anger.

THE PARDONER'S PUZZLE

The gentle Pardoner, "that straight was come from the court of Rome," begged to be excused, but the company would not spare him. "Friends and fellow pilgrims," said he, "of a truth the riddle that I have made is but a poor thing, but it is the best that I have been able to devise. Blame my lack of knowledge of such matters if it be not to your liking." But his invention was very well received. He produced the accompanying plan and said that it represented sixty-four towns through which he had to pass during some of his pilgrimages, and the lines connecting them were roads. He explained that the puzzle was to start from the large black town and visit all the other towns once, and once only, in [a single pilgrimage consisting of fifteen straight lines]. Try to trace the route … with your pencil. You may end where you like, but note that the apparent omission of a little road at the bottom is intentional, as it seems it was impossible to go that way.

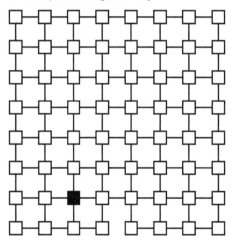

— Henry Ernest Dudeney

They fought up to the ankle in their blood.
And in this manner I leave them to remain fighting,
And forth I will tell you of Theseus.

and

But I will stop speaking of Theseus
a little while,
And speak of Palamon and of Arcite.

and

Now I will stop (speaking) of the gods above,
Of Mars, and of Venus, goddess of love,
And tell you as plainly as I can
The essential part, for which I began.

In each case, the Knight could simply stop talking about one character or scene and begin talking about the next. Instead, Chaucer deliberately draws our attention to severed threads, dropped lines, in order to create a sense of stories that could continue and stories that have already begun. In doing so, he actively encourages us to imagine a whole larger than what is on the page—something like the way those stone slabs extending nearly across the stream invite us to imagine another type of bridge. The rhetorical gesture creates the impression of interruption and digression, a sense that a narrative line has been abandoned or abruptly ended—though if he hadn't drawn our attention to them, we would have thought the narrative to be unbroken. Often, fiction both draws us into a specifically depicted series of thoughts and events and encourages us to imagine more. For a contemporary example, see Anne Carson's *Nox*, an elegy to her brother, which includes reproductions of partial documents and deliberately obscured and illegible text to convey both a sense of loss and the impossibility of fully comprehending the departed.

Is there such a thing as a linear story?
    There is; I've written one.

The Box
Once there was a boy who wanted a bike. One day a man knocked on the door. He was holding a box. It was a bike!

Granted, I was five years old, but I think you'll agree it shows promise. Note the expression of the character's desire (clearly anticipating years of workshops in which someone would say, "But what does this guy *want*?"); note the economical shift from exposition into scene, and the deliberately withheld information about the secondary character. (What man? My father? No, my father had already vetoed the bike.) And then, in the third sentence, the introduction of suspense. If only I had stopped there . . .

So: a pretty poor excuse for a story. The voyage from introduction to climax to (happy) catastrophe does not offer much to the reader. But there are fairly straightforward-seeming stories that have engaged readers, and those include fables and folktales. "Petie Pete versus Witch Bea-Witch,"[30] from Italo Calvino's landmark *Italian Folktales*, goes like

---

30 *Petie Pete versus Witch Bea-Witch*

Petie Pete was a little boy just so tall who went to school. On the school road was a garden with a pear tree, which Petie Pete used to climb and eat the pears. Beneath the tree passed Witch Bea-Witch one day and said:

  "Petie Pete, pass me a pear
  With your little paw!
  I mean it, don't guffaw,
  My mouth waters, I swear, I swear!"

Petie Pete thought, Her mouth waters not for the pears but for me, and refused to come down the tree. He plucked a pear and threw it to Witch Bea-Witch. But the pear fell on the ground right where a cow had been by and deposited one of its mementos.

Witch Bea-Witch repeated:

  "Petie Pete, pass me a pear
  With your little paw!
  I mean it, don't guffaw,
  My mouth waters, I swear, I swear!"

this: Young Petie Pete is in a pear tree when he's called by a witch, who asks him to hand her a pear. In fact, she wants to kidnap him, take him home, and eat him. Petie Pete falls for her devious ruse but then, through cunning, he escapes.

That's pretty much it. In summary, the tale doesn't seem any more promising than "The Box." In basic plot the narrative would seem to be depicted nicely by Freytag's pyramid. At the outset, Petie Pete is, implicitly, enjoying himself in the pear tree (introduction). The witch appears, confronts him with her request and bad intent, and when he climbs down, pops Pete into a bag and takes him to her home, where her daughter will cook him (climax). In the final scene, Pete prevails over both the witch and her daughter (catastrophe). We can also identify rising and falling action—which is to say, if we want to pretend that "Petie Pete versus Witch Bea-Witch" is aptly illustrated by Freytag's pyramid, we can. But that illustration of the basic story line, the essential sequence of events, does very little to help us understand why the story of Petie Pete has held listeners' interest for over a century.

The tale divides neatly into three sections. (1) Witch Bea-Witch convinces Petie Pete to come down from his tree and stuffs him into her bag, but when she stops to relieve herself, Petie Pete gnaws through the cord holding the bag shut and puts a large stone inside. When the witch gets home, she has her daughter heat water in their cauldron and opens her

---

But Petie Pete stayed in the tree and tossed down another pear, which fell on the ground right where a horse had been by and left a big puddle.

Witch Bea-Witch repeated her request, and Petie Pete thought it wiser to comply. He scampered down and offered her a pear. Witch Bea-Witch opened up her bag, but instead of putting in the pear, she put in Petie Pete, tied up the bag, and slung it over her shoulder.

After going a little way, Witch Bea-Witch had to stop and relieve herself; she put the bag down and went behind a bush. Meanwhile, with his little teeth as sharp as a rat's, Petie Pete gnawed the cord in two that tied the bag, jumped out, shoved a heavy rock into the bag, and fled. Witch Bea-Witch took up the bag once more and flung it over her shoulder.

"O Petie Pete,
To carry you is a feat!"

she said, and wound her way home. The door was closed, so Witch Bea-Witch called her daughter:

"Maggy Mag! Marguerite!
Come undo the door;
Then I ask you more:
Put on the pot to stew Petie Pete."

Maggy Mag opened up, then placed a caldron of water over the fire. When the water came to a boil Witch Bea-Witch emptied her bag into it. *Splash!* went the stone and crashed through the caldron. Water poured into the fire and spattered all over the floor, burning Witch Bea-Witch's legs.

"Mamma, just what do you mean
By boiling stones in our tureen?"

cried Maggy Mag, and Witch Bea-Witch, dancing up and down in pain, snapped:

"Child, rekindle the flame;
I'll be back in a flash with something tame."

She changed clothes, donned a blond wig, and went out with the bag.

A MUSE AND A MAZE

bag, only to find the rock. (2) Witch Bea-Witch goes back to the pear tree and again convinces Petie Pete to come down. Again, the witch stops to relieve herself; this time, Petie Pete finds the bag tied too tightly to gnaw his way out, so he attracts the attention of a quail hunter who happens to be passing by, and convinces the hunter to put his dog in the bag. At home, after her daughter heats the water, the witch opens the bag and the dog eats up their hens. (The attentive reader might wonder why the witch and her daughter don't simply boil a chicken for dinner; but we might as well ask why the witch doesn't treat her apparent urinary tract infection.) (3) The witch returns to the pear tree, persuades Petie Pete to come down, goes home with "no rest stops," and shuts him up in the chicken coop. The next morning, Petie Pete fools the daughter and chops off her head. When the witch comes back, she sees Petie Pete on the hood above the fireplace; she tries to climb up after him, but falls into the fire and burns to ashes.

Each of the three sections has the same three components: Petie Pete is approached by the witch, Petie Pete is fooled by the witch, and Petie Pete outwits the witch. Having something occur twice illustrates either simple repetition or contrast; having something happen three times creates pattern. Pattern creates anticipation. (In the film *Groundhog Day*, the first time we see Phil Connors, the TV weatherman played by Bill Murray, walk through Punxsutawney, we're simply watching what

---

Instead of going on to school, Petie Pete had climbed back up the pear tree. In disguise, Witch Bea-Witch came by again, hoping he wouldn't recognize her, and said:

"Petie Pete, pass me a pear
With your little paw!
I mean it, don't guffaw,
My mouth waters, I swear, I swear!"

But Petie Pete had recognized her and dared not come down:

"Pears I refuse old Witch Bea-Witch,
Who would bag me without a hitch."

Then Witch Bea-Witch reassured him:

"I'm not the soul you think, I swear,
This morning only did I leave my lair.
Petie, Pete, pass me a pear
With your little paw so fair."

She kept on until she finally talked Petie Pete into coming down and giving her a pear. At once she shoved him down into the bag.

Reaching the bushes, she once again had to stop and relieve herself; but this time the bag was tied too tight for Petie Pete to get away. So what did he do but call "Bobwhite" several times in imitation of quail. A hunter with his dog out hunting quail found the bag and opened it. Petie Pete jumped out and begged the hunter to put the dog into the bag in his place. When Witch Bea-Witch returned and shouldered the bag, the dog inside did nothing but squirm and whine, and Witch Bea-Witch said:

"Petie Pete, there's nothing to help you,
Bark like a dog is all you can do."

She got home and called her daughter:

"Maggy Mag! Marguerite!
Come undo the door;

---

happens; the second time, we're understanding, along with the character, that he's essentially reliving the same day, and that the people around him don't know that; the third time he awakens to Sonny and Cher singing "I Got You, Babe," we immediately begin to anticipate what might follow.)

While it's tempting to say that Petie Pete's three sections each take the shape of Freytag's pyramid, no one of them stands as a complete story; the three together are the story. The three sections escalate in tension and outcome. At the same time, they grow shorter, because we already know the essential situation; the teller of the tale can focus on the variation. In *Italian Folktales*, the first section is about a page and a third, the second slightly shorter, the third just half a page.

As retold by Calvino, the tale invokes other threes. In the first section, the witch calls to Petie Pete three times. The first two times he throws her a pear; the third time he hands it to her, and she snatches him up. The first time he throws a pear, it lands where "a cow had ... deposited one of its mementos"; the second time, it lands where "a horse had ... left a big puddle"; after she ties Petie Pete into her bag, the witch stops to relieve herself. In the first section, the witch presumably has black hair; in the second, she disguises herself by wearing a blond wig; in the third, she disguises herself by wearing a red wig. The witch's incantatory

---

Then I ask you more:
Put on the pot to stew Petie Pete."

But when she went to empty the bag into the boiling water, the angry dog slipped out, bit her on the shin, dashed into the yard, and gobbled up hens left and right.

"Mamma, have you lost your mind?
Is it on dogs you now want to dine?"

exclaimed Maggy Mag. Witch Bea-Witch snapped:

"Child, rekindle the flame;
I'll be back in a flash."

She changed clothes, donned a red wig, and returned to the pear tree. She went on at such length that Petie Pete fell into the trap once more. This time there were no rest stops. She carried the bag straight home where her daughter was waiting on the doorstep for her.
"Shut him up in the chicken coop," ordered the Witch, "and early tomorrow morning while I'm out, make him into hash with potatoes."

The next morning Maggy Mag took a carving board and knife to the henhouse and opened a little hen door.

"Petie Pete, just for fun.
Please lay your head upon this board."

He replied:

"First show me how!"

Maggy Mag laid her neck on the board, and Petie Pete picked up the carving knife and cut off her head, which he put on to fry in the frying pan.
Witch Bea-Witch came back and exclaimed:

"Marguerite, dear daughter,
What have you thrown in the fryer?"

"Me" piped Petie Pete, sitting on the hood over the fireplace.
"How did you get way up there?" asked Witch Bea-Witch.
"I piled one pot on top of the other and came on up."
So Witch Bea-Witch tried to make a ladder of pots to go after him, but when she got halfway to the top the pots came crashing down, and into the fire she fell and burned to ashes.

A MUSE AND A MAZE

request—"Petie Pete, pass me a pear / With your little paw! / I mean it, don't guffaw, / My mouth waters, I swear, I swear," is repeated three times; and so on. While some of these details are related to the tale's plot, the primary purpose of this patterning is to provide texture or surface interest; and the abundance of it helps explain why Calvino said the Italian folktale is characterized by "grace, wit, and unity of design."

The story doesn't simply keep breaking into thirds. It also alternates between prose and verse, as the characters often speak in rhyming couplets or quatrains. And we can't overlook the Looney Tunes logic of the characters: Witch Bea-Witch is intent on eating Petie Pete—never mind the fact that she has a yard full of chickens. Petie Pete understands from the outset that the witch wants to eat him, but when she repeats her request for a pear a third time, we're told "he found it wiser to comply." Why? This story answers no whys. The second time the witch confronts him, all we're told is that "she kept on until she finally talked Petie Pete into coming down." The third time, "She went on at such length that Petie Pete fell into the trap once more." Petie Pete may be clever, but he also appears to be an idiot. Lucky for him, Maggy Mag, the witch's daughter, is apparently related to Wile E. Coyote: on the verge of chopping off the boy's head, she says "Petie Pete, just for fun, / Please lay your head upon this board"; when he says "First show me how," she does. Poor decision. The basic conflict—the witch's bad intent and Petie Pete's desire for self-preservation—makes perfect sense. Within that conflict, the character's actions and responses are nonsensical, unpredictable, and comic.

Repetition creates anticipation; surprise creates uncertainty. By combining the two, this little tale produces both forward momentum and tension. It's important to note that the characters' "logic" has no answer—it's never explained. In fact, the story ends with a bit of nonsense: Petie Pete sits on the hood above the fireplace, the witch asks how he got there, and somehow she falls from a stack of pans and burns to death in her fireplace. She might just as easily have fallen into a well, or been shot by a passing quail hunter. While the basic plot might seem as straightforward as the plot of "The Box," this irrationality provides a quavering strangeness, a kind of mystery. At the same time, our basic expectation is satisfied, as young Petie Pete prevails.

Again: can Freytag's pyramid be found in this folktale? Sure. But to

The Russian abstract artist Wassily Kandinsky said that the fundamental elements of painting are the point and the line. In *Point and Line to Plane*, he says the point "represents the briefest, constant, innermost assertion." He explains the importance of size and placement of the point, and demonstrates how a dancer's leap can be expressed as a "five-pointed plane."

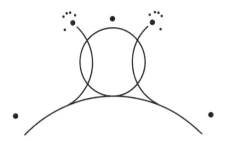

The line, Kandinsky goes on to say, "is the track made by the moving point." A point has no direction; it becomes a line when one or more forces are applied. So: Petie Pete in the pear tree is at rest; he is a point; he is silent. That point turns to a line when force is applied—when the ill-intentioned witch makes her request.

Rhythm, Kandinsky says, is created through repetition of the line. His examples, below, illustrate repetition at equal intervals, repetition at uniformly increasing intervals, and repetition in unequal intervals.

The basic action of "Petie Pete versus Witch Bea-Witch" could, then, be described in terms of a line—the witch's encounter with Petie Pete—repeated at uniformly increasing intervals. In Kandinsky's terms, the repeated elements in each of those encounters provide both quantitative and qualitative reinforcement—the exact repetition is quantitative, the gradual changes are qualitative. If each section of the tale reminds us of Freytag's pyramid, we might illustrate the entire narrative like this:

Or, to recognize that each of the first two episodes resolves that episode but not the story,

But that would still account only for the essential action, and not for the other elements that make the story memorable.

Kandinsky classifies lines as straight or curved. A straight line, he says, is the result of a single force being applied to a point; a curved line results from two forces being applied simultaneously. A straight line can be redirected to form angles, or zigzags, and a curved line can change direction as the forces applied to it change. A painting can be composed of both straight and curved lines.

The straight-lined angles in the illustration above represent the three encounters between Petie and the witch. We need a curved line to represent the curious, surprising, and comic logic of the characters. The curved line overlaps the straight lines, as the basic events and the characters' surprising actions and responses are simultaneous— and it's the combination of the familiar, repeated action and the unique details of Petie's interactions with the witch that make the tale distinct. Kandinsky says the "contrasting combination of a curved line with an angular line [results in] the characteristics of both [acquiring] a strengthened sound."

see the tale as an illustration of that pyramid at work overlooks virtually everything that makes it interesting.

The predictability and anticipation of a repetitive structure as well as the repetition of detail, with variation, combines with an ongoing chain of unpredictable elements. On their own, neither the tidy, nearly symmetrical structure nor the apparently random and inexplicable actions and decisions would be as effective.

We see—or hear—something similar in music all the time. We happily sing a song whose refrain includes the syllables "Goo goo ga joob" in part because the sounds of the words and syllables give us pleasure, in part because the music is so rhythmic and melodic that we are carried along by the nonverbal qualities of the song. We accept this combination of rigid pattern (especially in popular music, but to some extent in virtually all music) and surface irregularity. Children accept, even delight in, some degree of nonsense; the reading habits of adults sometimes veer dangerously to the reductive. As writers, we have the opportunity to remind readers of the pleasure that can come from not knowing and from partial understanding: the pleasure of mystery. Despite the familiarity of its basic story—clever boy outwits witch, or hero outwits oafish bully (think Odysseus and the Cyclops), "Petie Pete" ultimately illustrates not simplicity but the kind of complexity at work in most satisfying fiction.

MAZE OR LABYRINTH?

While some board games complicate the route from beginning to end, others have neither a beginning nor an end—and some do away with the route. Progress is measured by other means. In Monopoly, players could, theoretically, make infinite loops around Atlantic City accumulating wealth, though the game's constraints are designed to put an end to things, eventually: (a) each trip becomes more hazardous as rents increase, (b) players are required to continue moving around the board, which becomes a financial minefield to the extent that being incarcerated can come as a relief, and (c) the money supply is limited. Clue has its own rules for the way tokens may be moved on the board, but players

31 The North American game was developed from the British Cluedo, invented in 1944 by Anthony E. Pratt as a diversion during air raid drills. In recent years a number of variants have been published, including one where the conservatory and billiard room are replaced by a spa and home theater.

are like wayfarers, heading off to various locations to try to determine who killed poor Mr. Boddy, where, and by what means.[31] The goal isn't to follow a path so much as to explore a space, making Clue a precursor to many video games. Rather than reach a finish line, or the square numbered 100 in Chutes and Ladders, players are trying to obtain information. While Clue is referred to as a murder mystery, by our definition it's a puzzle players compete to solve. The number of rooms, suspects, and weapons is limited, and these constraints combine with the rules of the game to ensure that the solution can be deduced.

As readers, we move through a story identifying significant information, accumulating understanding about characters and events. While in some cases the focus of the story is apparent from the outset, in others the challenge is intensified by the fact that, on first reading, we don't know what we're looking for: we can see where we're starting, but we don't know where we're headed. In this way, certain stories are like mazes: the characters, events, images and information we're given offer a variety of possible routes, and as we read we realize that some end, others are less likely to be pursued, while still others continue to lead us forward. This is complicated by the fact that stories accumulate meaning in a variety of ways: so while we might identify one or more main characters fairly quickly, and the importance of some scenes and actions will be clear immediately, the significance of various gestures, speeches, images, and metaphors may become evident only gradually. The reader is Theseus in the labyrinth, unspooling thread in order to find his way out of what he's getting himself into.

While Alice Munro is regarded by many as one of the greatest living short-story writers, and she recently received the Nobel Prize in Literature, some readers have trouble appreciating her work. Those readers find her stories confusing: without clear direction, without emphatic conclusion. Her stories seem to be about something, as Allen Grossman said about poetry, the way a cat is about a house. Chekhov tells us not to look to artists for answers to life's problems, but readers who struggle with Munro's work sometimes have trouble identifying the question.

Even more than most literary writers, Munro is less interested in transporting us from a beginning to an ending than she is interested in encouraging us to dwell. This doesn't mean her stories are shapeless or

A MUSE AND A MAZE

pointless; far from it. But Freytag's pyramid is not the best tool to use to understand how her stories work. In her case, it might be more helpful to think of a story as a labyrinth.

To refresh your memory: In Greek mythology, King Minos made an error in judgment and, as a result, his wife gave birth to a creature half-man, half-bull: the Minotaur. Minos had Daedalus design and build a labyrinth to encage the beast. Each year, the seven most courageous young men and seven most beautiful young women of Athens were sent in, sacrificed to the monster. Theseus, an Athenian with a good track record of setting things straight, volunteered to descend into the labyrinth and kill the Mino-taur—the problem then being to make his way back out, as even Daedalus had trouble finding his way free. As luck would have it, Ariadne, King Minos's daughter, fell in love with Theseus and passed along two bits of advice from Daedalus. The first was that Theseus should tie one end of a skein of thread to the door as he entered, and unravel the rest as he traveled. The second was to go forward and down, never left or right. The-seus famously slew the beast and found his way out of the labyrinth. After that, in most versions of the myth, things go south: in one, he marries Ariadne but they're unhappy; in another, he dis-covers Ariadne was already married; in another, he unaccountably forgets about her and sails back to Athens. The story has been retold in various ways over a very long time in part because it is

A labyrinth: elaborate, time-consuming, with changes of direction difficult to predict if you're walking in it, but a single path, with no possible wrong turns.

metaphorically potent. We have all journeyed into the darkness, we have all grasped for the threads that will help us find our way; and the biggest challenges seem to require going further into the dark, complex, threat-ening unknown.

While the terms "labyrinth" and "maze" are often used interchange-ably, some reserve "labyrinth" to refer to a single (albeit indirect) path that leads, eventually, to one destination, and "maze" to refer to a branching puzzle with choices of path and direction. This is a useful distinction: a

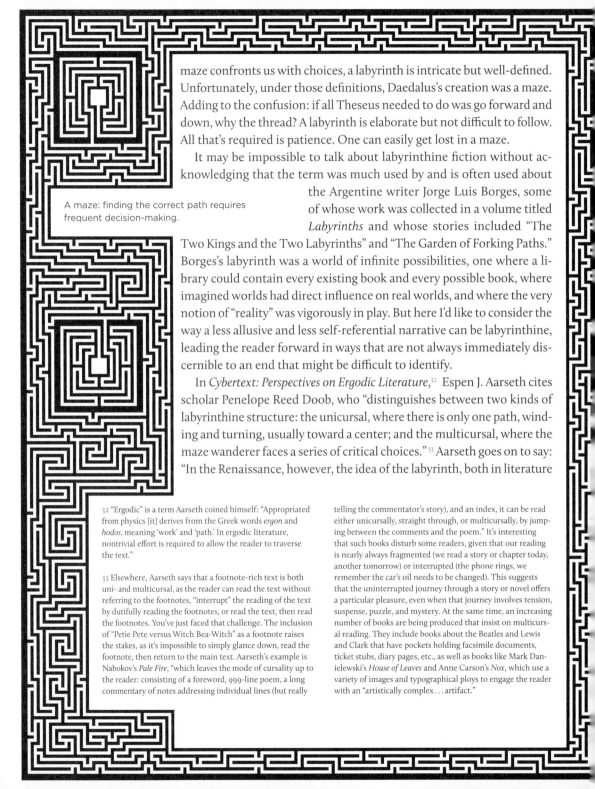

maze confronts us with choices, a labyrinth is intricate but well-defined. Unfortunately, under those definitions, Daedalus's creation was a maze. Adding to the confusion: if all Theseus needed to do was go forward and down, why the thread? A labyrinth is elaborate but not difficult to follow. All that's required is patience. One can easily get lost in a maze.

It may be impossible to talk about labyrinthine fiction without acknowledging that the term was much used by and is often used about the Argentine writer Jorge Luis Borges, some of whose work was collected in a volume titled *Labyrinths* and whose stories included "The Two Kings and the Two Labyrinths" and "The Garden of Forking Paths." Borges's labyrinth was a world of infinite possibilities, one where a library could contain every existing book and every possible book, where imagined worlds had direct influence on real worlds, and where the very notion of "reality" was vigorously in play. But here I'd like to consider the way a less allusive and less self-referential narrative can be labyrinthine, leading the reader forward in ways that are not always immediately discernible to an end that might be difficult to identify.

In *Cybertext: Perspectives on Ergodic Literature*,[32] Espen J. Aarseth cites scholar Penelope Reed Doob, who "distinguishes between two kinds of labyrinthine structure: the unicursal, where there is only one path, winding and turning, usually toward a center; and the multicursal, where the maze wanderer faces a series of critical choices."[33] Aarseth goes on to say: "In the Renaissance, however, the idea of the labyrinth, both in literature

A maze: finding the correct path requires frequent decision-making.

[32] "Ergodic" is a term Aarseth coined himself: "Appropriated from physics [it] derives from the Greek words *ergon* and *hodos*, meaning 'work' and 'path.' In ergodic literature, nontrivial effort is required to allow the reader to traverse the text."

[33] Elsewhere, Aarseth says that a footnote-rich text is both uni- and multicursal, as the reader can read the text without referring to the footnotes, "interrupt" the reading of the text by dutifully reading the footnotes, or read the text, then read the footnotes. You've just faced that challenge. The inclusion of "Petie Pete versus Witch Bea-Witch" as a footnote raises the stakes, as it's impossible to simply glance down, read the footnote, then return to the main text. Aarseth's example is Nabokov's *Pale Fire*, "which leaves the mode of cursality up to the reader: consisting of a foreword, 999-line poem, a long commentary of notes addressing individual lines (but really telling the commentator's story), and an index, it can be read either unicursally, straight through, or multicursally, by jumping between the comments and the poem." It's interesting that such books disturb some readers, given that our reading is nearly always fragmented (we read a story or chapter today, another tomorrow) or interrupted (the phone rings, we remember the car's oil needs to be changed). This suggests that the uninterrupted journey through a story or novel offers a particular pleasure, even when that journey involves tension, suspense, puzzle, and mystery. At the same time, an increasing number of books are being produced that insist on multicursal reading. They include books about the Beatles and Lewis and Clark that have pockets holding facsimile documents, ticket stubs, diary pages, etc., as well as books like Mark Danielewski's *House of Leaves* and Anne Carson's *Nox*, which use a variety of images and typographical ploys to engage the reader with an "artistically complex…artifact."

and visual art, was reduced to the multicursal paradigm that we recognize today. Consequently, the old metaphor of the text as labyrinth, which in medieval poetics could signify both a difficult, winding, but potentially rewarding linear process *and* a spatial, artistically complex, and confusing artifact, was restricted to the latter sense." Here we'll reclaim that old metaphor and examine the "difficult, winding, [and] potentially rewarding process" of a narrative that takes us on a journey that often has us wondering about the nature of our destination.

Mazes can be traced back at least 2,500 years, and have often been associated with great spiritual power and with the underworld. Some prehistoric labyrinths are thought to have been designed to trap evil beings or spirits, while other labyrinths appeared on church walls and floors as symbolic pilgrimages. Labyrinths are sometimes used for meditation, the physical journey representing an emotional, psychological, or intellectual one. In Arizona I lived near the Salt River Pima-Maricopa Indian Community, so routinely passed buildings and gateways bearing the community's Great Seal. The Great Seal features a version of an ancient image, often seen as a petroglyph, on pottery and in baskets, that depicts a figure standing at the opening of a winding path.

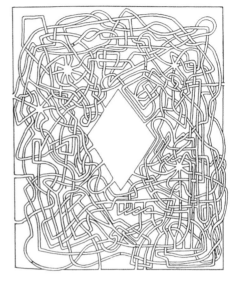

A maze drawn by Lewis Carroll. The object is to move from the inner diamond to the exterior. The successful path can go under and above other paths, but a line drawn across a path blocks the way. If you find this maze less than aesthetically pleasing, it might be useful to think about why. What makes one maze engagingly complex and another simply annoying? What does a writer need to do to lure a reader into, and through, a "difficult" book?

The "Man in the Maze," or house of "Se-eh-ha," represents the choices one makes along the journey of life, including, in turns, happiness and sadness, successes and failures. According to legend, the center represents the culmination of dreams and goals in a meeting with the Sun God before the passage to the next life. Other cultures use similar designs to illustrate the journey outward, with birth at the center. The universality of the spiral—one of the most common petroglyphs worldwide—and the maze, over millennia, suggests that, in contrast to the

straight lines and simple angles of Aristotle and Freytag, many people believe a curving or indirect path best describes the stories of our lives.

Which brings us back to Alice Munro. If her story "Royal Beatings" is a labyrinth, it's not because she wants us to feel lost or confused. She means to lead us somewhere, but the route is indirect. The heart of her stories is often somewhere in the center, and while we're on our journey it can be difficult to comprehend the whole—the hedges are too high for us to see over, the turns too unpredictable. But this doesn't mean her stories are disorganized or that we can't, once we've finished them, perceive their shape.

"Royal Beatings" is typical of Munro's work in that while it offers the reader at least one central subject, or primary conflict, it is much less interested in illustrating that conflict, or resolving it, than in exploring it.

A brief outline of the story might look like this:

1. We're introduced to the term "royal beatings" and to the main characters: Rose, Flo (Rose's stepmother), and Rose's father.
2. We learn that Rose's mother died when she was very young.
3. We learn more about Flo, particularly that she's a gossip.
4. We learn more about Rose's father, a furniture repairman, who in some ways seemed mysterious to both Flo and Rose.
5. We learn that while the family was poor, they were able to install an indoor bathroom.
6. We meet Becky Tyde, "a big-headed loud-voiced dwarf" who had polio as a child. We see her talking with Flo in a scene set in an unspecified time.
7. We're told that Becky's father beat her and her siblings, and there was a rumor that her father had impregnated her and "disposed of" the child. Later, three men were hired by "more influential and respectable men" to give Becky's father a horse-whipping; they beat him so badly that he died as he tried to leave town.
8. We learn more about Rose and Flo: the way Flo talks and dresses,

Rose's earliest memories of her, and what Rose imagines of Flo's life before Flo married her father.

9. Finally, we return to the royal beatings. We see one illustrated: a petty dispute between Flo and Rose leads to Flo's anger and Rose's defiance; Flo calls for Rose's father; and, almost reluctantly, he beats her, hitting her with his hands, whipping her with his belt, and kicking her. The buildup, the beating, and the aftermath constitute the largest section of the story.

10. We see an evening when the family is something like happy together.

11. Then we leap to a day, many years later, when Rose hears a man interviewed on the radio. He's 102 and is being asked about the old days. At the end of the interview, we learn that the man was one of the three who beat Becky Tyde's father to death. Rose imagines Flo would like to hear about it, but Flo is now in a nursing home, and has succumbed or nearly succumbed to dementia. The End.

Or at least that's the end if you believe a story begins at the beginning and ends at the ending, like a piece of string. And if we're inclined to look for a simple progression from beginning to end in a story, "Royal Beatings" is not very satisfying—in fact, to the reader looking for an emphatic conclusion, a "catastrophe," an epiphany, or a "point," "Royal Beatings" is deeply frustrating. It might seem to be told by someone who has a story in mind but gets distracted, or who puts the pieces in the wrong order and leaves some out.

Rather than leading directly to a particular event or moment of insight, a type of dramatic climax familiar from fiction but not so common in life, Munro's story circles something dark and confounding, a difficult truth beneath the surface. If we feel a bit lost, it's because we aren't sure quite what story we're meant to pursue. Initially, the narrator seems intent on explaining the "Royal Beatings" of the title, but that doesn't justify all the other information we're given.

The first clue—the piece of thread we need to recognize and follow—is in that title, which is repeated, in italics, as the story's first sentence: *Royal Beatings*. We're told this is Flo's term and that it evoked images of grandeur in Rose, as if it were "an occasion both savage and splendid," with "formal spectators"—a dramatic performance. But "in real life [the beatings] didn't approach such dignity." The story opens, then, by directing our attention to the gap between appearance and reality. Once we recognize that, we start to see this thread everywhere.

In an apparent aside, what might seem to be a dead end, we learn that after Rose's father died, Flo went out to the shed where he worked and found a variety of notes and scraps of paper that make no sense to her:

> Ate new potatoes 25th June. Record.
>   Dark Day, 1880's, nothing supernatural. Clouds of ash from forest fires.
>   Aug 16, 1938. Giant thunderstorm in evng. Lightning str. Pres. Church, Turberry Twp. Will of God?
>   Scald strawberries to remove acid.
>   All things are alive. Spinoza.

We're told "[Rose] had reached an age where she thought she could not stand to know any more, about her father, or about Flo; she pushed any discovery aside with embarrassment and dread." That leads to Rose's memory of hearing her father talking to himself, saying "words [that would] hang clear and nonsensical on the air: "Macaroni, pepperoni, Botticelli, beans—" She wonders what that might mean, but

> she could never ask him. The person who spoke these words and the person who spoke to her as her father were not the same, though they seemed to occupy the same space. It would be the worst sort of taste to acknowledge the person who was not supposed to be there; it would not be forgiven. Just the same, she loitered and listened.

Here we're presented with a true mystery—we will never, in this story, learn why Rose's father said the things he did, we won't learn anything more about the mind that kept that variety of notes, and we won't meet a character who knows any more about him. The crucial information is not something we should deduce about Rose's father, but rather the assertion that "the person who spoke these words and the person who spoke to her as her father were not the same."

As if to explain her point, the narrator tells us, "This was something the same as bathroom noises."

> Flo had saved up and had a bathroom put in, but there was no place to put it except in a corner of the kitchen. The door did not fit, the walls were only beaverboard. The result was that even the tearing of a piece of toilet paper, the shifting of a haunch, was audible to those working or talking or eating in the kitchen. They were all familiar with each other's nether voices, not only in their more explosive moments but in their intimate sighs and growls and pleas and statements. And they were all most prudish people. So no one ever seemed to hear, or be listening, and no reference was made. The person creating the noises in the bathroom was not connected with the person who walked out.

It's like a villanelle, this inclination of going back to events in our past, the way the villanelle's form refuses to move forward in linear development, circling instead at those familiar moments of emotion.... We live with those retrievals from childhood that coalesce and echo throughout our lives, the way shattered pieces of glass in a kaleidoscope reappear in new forms.... We live permanently in the recurrence of our own stories, whatever story we tell.

— *Michael Ondaatje*

That paragraph does several things at once. It underscores our sense of the family's living conditions in a way that we're unlikely to forget. It focuses our attention on something we connect to our own experience that seems never to have been said before, or at least not quite this way. It suggests more than it states, through deliberate diction. Munro avoids both the vulgar and the clinical. This is important for consistency of tone, and the diction encourages us to consider the topic in a way we probably would not if she used a colloquial term like "fart" or the more objective "passing gas." Her choices evoke the animal ("haunch") and metaphorical ("nether voices" summons "nether world"). Finally, the passage illustrates persuasively a way in which nearly all of us turn a blind eye, or a deaf ear, to certain events, and so helps us to understand how we separate a person from some of his or her actions.

Munro's interest in telling this story is not to elicit our sympathy for a physically abused girl or for the adults responsible for her abuse, and it isn't to argue that everyone aware of some wrongdoing is complicit; her interest goes beyond those commonplaces. Instead, we come to learn, she's interested in deceptive appearances, in our sordid desire for dramatic event, no matter how ugly—and, ultimately, in the darkness that we embrace but never acknowledge. This story means to lead us to contemplate our own metaphorical "nether voices," as they are often wordless and, like Rose's father's mutterings, difficult to comprehend. In the labyrinth that is the story, the paragraph about bathroom noises is not the very center, but it is a place of discovery. When we read this paragraph the first time, we can't possibly know how important it will be, but we will not forget it.

The more closely we look, the more references to false or deceptive appearances we find. The word "Royal" on Flo's tongue "took on trappings." Rose likes to think that her family lives on the border between the good and bad sections of town, "but that was not true." A sign for a tea company is in the window of a building across the street, "a proud and interesting decoration," but there is no tea to be had. Becky Tyde, the dwarf with polio, wears "little polished high-heeled shoes, real lady's shoes." The men who want to beat Becky's father hire other men to do it; those men blacken their faces to disguise themselves. The house where Mr. Tyde was beaten to death "would never look sinister, in spite of what had happened in it"—and on and on and on. Everywhere we look in this story, there's a darkness that someone is trying to hide, suppress, or ignore.

The most obvious example of this would seem to be the beatings Rose's father administers—but Munro does not use the longest sequence of her story simply to confirm everything she's conveyed subtly. Instead, she's delayed the scene because it does a great deal more than continue our journey from the story's opening lines to its final sentence.

The description of the beating is ceremonial, ritualistic. We're told Rose "displays theatrical unconcern," that "Flo becomes amazingly theatrical herself," that Rose's father seems to be "on the verge of rejecting the role he has to play." Somehow this family has fallen into a pattern of behavior that controls all three of them. Rose's father is "out of character... like a bad actor.... He is acting, and he means it." Then, just before the physical beating finally begins, Rose looks "at the kitchen floor, that clever and comforting geometrical arrangement." (That geometrical arrangement is no labyrinth, but it's a fortuitous echo.) Rose thinks, "Pots can show malice, the patterns of linoleum can leer up at you, treachery is on the other side of dailiness." Then Rose succumbs; she "plays his victim."

The story's greatest surprise, perhaps its most moving insight, comes after the beating is finished. Rose goes up to her bedroom. She isn't bleeding, no bones are broken—Munro deliberately deemphasizes the physical. Instead she focuses on Rose's mental and emotional circumstances:

> She has passed into a state of calm, in which outrage is perceived as complete and final. In this state events and possibilities take on a lovely simplicity. Choices are mercifully clear. The words that come to mind are not the quibbling, seldom the conditional.... She will never speak to them, she will never look at them with anything but loathing, she will never forgive them.... Encased in these finalities, and in her bodily pain, she floats in curious comfort, beyond herself, beyond responsibility.... She floats in her pure superior state as if drugged.

This is the darkness behind the darkness: the beatings, awful as they might be, do in fact give the lives of Flo, Rose, and her father a brief, theatrical grandeur. After she is beaten, when she is simply a victim, Rose "floats in curious comfort ... [a] pure superior state."

But nothing that good can last. Flo comes to the room with cold cream and some of Rose's favorite foods. Rose tries to resist, but "soon, in helpless corruption, she will eat them all.... All advantage will be lost.... Life has started up again." This is the unexpected turn, the shameful discovery: to be the victim is, in some ways, to have something to savor, and to heal is to lose the distinction that comes with being wronged.

The story continues to the day many years later when Rose hears the interview with Hat Nettleton, the murderer treated as a distinguished town elder, and ends with the information that, in the nursing home, Flo "occasionally showed her feelings by biting a nurse." In this story, that's a comic coda. It has nothing to do with plot; it doesn't resolve anything.

Instead, it sends us back into the story, looking for the path we might have missed. And like that first sentence, it contains a clue, a wisp of thread: "Flo occasionally showed her feelings." That use of "show," and the implication that her feelings are often hidden, resonates off all the other deceptive appearances, all the false surfaces. Eventually, starting at the beginning or at the end, we find our way to the heart of the story, an underworld.

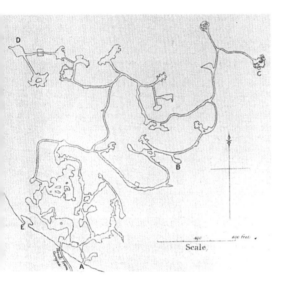

A map of the caves of Crete, believed to be the inspiration for the labyrinth of myth.

NOT A LINE, BUT A WAY

Like the river itself, [*Life on the Mississippi*] is labyrinthine, a succession of meanders, chutes, and cutoffs; it turns digression into a structural principle.

— JONATHAN RABAN

The point here isn't that we should use Kandinsky's remarkable line drawings, reindeer hunters' paths, mazes, or labyrinths as models for the structure of our stories—though we might. Munro's gradual unwinding of information isn't an intrinsically better structural model than the explicit three-part story of "Petie Pete," and it isn't better, as a general model, than Freytag's pyramid. But it's better for the story that she wants to tell, one that is based not on a sequence of actions leading to an ultimate dramatic conflict, not on a sequence of actions leading to a character's epiphany or moment of insight, but on a combination of events, images, and information that the writer arranges to lead the reader to a moment of recognition in a way that seems particularly true to life.

If we want fiction to be vital—alive and changing, with the ability to surprise us, and to transcend our expectations—we need to avoid surrendering to any one sense of how a story or novel progresses, of how a narrative unfolds. "The content of a work of art," Kandinsky wrote, "finds its expression in the composition: that is, in the sum of the tensions inwardly organized for the work." Narrative need not be dictated by chronology, or by plot, or by a character's movement toward insight. A story doesn't need to take the reader where he thinks he wants to go, or where he expects to go; and as writers we need to be wary of the pressure we sometimes feel to deliver the reader to some particular kind of destination in some particular way. Truly memorable fiction often defies our notion of what a story is.

We live in an age that not only allows us to travel great distances with relative ease but often puts us in situations where we are expected to be mobile, even if we're simply commuting to school or work. Most of the time we spend moving from place to place, we're intent on our destination. When we're between places, in the car, train, or plane, or on the bus or bike, we might feel we're nowhere, we're losing time: we're being transported. As Tim Ingold puts it, we are simply being carried along lines. But if we take on the role of wayfarers, we are always somewhere, always inhabiting the moment.

When our son was young, he enjoyed having me or my wife read to him as he fell asleep. If, when the story ended, he was still awake, he'd ask for more. It wasn't that he wanted to work his way through a particular number of stories, or get to the end of a book, or even, I eventually understood, that he wanted to stay awake. What he wanted was to fall asleep as we read. Or rather, he wanted us to be by his side, telling him stories, as he drifted off.

At that time I didn't know about the Khanty people of western Siberia. Apparently, old Khanty storytellers continue their stories after dinner, late into the darkness, until everyone else is asleep. Their word for story translates as "a way," as in a path to be followed, one that can go on indefinitely.

Everyone who's made the voyage knows that what's to be found in a labyrinth isn't at the end; the power is in the passage, in the darkness and light and in the discoveries we make. When we emerge, we're essentially in the same place, the same external world, where we began—but changed by where we've been.

THE PLEASURES
OF DIFFICULTY

The spur and burden of the
contract are intolerable to me.
I can endure the irritation of it
no longer.... I never had such
a fight over a book in my life
before ... this wretched God-
damned book.

— MARK TWAIN, on *Life on the Mississippi*

My wife has a fantasy, a desire she often expresses, which I feel certain she would be delighted to have me share with you.

"Let's just float in the pool and drink gin and tonics," she'll say. "Let's bake like lizards."

We live in Arizona, where we have a pool, and where gin is sold in every grocery store, and where it is no challenge at all to bake like a lizard.

From this you might understandably presume that my wife is an aspiring alcoholic, or an idle and frivolous person. But in fact the -holic my wife is closest to becoming is a worka-; and as I am writing this, at eleven o'clock at night, she is standing in her study, playing her viola. She'll do this for an hour, maybe longer; she does it virtually every night. My wife is not a professional musician. While she's played violin or viola since she was eight years old, and she has played in any number of quartets and chamber groups and orchestras, the vast majority of her playing is not for other people to hear. For a while, when we lived in Asheville, North Carolina, she was a regular on the wedding circuit, making pocket money playing, as she cheerfully put it, "the same damned tunes. Pachelbel's *Canon*, Handel's *Water Music*, and the Mendelssohn. Most of the time people wouldn't know if it was us playing or a radio." She stopped playing weddings not because we became independently wealthy, not because she didn't enjoy the other musicians, not, she assures me, because she's become cynical about marriage, and not because "playing" had become work—but because the work had become tedious.

In contrast, the other night she drove to a church where, with about sixty other musicians she had never met, she sight-read Mahler's Fifth Symphony. They played it beginning to end, without a break, without an audience. She came home exhausted. "That was glorious," she said. "It's so complicated."

"Complicated," I said, trying to look sympathetic in a knowing way, when in fact I am a heathen. I can sing along with "Morning, Noon and Night" and "Chug-a-lug," but I can tell you nothing about Mahler's Fifth Symphony. I can't even tell you with complete confidence that Mahler had previously written four other symphonies. I asked my wife, "But you had a good time?"

"Glorious," she said again. Then, shaking her head: "It was terrifying."

I would have given her a hard time about the apparent contradiction except for the fact that I am currently learning how to ride a bike. I exaggerate only a little; I never rode much as a child, I have virtually no sense of balance, and my feet are attached to my legs nearly perpendicular to the desired angle for feet, so situating myself on a potentially fast-moving foot-powered object requiring some combination of balance and dexterity never seemed like a good idea. A month or so ago, though, my doctor suggested I take up swimming or biking.

Not many people would buy a book of sudoku that looked like this:

4	5	2	3	9	1	8	7	6
3	1	8	6	7		2	9	3
6	7	9	4	2	8	3	1	5
8	3	1	5	6	4	7	2	9
2	4	5	9	8	7	1	6	3
9	6	7	2	1	3	5	4	8
7	9	6	8	5	2	4	3	1
1	8	3	7	4	9	6	5	2
5	2	4	1	3	6	9	8	7

My wife would not look kindly on my splashing and making a lot of commotion in the pool; it dilutes the gin. So for the past week I've been riding out to a desert park in 104 degree heat, then turning around and riding back. Most of the last mile is uphill, part of it fairly steep, and I have not yet been able to make it to the top without pausing. There are many other places I could bike, flat places; but I ride out to the park every day now, then turn around and try to climb that hill.

"Did you have fun?" my wife says from her blue pool float, glass in hand. "You look like you're going to have a heart attack."

"Nah, it's great," I tell her before going under. "Damn it."

I don't think my wife and I are unusual in this: most of us lie to ourselves. We say we want the good life, we say we want to live on Easy Street, but we suspect it's true that heaven is a place where nothing ever happens, and it sounds pretty dull. So while we might lounge in the sun for a while, or have a drink, before long we dry off and make trouble for ourselves.

Not everyone is like this, but most writers (and other artists) are. Most of us are, at least for periods, unsatisfied with our current degree of fluency. Sometimes—maybe often—we find writing frustrating, even aggravating. Absolutely no one is telling us to do it. The financial rewards are, for nearly all of us, modest. And yet we continue, trying to do a difficult thing well.

To argue for the pleasures of difficulty is not to promote the products of laziness, self-absorption, or hostility—that is, work that is intentionally vague, obscure, or encoded to prevent accessibility, work that doesn't intend to communicate with readers but which instead exists as a fortress without doors. This is the sort of writing some of us produced as teenagers in a misguided display of (we thought) superiority that was, in fact, a fear of being understood, and so revealed to be not unlike other people. (Tom Wolfe argued against that kind of elitism years ago in *The Painted Word*.) I am not arguing here for fiction or poetry that only certain trained readers can hope to understand and admire. While we may say that we read to be entertained or enlightened, often we find that the books we return to, the books we find most valuable, are the books that disturb or elude us, defy us in some way, even as they appeal to us.

And the casual sudoku solver may be put off by the challenge presented by this:

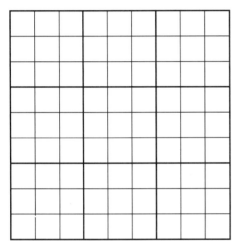

But somewhere in between are a great many variations of the puzzle, with varying degrees of difficulty, which occupy a remarkable number of people.

I first read Vladimir Nabokov's *Lolita* as an undergraduate English major. Over the years I've reread it many times; I've read and reread *The Annotated Lolita*; and I've taught the novel to undergraduates and graduates. I've referred to the novel enough that one student, only partly kidding, said she wondered if I could teach an entire course without mentioning it. "You must love that book," more than one person has said to me. But "love" is a word I would never use to describe my feelings toward it. "You really understand that book," one or two people have said to me, but I strongly doubt my understanding of the novel—which is to say, I have *an* understanding of the novel, but that understanding has certainly changed over time, and is very much open to interrogation; I feel challenged every time I return to it. Poet C. Dale Young described a similar—though superficially opposite—experience

A MUSE AND A MAZE

reading Joseph Conrad's *Heart of Darkness*. The first time he read it, he said, the book seemed perfectly clear. Why did people make such a fuss? Moved to reread it, he found Conrad's tale increasingly elusive, more complicated. Richer. However it happens, the appeal of the books we return to is often, at least in part, a fascination with what we can't quite reach.

Many writers seem to be mathphobes. I've known writers who complain at length (and with good reason) about the shocking decline of literacy both in and outside of classrooms, but who laugh at the impossibility of calculating numerical grade averages or the tip on a restaurant bill. Many people who feel an aversion to math think of it as a foreign language, or a system of rules to be memorized and applied to abstractions. But while one of the appealing qualities of math is the consistency or purity of the knowledge it offers—$2 + 2 = 4$ all day long, no matter the weather or the majority party in Congress—most dedicated mathematicians are passionate about the unknown, the problems unsolved. A delightful illustration is Simon Singh's *Fermat's Enigma*, about the many people who dedicated some large part of their lives to proving that something isn't mathematically possible.

Pythagoras is credited with the theorem that the longest side of any right triangle—the hypotenuse—always has the same relationship to the other two sides of that triangle. Specifically, if the two shorter sides are a and b and the hypotenuse is c, $a^2 + b^2 = c^2$. Mathematicians, being mathematicians, wondered if there are any positive integers for which it's true that $a^3 + b^3 = c^3$ (or, for that matter, $a^4 + b^4 = c^4$, and so on). Nobody could come up with numbers that satisfied the equation, but neither could anyone prove that there wasn't such a combination of numbers. Enter Pierre de Fermat, a French lawyer and amateur mathematician who, in 1637, jotted in the margins of his copy of Diothantus's *Arithmetica* that

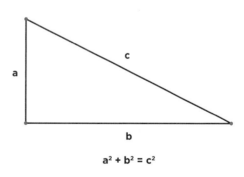

$a^2 + b^2 = c^2$

he had come up with a proof but didn't have space to write it out. Fermat did write out plenty of other proofs, so the combination of a very specific problem, or puzzle, and a mystery (what did Fermat see that no one else could see?) sent countless others off on a journey.

The pleasure of math, at least on one level, is not doing routine computations, or "plugging in numbers," but solving problems—and not the kind that are answered in the back of the book.

> Everything I have written up to now is trifling compared to that which I would like to write.... I am displeased and bored with everything now being written, while everything in my head interests, moves, and excites me.
>
> — *Anton Chekhov*

THE MILLER'S PUZZLE

The Miller took the company aside and showed them nine sacks of flour that were standing as depicted in the sketch:

"Now, hearken all and some," said he, "while that I do set ye the riddle of the nine sacks of flour. And mark ye, my lords and masters, that there be single sacks on the outside, pairs next unto them, and three together in the middle thereof. By Saint Benedict, it doth so happen that if we do but multiply the pair, 28, by the single one, 7, the answer is 196, which is of a truth the number shown by the sacks in the middle. Yet it be not true that the other pair, 34, when so multiplied by its neighbour, 5, will also make 196. Wherefore do I beg you, gentle sirs, so to place anew the nine sacks with as little trouble as possible that each pair when thus multiplied by its single neighbor shall make the number in the middle." As the Miller has stipulated in effect that as few bags as possible shall be moved, there is only one answer to this puzzle, which everybody should be able to solve.

— *Henry Ernest Dudeney*

THE STRATEGIC RELEASE OF INFORMATION

Within a sentence, diction can be used to clarify or to strategically obscure. The first sentence of Antonya Nelson's short story "Strike Anywhere" is, "This was the next time after what was supposed to be the last time."

There's nothing about that language or its arrangement that is hard to comprehend; the difficulty comes from the fact that we have signifiers, but no specific content. What is "this"? we think. The next time for what? The last time for what? All we know for sure is that "this" is an occasion, and it's significant because it wasn't supposed to happen. The sentence appears to be telling us something, and we understand the logic of its grammatical construction, but we need to know more—a deliberate mystery pushes us forward.[33]

A MUSE AND A MAZE

The next sentence puts us at ease by offering clear and explicit information—two characters and a bit of action: "The father parked at the curb before the White Front, and the boy found himself making a prayer."

So we've got a boy and his father, and the boy seems to be worried. Despite the matter-of-factness and absolute clarity of the sentence, tension is maintained, as is the mystery—we still don't know what's going on, or why it's important. The boy's worry mirrors our own unease about not knowing what the narrator is referring to.

The paragraph continues, "It was Sunday, after all, and this was what his mother did when faced with his father's stubborn refusal to do what he said he'd do. Or not do what he said he'd not do."

We understand that "this" refers to prayer, but all that doing and not doing conveys more sound than sense—and echoes, it's worth noting, the first sentence. The first sentence created a desire to know certain information: What is this significant event? And why isn't it supposed to happen? We still don't have answers, but the context for the questions is becoming increasingly clear—so while we're eager to have those initial questions addressed, we're content to wait a little longer, because we're getting what seems to be important information. By the third paragraph, when we learn that the White Front is a bar, we've got a clue regarding the source of the trouble; yet by that time the focus of the narrative is no longer the simple fact of what's going on, but the difficult situation the boy is in, and his father's obliviousness, or self-interest, and the mother's influence, or lack of it. (This opening would unfold much differently if Nelson had chosen to call the establishment the White Front Tavern; even the specific information she releases is calibrated to sustain curiosity.) The opening passage ends with these two sentences:

> "Not one inch," his father reminded him, face looming at the window before locking the truck door, slamming it, and crossing the sidewalk. He slapped the wallet in his back pocket, cinched his hat, drew breath to make himself tall, and disappeared through the dark entryway of the bar.

The dilemma has—or rather, the dilemmas have—been set up with

33 The ideal reader is thinking, "Don't you mean 'puzzle'? Because the author knows the answers, and before long, we will." Yes: this is, in the story as a whole, a puzzle—and barely even that, because the answer is going to be handed to us. In the moment that we read the sentence, though, it raises questions we can't possibly answer, what we might think of as localized, or small-scale, or short-term mysteries.

tremendous economy, and that's possible because, while the situation is familiar, a classic—we're told something bad has happened, that there will be hell to pay if it happens again, and then we're shown strong indicators that it's about to happen—as readers we have been artfully misdirected. The author has put the opening cards on the table, but at least some of them are face down. The opening of "Strike Anywhere" shifts our attention from a minor mystery to a more significant one.

On some level or another, nearly every successful story works this way, leading us from one specific unknown to another, like stepping stones across a river. But just as important as the stepping stones—those secure places to rest our feet that make our progress possible—are the spaces between those stones, and the water rushing through those spaces. In Nelson's story, omitted and withheld information represents the difficulty. And while this might seem like a narrow, shallow stream to cross—few if any readers would be inclined to give up in frustration—by increasing the span of the river, by increasing the spaces between the stones, by deepening and hastening the water, difficulty can be increased.

We might tell ourselves that every sentence in a story should be beautiful, or finely wrought, or exquisitely detailed, or should present the reader with a new and brilliant figure of speech. But that first sentence—"This was the next time after what was supposed to be the last time"—taken on its own, out of context, might seem vague or confusing, and in a draft by a lesser writer, it would probably be followed by similarly abstract assertions. The combination of the abstract and the concrete, coupled with the deliberate release of contextualizing information, is what makes this writing strategic. In that first sentence, Nelson is not trying to find her way into the story—she's creating questions she knows we'll want answered.

Simply omitting information doesn't create a sense of mystery or tension (you don't know my shoe size, but you don't care). The reader needs

Letters in the sentences "Roses are red, violets are blue" are scrambled by the following procedure. The words are written one below the other and flush at the left:

roses
are
red
violets
are
blue

The columns are taken from left to right and their letters from the top down, skipping all blank spaces, to produce this ordering: rarvaboreirlsedoeuelesets. The task is to find the line of poetry that, when scrambled by this procedure, becomes tinflabttulahsoriooasaweikoknargedyeaste.

A MUSE AND A MAZE

to be made to want to know what's being withheld or obscured. If the reader isn't provoked to *want* to know more, the story has no forward momentum, no sense of urgency.

Virtually no one is likely to find "Strike Anywhere" difficult to read. And that's the point: even when it seems most accessible, good fiction is rich with minor complications, interruptions, suspensions—all of which serve to engage us and, perhaps perversely, increase our reading pleasure.

A more complex example is Charles D'Ambrosio's "The Scheme of Things." The story opens with a young man and a young woman who, we gradually learn, are going door to door to raise money, presumably for a charity. That scheme eventually leads them to the home of a generous older couple who takes them in and feeds them, and whom the two end up robbing in surprising and revealing ways. The young woman, Kirsten, has visions. She isn't just perceptive; she sees things that aren't visible to other people. Most significantly, she sees a young girl, talks to her, and offers to take her home, whereupon the girl runs off. Only several pages later do we find out that the girl has been dead for several years. While the story doesn't use this word to describe her, the young girl Kirsten sees is a ghost.

Here's the writer's problem: he doesn't want to introduce the girl as a ghost. That would give away the surprise and, more important, distance us from Kirsten's experience, since Kirsten thinks the girl is real. Neither does the writer want us to feel cheated when we learn the girl is a ghost. But the story is told in the omniscient third person. An omniscient narrator, by definition, knows everything. So the omniscient narrator knows the girl Kirsten sees is a ghost. If the omniscient narrator asserts that the girl is alive and then, several pages later, tells us she has been dead for years, there's at least a chance we'll start doubting all sorts of things the narrator tells us, and that the story will lose its authority.

So: How to tell the reader the young girl is a ghost but not tell the reader the young girl is a ghost.

As any lover of logic problems knows, the first step to solving one is to make sure you've defined it correctly. You remember the old story about

34 If the answer seems obvious,
you probably also know why a
barber in Geneva would rather
cut the hair of two Frenchmen
than of one German.

the plane that crashed exactly on the Texas/Oklahoma border, and the legal dispute regarding which state the survivors should be buried in.[34] The point of the joke is that we focus on a false problem. The question beginning "Which state . . ." begs one of two answers: Texas or Oklahoma. In that way, the joke is like a magic trick—say, the one where a magician asks a member of the audience to select a card and then, toward the end of the performance, the card is revealed in a sealed envelope, or a block of ice. The astonished/delighted/exasperated audience member asks, "How did he know what card I would choose?"—which is the wrong question.

We often bang our heads against our laptops—or bang our laptops against our heads—because we're focusing on the wrong problem. "I need to fix this ending!" we say to ourselves, when we know by now that any serious problem with an ending is almost certainly a problem that begins much earlier. We keep trying to bring a dead scene to life, only to realize the scene has no reason for being. Or, as in the case of "The Scheme of Things," we think the problem is how to introduce a character, when in fact the problem is how to incorporate a specific incident into the larger aims of the story.

Here's how D'Ambrosio does it. The story begins with description of one of the two main characters:

> Lance vanished behind the white door of the men's room and when he came out a few minutes later he was utterly changed. Gone was the tangled nest of thinning black hair, gone was the shadow of beard, gone, too, was the grime on his hands, the crescents of black beneath his blunt, chewed nails. Shaving had sharpened the lines of his jaw and revealed the face of a younger man. . . . He looked as clean and bland as an evangelist.

That first sentence—"Lance vanished behind the white door of the men's room and when he came out a few minutes later he was utterly changed"—and especially the use of "vanished" and "utterly," might suggest something of a magic trick. Lance didn't simply open the door or go into the men's room—he "vanished." He didn't just look different; he was "utterly changed." The next sentence is a nice bit of sleight-of-hand, as D'Ambrosio tells us what Lance looked like earlier by telling us what's missing: gone was the black hair, gone was the beard, and so on. That emphasis on what has disappeared makes ominous the otherwise simple statement, "He looked as clean and bland as an evangelist." One thing we immediately understand: Lance is no evangelist. We suspect he is up to no good.

Having established that possibility, the story introduces the other main character, Kirsten, and the boy at the service station who inspects their damaged car. In what might appear to be a throwaway gag, Lance assumes the boy's name is Randy—the name on the oval patch above his shirt pocket—only to learn that it's Bill. When the boy goes to get parts for a temporary repair, Lance sits on the hood and looks around. We see brown clouds of soil, dust on the leaves of a few dying elms, some trailers across the street, and then this:

> One of the trailer doors swung open. Two Indians and a cow-girl climbed down the wooden steps. It was Halloween.

On first reading, this arrangement of information feels like another deadpan joke. The narrator could have told us earlier that it was Halloween—that certainly would have given us a different context for Lance's transformation. But it would have been a wasted gesture in the first paragraph, given the story's purposes. Here are those plain and direct sentences again:

> One of the trailer doors swung open. Two Indians and a cow-girl climbed down the wooden steps. It was Halloween.

Notice what the second sentence doesn't say: "Three children, two dressed as Indians and one as a cowgirl, climbed down the wooden steps." No, the omniscient third-person narrator asserts that what exits the trailer are "two Indians and a cowgirl." Also absent: the word "costume."

So on the next page we accept the narrator's assertion that when Kirsten, the other main character, walks toward the intersection, "ghosts and witches crossed from house to house, holding paper sacks and pillowcases." Not children dressed as ghosts and witches, not people in costumes.

The narrator then rewards our close reading by adding to the motif: "The street lights sputtered nervously in the fading twilight.... The casual clothes that Lance had bought her in Key Biscayne, Florida, had come to seem like a costume and were now especially flimsy and ridiculous here in Tiffin, Iowa." Lance vanishes and reappears, looking as bland as an evangelist; Indians and cowgirls and ghosts and witches walk the streets, but Kirsten feels as if her clothes are a costume.

Subtext is beginning to take shape, but we have no way to see that the next lines are part of it: "A young girl crossed the road, and Kirsten followed her. She thought she might befriend the girl and take her home..."

The interaction with the little girl transpires over the course of two pages; then there's some other action; and so quite some time passes before we learn that the little girl Kirsten met was actually killed in an accident years ago.

If there were no preparation for that revelation, the story would feel like a cheat. But from its very first sentence, the story has announced that people are not what they appear to be; and by introducing those two Indians and a cowgirl before we know it's Halloween, the story has essentially telegraphed the illusion that's about to follow. Rather than feel tricked, when we realize that the little girl was a ghost, we recognize that the narrator was telling us more than we could understand, withholding information but also drawing our attention to the very thing we should be looking at.

When we learn the little girl had been killed in an accident years earlier, and when we realize those lines about the two Indians and a cowgirl that caught our attention were *designed* to catch our attention, for a reason we couldn't have anticipated, we might feel something like glee. Our pleasure is not in being fooled, but in realizing that our careful attention has been anticipated and rewarded by the author. As a result, the solution to a problem that could have undermined the narrative's authority instead enhances that authority; and as we continue reading, we are alert for other subtle clues the writing might offer.

You come to these places and say to yourself, I can't do this, I know I can't do this, I'm certain I can't do it, but I have to do it, I know I have to. You would give anything to be somewhere besides there, but there's no use thinking about it. You have to go on. In the end it uplifts you somehow.

— JAMES SALTER

Even among gatherings of thoughtful readers and writers, there are a number of terms, like "narrative line," that come up fairly often without being carefully defined or investigated. These terms are assumed to have meaning that everyone understands, even if no one bothers to explain exactly what that meaning might be.

One of those terms is "flow." It's not uncommon for someone to say that a story, or a passage in a story, "flows." This is meant as praise. But if someone asks, "What do you mean by flow?" the response is often either an awkward hemming and hawing or the classic, desperate, "You know what I mean." What is it that we know? That fiction flows or doesn't flow. Or it flows in places. In any case, to flow is good; not to flow is bad.

My father, who sold industrial equipment designed to control and measure water and steam, knew what flow was and how to measure it. In that world, flow is a matter of volume, speed, and pressure, and is controlled by various valves and regulators. While that might seem far removed from writing, in the essay "What We Talk About When We Talk About Flow," David Jauss makes a strong case that, on the microlevel, syntax serves as a kind of regulator. While he offers no formula for achieving ideal flow in fiction, he suggests that varying syntax is key. On the macrolevel, he argues for variety in the length and structure of scenes. Interestingly, this suggests that smoothness, regularity, and uniformity—virtues when we try to control the flow of water through pipes—are not the methods or goals of aesthetic flow.

Some insight into this apparently counterintuitive feature of effective flow in writing is offered by a Hungarian psychologist with the conversation-stopping name of Mihaly Csikszentmihalyi. Csikszentmihalyi defines flow as "the mental state of operation in which a person in an activity is fully immersed in a feeling of energized focus, full involvement, and success in the process of the activity." This could apply to reading, or presumably writing, but also to playing air hockey or slide guitar. It's a state often discussed by the designers of video games and people who study them. To maintain "flow" is the ideal. If you've been around a teenager or teenager-at-heart who seems zoned out, comatose, except staring at a monitor with a controller in hand, he is, possibly, experiencing flow.

Game designer and Carnegie Mellon professor Jesse Schell discusses the "flow channel" in his book *The Art of Game Design*, which offers an interesting perspective on the creation of narratives. According to Schell, the four requirements necessary to put a game player—or, for our purposes, a reader—into the "flow state" are (1) clear goals, (2) no distractions, (3) direct feedback, and (4) continuous challenge. He discusses all of those, but our immediate interest is that last item: continuous challenge. "If we start to think we can't achieve [the goal]," he writes, "we feel frustrated, and our minds start seeking an activity more likely to be rewarding. On the other hand, if the challenge is too easy, we feel bored, and again, our minds start seeking more rewarding activities." So: challenging is good, easy is bad, too hard is too bad. Never mind, for the moment, how we measure degrees of challenge, ease, or difficulty in a poem or story. And we shouldn't get our hopes up for an answer, because of course all those qualities are relative. What's too easy for you is nearly impossible for me.

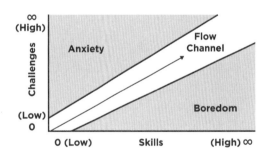

Simply establishing a constant state of challenge turns out not to be effective for long. Instead, the ideal situation, flow-channel-wise, is to keep the game player or reader moving within a tolerable range of new challenge and acquired skill—or, as Csikszentmihalyi puts it, between anxiety and boredom.

A child might be challenged by playing tic-tac-toe, for instance; but once someone learns how to win or force a draw every time, the game holds less interest. Books of sudoku and crossword puzzles are often labeled easy, medium, or hard because few people will pay for a book of puzzles they can't do, and not many more will spend time with puzzles that are too simple. With a game like chess, new players might have trouble remembering how the different pieces move; after that, the level of difficulty changes with the opponents they play. Of course, all this varies with the individual. Some people get pleasure from winning all the time, some people might persist despite losing all the time, but most people will be stimulated by a cycle of success and failure, by ongoing challenges. The player moves from frustration, or anxiety, to satisfaction, or competency, then to a new level of frustration, and so on.

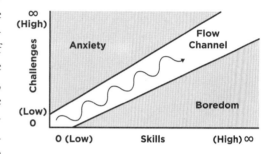

This cycle of satisfaction and frustration is familiar to every writer. We write sentences or drafts that disappoint us, and we feel frustrated. But then a sentence or paragraph or image delights us, and that success encourages us to continue. If we never felt pleasure from anything we wrote, we'd stop; but if we were completely satisfied, if we didn't feel the urge to move beyond what we have accomplished or to take on a new challenge, we'd lose interest.

Most serious poetry and fiction is unlike a game in that it doesn't intend to become increasingly difficult, but it is like a game in that we want the reader to be engaged and to experience some combination of intrigue, delight, challenge, surprise, provocation, and satisfaction. The ideal reading experience might be comparable to that flow state. The books that give us the most pleasure, the deepest pleasure, combine uncertainty and satisfaction, tension and release.

Schell says that the key to a successful game is to let players progress quickly to the point where they find themselves challenged, and to make sure that every significant success leads to an increase in difficulty. It isn't enough for the story to be somewhere in between too hard and too easy;

ideally, the story will provide the reader an ongoing series of challenges and satisfactions. If, on a hike, all we care about is convenient travel—the physical equivalent of reading a kitchen appliance manual—we're happy to have big stepping stones, close together, and a quietly flowing stream.

But if we're looking for an interesting experience, if the stream is quiet, the stepping stones can be smaller or farther apart. If the stream is wide and the water is rushing by, we want the security of flat, broad stones. Eventually, some of us will seek out greater adventure—a deep, rushing stream and small, uneven stones that are a long, uncertain stride apart—but if that experience goes on too long, we're likely to grow exhausted (or fall and be swept to our death; happily, such a dire fate is unlikely when we tackle *Absalom! Absalom!* or *Ulysses*).

Michael Ondaatje's *Coming Through Slaughter* is a fictionalized biography of the trumpet player Buddy Bolden, a mythic and enigmatic figure sometimes credited as a founder of jazz. No recording of his music is known to exist, and the verifiable historical record of Bolden's life is full of blanks; even the most scholarly biography of him contains numerous conjectures. Ondaatje's novel is based on the historical record but also on apocryphal tales, misinformation, and original research that has nothing to do directly with Bolden. The novel's narrator has access to Bolden's thoughts. Ondaatje moves historical figures through time and space for his own purposes, and he invents a number of characters, including a writer Ondaatje's age who sees his own artistic trials reflected in Bolden's life story.

What makes the book difficult? Let's start at the beginning.

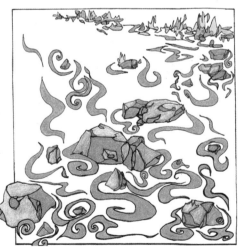

Ondaatje's novel is not titled "The Buddy

Bolden Story," or "The Founder of Jazz." It's titled *Coming Through Slaughter*, and the meanings of that title remain unclear for quite a long time.

The first page of the novel features a distressed historical photograph of six musicians holding their instruments.

Beneath the picture is a paragraph that is not a caption:

Buddy Bolden began to get famous right after 1900 come in. He was the first to play the hard jazz and blues for dancing. Had a good band. Strictly ear band. Later on Armstrong, Bunk Johnson, Freddie Keppard—they all knew he began the good jazz. John Robichaux had a real reading band, but Buddy used to kill Robichaux everywhere he went. When he'd parade he'd take the people with him all the way down Canal Street. Always looked good. When he bought a cornet he'd shine it up and make it glisten like a woman's leg.

Beneath that paragraph and to the right is the name "Louis Jones."

The photograph looks like an actual historical document (and it is, although the negative has been flipped). The paragraph implies that Buddy Bolden is a significant figure in the book, and the last sentence might lead the reader to assume he is the man in the photograph holding a cornet. "Louis Jones" is not identified. Even so, the photograph and the paragraph seem to work together. They make sense.

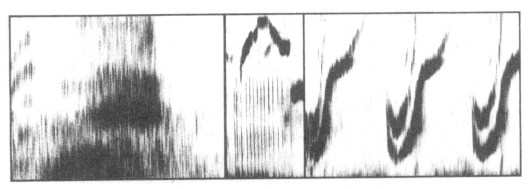

The second page of the novel holds, at the top of the page, a curious black-and-white image. A paragraph at the bottom of the page tells us that the image represents three sonographs of dolphin sounds, or "squawks." It ends, "No one knows how a dolphin makes both whistles and echolocation clicks simultaneously."

Most readers will not see much immediate connection between the information on the first two pages, beyond the fact that they are both about sound or music. An energetic reader with a passion for metaphor might begin wondering how Buddy Bolden is and is not like a dolphin. The game has begun, but it feels a little as if we've been given one piece of a jigsaw puzzle and one Scrabble tile.

The third page of the novel features the number 1.

The fourth page begins with the two-word paragraph, "His geography."

By this point, as readers, we understand that we will be required to do some heavy lifting. We might tentatively decide that "His" refers to Buddy Bolden, but not with much confidence. There has been no explicit repetition, no patterns have been established, and the narrator who offered up the photographs and quotations doesn't even provide us the comfort of a complete sentence.

The next paragraph begins, "Float by in a car today and see the corner shops. The signs of the owners obliterated by brand names. Tassin's Food Store which he lived opposite for a time surrounded by Drink Coca Cola in Bottles, Barq's, or Laura Lee's Tavern.... This district, the homes and stores, are a mile or so from the streets made marble by jazz."

This description begins to ground us. We're still off-balance, but we feel something like gratitude for this coherent paragraph that looks more like the beginnings of other novels we know.

The next paragraphs are unsettling. There is no more reference to Buddy Bolden, to "him," or, for that matter, to dolphins. The narrator tells us, "Here there is little recorded history," then proceeds to offer colorful details and anecdotes—about a woman beaten to death with her own wooden leg, about prostitutes selling "Goofer Dust and Bend-Over Oil," and about the notorious Oyster Dance. While those opening photographs and the prose near them seem to have been forgotten, we're getting what feels like background for a long story; we're content to wait.

The narrative begins leaping back and forth through time, shifting between glimpses of Bolden's daily life and more distant discussions of the era. While the shifts are sometimes disorienting, we understand that everything we're reading either helps to convey a sense of New Orleans during the time Bolden lived or shows us a fragment of Bolden's imagined life. If it weren't for that sonograph, we might even feel comfortable. But then, on page 17, we see, in italics, the words "Nora's Song" and something that does not look like a song lyric:

> Dragging his bone over town. Dragging his bone over town.
> Dragging his bone over town. Dragging his
> Bone over town. Dragging his bone
> Over and over dragging his bone over town.
> Then and then and then and then
> Dragging his bone over town

And then

> Dragging his bone home.

We can make at least provisional sense of this. "Bone" is a colloquial reference to a brass instrument, in this case Bolden's cornet; and as he is nonmonogamous, the word may carry another meaning. At the same time, the passage departs from the conventions of prose and presentation that have been established. The anxious reader might hesitate to turn the page, scared of what she might find. The more adventurous reader is eager to go forward, not only assuming but hoping for both coherence and more surprises. And that latter reader is not disappointed. *Coming Through Slaughter* is unusual in that it offers new challenges very nearly to the last page. While the narrative follows Bolden to the end of his life, the final pages also include "Selections from *A Brief History of East Louisiana State Hospital* by Lionel Gremillion," a variety of quotations, what could be song lyrics, and notes juxtaposed on nearly blank pages, followed by three pages of summaries of transcripts of a recorded interview we're told is stored in the Tulane library. Almost nothing in those three pages speaks directly about the characters or plot of the novel, though at the end there is an oblique reference to Bolden. In this way, Ondaatje enacts Bolden's becoming a footnote in musical history, a figure about whom little is known aside from anecdote. Ondaatje's novel may look different from many books we know, in that it is composed of many small sections containing different kinds of information, with great variety in how words and blank spaces are deployed on the page, but the strategy it illustrates is common to many other books. By deliberately moving his readers between stages of frustration and satisfaction, of tension and release—or, let's say, between difficulty and ease—Ondaatje keeps the reader in the flow state.

Words in the first column are synonyms, of a sort, of words in the second column. In the same way that a bit of melted butter could be called an expat, you may need to imagine the words respaced or hyphenated.

(1)

stagecoach	beach bum
battle cry	automate
hearing aid	drama teacher
tangent	chieftain
carpooler	warrant
clanking	gavel

(2)

opts	bowl over
Robin Hood	say a blessing
coquette	tower
adverse	at ease
dog race	jingle
tugboat	shutout score

(3)

decimal	Lilliputian
domain	seafood seller
standoffish	searing
atoll	off the old lady
bedroll	often
minuteman	act funny

You know, I order everything.
You know everything I order.
I know everything you order.
You order everything—and I know.
I order everything—and you know.
Everything I order, you know.
Everything I know, you order.
I order you: know everything.
Order everything! I know you.

The most basic level on which the order of information influences our comprehension is the arrangement of letters and spaces. The sequence of letters is crucial to the word, as any jumble-solver knows, and as most of us recognized at an early age with dismay (as we struggled with lessons in spelling) and pleasure (as we mastered those lessons and began to play games with the arrangement of letters). A child doesn't need to be named Hannah or Otto to recognize the strange delight of palindromes; Mom and Dad know the midcentury classic "A man, a plan, a canal: Panama," but they may not know the comic response "A dog, a plan, a canal: pagoda," the more exotic "Satan, oscillate my metallic sonatas," the potentially erotic "Kay, a red nude, peeped under a yak," or the elegant lament, "'Reviled did I live,' said I, 'as evil I did deliver.'"

Other letter-arrangement games include finding as many words as possible in a larger one (when I was in elementary school, that longer word was one constant, pliant *Constantinople*), Word Golf (*word wood good gold golf*—How easily can *love* turn to *hate*? How close is *dirt* to *bath*? Word Golfers know), and codes (even Homastay Effersonjay wrote youthful letters in pig Latin). We all know about the dyslexic atheist who doesn't believe in *dog*, we *dare* to *read*, and Nabokov revealed that *therapist* is *the rapist*.[35] A single omission changes everything: a young student discovered that an unfortunate typing error turned a quite serious story into something else when a woman requested a private meeting with her counselor so they could discuss her elf-inflicted wounds.

But typically we think of words as our most fundamental elements,

35 Poet Heather McHugh, a fan of anagrams, set some sort of record when she created a sonnet that is an anagram of Shakespeare's sonnet 23.

and we use them to create phrases and sentences. Syntax creates meaning. It can provide clarity, but it can also create mystery and tension. Mystery and tension, syntax can create. Created is mystery; also . . . tension.

Here is the first sentence of Thomas Bernhard's novel *Correction*:

> After a mild pulmonary infection, tended too little and too late, had suddenly turned into a severe pneumonia that took its toll of my entire body and laid me up for at least three months at nearby Wels, which has a hospital renowned in the field of so-called internal medicine, I accepted an invitation from Hoeller, a so-called taxidermist in the Aurach valley, not for the *end* of October, as the doctors urged, but for *early* in October, as I insisted, and then went on my own so-called responsibility straight to the Aurach valley and to Hoeller's house, without even a detour to visit my parents in Stocket, *straight* into the so-called Hoeller garret, to begin sifting and perhaps even arranging the literary remains of my friend, who was also a friend of the taxidermist Hoeller, Roithamer, after Roithamer's suicide, I went to work sifting and sorting the papers he had willed to me, consisting of thousands of slips covered with Roithamer's handwriting plus a bulky manuscript entitled "About Altensam and everything connected with Altensam, with special attention to the Cone."

None of the information in that sentence is difficult to comprehend, but the arrangement is disorienting. A variety of information passes by that seems quite worthy of being the subject of the sentence—or of *a* sentence—and of our attention, but the syntax, as well as the length of the sentence, seems to make everything subordinate. We're confronted with surprising qualifiers: "the field of so-called internal medicine," "a so-called taxidermist." There's even a syntactical joke, via a parenthetical clause: "went on my own so-called responsibility straight to the Aurach valley and to Hoeller's house, without even a detour to visit my parents in Stocket, *straight* into the so-called Hoeller garret." That mention of not taking a detour *is* a detour on our voyage

What four consecutive letters of the alphabet can be arranged to spell a familiar four-letter word?

through the sentence. The end of that voyage—the mention of Roitham-er's manuscript—feels oddly anticlimactic. We might think of a sentence as carrying us forward in our progression through a narrative, but this sentence seems at least as interested in going sideways; it feels as wide as it is long. After a rush of relief that the sentence has finally ended, our first impulse might be to go back and look again at all the things the narrator has alluded to, the narrative premise he's suggested.

Long sentences, unorthodox punctuation, repeated words and phras-es, and the use of attributives as a rhythmic device are defining elements of Bernhard's prose. He requires readers to choose their own places to stop and reflect. In the Vintage paperback edition, *Correction* is 271 pages long. It's divided into two chapters, each of which consists of a single paragraph.

The syntax of the sentences draws us forward, and the lack of para-graphs creates some anxiety about where to pause; at the same time, the length and structure of the sentences forces us to slow down to make sense of what we're reading. We need to be patient with this prose; we need to attend carefully to repetition and significant variation; and we need to be prepared to engage with abstractions since, as is often the case in Bernhard's work, there is very little action, at least in the present. In *Correction*, the narrator arrives at Hoeller's garret, has dinner with the family, contemplates his friend's papers, and reflects on the past. In the second half he sorts and orders excerpts from Roithamer's writings, quoting from and revising—"correcting"—them at length. At the end of the book, so far as we know, the narrator is still sitting with Roithamer's papers. The narrative's drama has little to do with physical movement, everything to do with expression—conveying understanding and emo-tion in words.

Sixteen pages into the novel, our narrator is standing in Hoeller's gar-ret, contemplating the task ahead of him—going through his deceased friend's papers and, more important, trying to comprehend his life's work. The narrator says,

> As I stood there looking around Hoeller's garret it was instant-
> ly clear to me that my thinking would now have to conform to
> Hoeller's garret, to think other than Hoeller-garret-thoughts

in Hoeller's garret was simply impossible, and so I decided to familiarize myself gradually with the prescribed mode of thinking in this place, to study it so as to learn to think along these lines, entering Hoeller's garret and learning to adjust, to entrust and subject oneself to these mandatory lines of thought and make some progress in them is not easy.

Even as the narrator is explaining his own actions, Bernhard, the author, is talking to us, his readers, about the challenge he knows he's given us; and he is, in his way, offering instruction, encouragement.

It may be obvious that to read Bernhard we must, like his narrator, familiarize ourselves "with the prescribed mode of thinking in this [book], to study it so as to learn to think along those lines . . . [because] to entrust and subject oneself to these mandatory lines of thought and make some progress in them is not easy." This is what we discovered for ourselves, but may not have articulated in the same way, as we learned to read "difficult" writers, which, depending on your own tastes, could mean Joyce, Faulkner, Borges, Proust, Pynchon, Gertrude Stein, or even, for some readers, Alice Munro or Mavis Gallant. Work commonly described as difficult decades ago might seem less so now, as other, similar work has served to make its techniques and strategies less exotic. Similarly, writing we found difficult earlier in our reading lives is likely to seem less so now, because its methods have grown familiar to us.

I once heard a respected teacher and writer bravely admit to having been unable to read Hemingway for many years, not because she disagreed with his attitudes or disliked the stories; she just didn't get it, didn't understand what the stories were doing. I say "bravely" because it can be embarrassing to admit that we don't understand something that everyone else seems to have read and understood. This is a kind of embarrassment we need to outgrow if we're to develop as readers and as writers. Teachers—and, for that matter, parents—see the other side of this experience. We urge a poem or story on someone because we "think they're ready for it," the way we might put a child on a bike without training wheels because it's time to take the next step—or rather, to discover what it means to be balanced on two wheels. Yes, it's difficult at first; it might even seem impossible. But then the reader/rider gets accustomed to it and moves on to the next challenge (pedaling up a steep hill, for instance). That's life.

Or at least, that's a life of growth. All of us have the option of avoiding challenges, of looking for the easiest way to do what we've done before, to read what we've read before, write the sort of poem or story we feel comfortable writing. Novelist, short-story writer, and essayist Francine Prose—such a prolific writer that we might assume she has gained a mastery that makes writing at least a little bit easier—has said, "The challenge is to keep doing something different, something harder and scarier in every way than the thing you did before . . . to do something more difficult every time."

MOUNT EVEREST, SCHOOLING, DANGERS OF SUCCESS, AND THE LONG JOURNEY WE'VE CHOSEN TO MAKE

So far so well, but the most and the best of the Poem I perceive remains unwritten, and is the work of my life, yet to be done. . . . The paths to the house are made—but where is the house itself?

— WALT WHITMAN, in notes for a preface made on May 31, 1861, his forty-second birthday

The making of poems is so mysteriously tied up with not-knowing that in some sense the poet is a perpetual amateur, a stranger to the art, subject to ineptitude, failure, falsity, mediocrity, and repetitiveness. Even to remember what a poem *is* seems impossible for a poet—one suspects that professors, or professionals, rarely have that problem. Nonetheless, some poets . . . make you want to use the word *professional* because their careers are testaments to their stamina of craft and spirit. Having found an initial place for themselves to stand and a way to speak, they have lost and found it again and again; they have reconceived themselves, gone past their old answers into the new questions.

— TONY HOAGLAND

Conductor Marin Alsop has called Mahler's Fifth Symphony "the Mount Everest of music." "It's a large-scale journey," she writes.

> Even as a young man, Mahler was after the big picture. When other twentysomethings might have been writing lighthearted music, Mahler was trying to solve the riddles of the universe through his epic symphonies.... The first two movements explore this struggle between darkness and light with no resolution. The third is a miniature journey unto itself, a kind of commentary by Mahler on popular culture past, present and future. For a conductor and the orchestra musicians, it's extremely challenging on many levels.... Just like the Everest climb, pacing is critical to the outcome. My goal is to give our journey a sense of structure, arrival and resolution. Mahler loves conflict, contrast, obsession and excess. But I always have to temper and monitor the indulgence so that it doesn't become *self*-indulgence. I have to feel as one with the musicians, and be vigilant about the path we navigate together.

To call a piece of writing difficult most often means that it challenges our ability to comprehend it in one way or another. To comprehend is "to grasp with the mind." The opposite of difficult work would be work that already lies within our grasp—work that is either immediately comprehendible or preconceived. This "easy" or easier work might still give us pleasure, especially when it satisfies our expectations, or works subtle variations on a familiar form we've come to enjoy; but, like my wife playing those weddings, eventually we're likely to find that simply clutching what's already in our hand is less interesting, less fulfilling, than extending our grasp.

Of course, we can't expect to grasp everything we reach for. Some work we read might elude us; some work we try to write might require understanding or skills we haven't yet developed. But even to make the attempt is to reach beyond what we can hold, what we can do, now.

Correction is about a life devoted almost entirely to perfecting one's art. We learn that Roithamer built the Cone for his beloved sister, whom he wishes to make "perfectly happy by means of a construction perfectly suited to her person." After six years of obsessive dedication, he completed the project and brought her to it. But this is no happy story of affirmation: soon after Roithamer showed his sister what he had made, she died, miserable. Roithamer wrote in his notes, "The effect of the finished Cone is not as anticipated." Shortly after that, Roithamer hanged himself. For Roithamer, the ultimate correction is annihilation, death. While *Correction* is by no means an instruction manual, it offers much to ponder about artistic ambition, difficulty, and dedication. Here are a few of the notions Bernhard offers us through his characters:

Every idea and every pursuit of an idea inside us is life. . . . The lack of ideas is death.

When we set out to do something we're constantly being sidetracked, we're thought to be crazy, our refusal to yield and to compromise. . . impels us onward. . . . The world around us is constantly balking and hindering us and it is precisely by this constant inhibiting and hindering action that it enables us to approach our aim and finally even reach it.

I have finished my Fifth [Symphony]—it had to be almost completely re-orchestrated. I simply can't understand why I still had to make such mistakes, like the merest beginner. (It is clear that all the experience I had gained in writing the first four symphonies completely let me down in this one—for a completely new style demanded a new technique.)

— *Gustav Mahler*

We have to go along with a crazy idea, our own, even when we don't remember how we got it, we must go along with this crazy idea all the way, bring it to realization in the teeth of all the doubts and all the rules and all the recriminations, despite *everything*. We bring this idea to realization in order to bring ourselves to realization.

The idea demands fulfillment, it demands realization, and never stops demanding to be realized. One always wants to give it up, but one ends by not giving it up because one is by nature disinclined to give it up and in fact one sets about realizing the idea. Suddenly one's head is full of nothing else, one has become the incarnation of one's idea. And now one begins to reap the benefits of all one's suffering, of one's origin and everything connected with one's origins. . . . It all turns out to be useful, and the worst of the horrors are most useful of all.

Resignation, weakness, emptiness, the failure to make it real. It's all a matter of schooling oneself, a school in which I am both the teacher and the pupil.

Conductor Herbert von Karajan has said that when one hears Mahler's Fifth, "you forget that time has passed. A great performance of the Fifth is a transforming experience. The fantastic finale almost forces you to hold your breath." And yet after its premiere, Mahler is reported to have said, "Nobody understood it. I wish I could conduct the first performance fifty years after my death."

Achieving the difficult thing by no means necessarily leads to the deep satisfaction, the recognition, or the life of bliss we might imagine. Andrew Wiles is the mathematician credited with proving Fermat's Last Theorem, which had stumped thousands of dedicated mathematicians for over three hundred years. Wiles devoted himself to the problem for nearly nine years; the final proof was over one hundred pages long. After it was verified, he said,

There's no other problem that will mean the same to me. This was my childhood passion. There's nothing to replace that. I've solved it. I'll try other problems, I'm sure. Some of them will be very hard and I'll have a sense of achievement again, but there's no other problem in mathematics that could hold me the way Fermat did. . . . Having solved this problem there's certainly a sense of loss, but at the same time there is this tremendous sense of freedom. I was so obsessed by this problem that for eight years I was thinking about it all the time—when I woke up in the morning to when I went to sleep at night.

That's a long time to think about one thing. That particular
odyssey is now over. My mind is at rest.

One can hear the resignation, almost as if Wiles is accepting death.
To have accomplished what he set out to do is not the ultimate source
of pleasure. The actual accomplishment, we'll assume, was a source of
pleasure; but the sustaining pleasure was the work itself.

People have told me that I've taken away their problem, and
asked if I could give them something else. There is a sense of
melancholy. We've lost something that's been with us for so
long, something that drew a lot of us into mathematics. Perhaps that's always the way with math problems. We just have
to find new ones to capture our attention.

Math problems, symphonies, building a house, and writing a story or
poem or novel are the same this way: we set goals, we progress, we set
new goals.

It's all a matter of schooling oneself. There is no reason to doubt Mark
Twain's expressions of frustration; they ring not of false modesty but of
sincere exasperation. We also know from his letters that, late in life, he
thought that "wretched God-damned book" was his best. Precisely why
he struggled so painfully, and why he valued the result so highly, is a
private matter. Though their letters and journals are sometimes revealing, for the most part we can't know what problems other writers give
themselves, or what makes a particular piece of work difficult for them.
On the rare occasions when it happens, it's a privilege to be in the company of writers so dedicated to their work that they willingly share their
challenges—both those they think they've met successfully and those
they're in the midst of struggling with. We each have our own sense of
the problems we've chosen—or the problems we've been offered, or the
problems we somehow find ourselves confronting. There's no point in
pretending that every moment of engaging them will be a joy. But our
deepest pleasures as artists result not only from surmounting but from
continuously engaging with the difficulties that represent our greatest
ambition.

SOURCES AND SOLUTIONS

Some puzzles are solved in solitude, others by groups. This book developed, slowly, from personal interests and from readers' responses to *Maps of the Imagination*. Some of those readers suggested related books and essays; others were kind enough to invite me to address various groups, ranging from professional designers and design teachers to object-oriented programmers, from a marketing team at General Mills to young game creators from around the world. All those interactions provided unanticipated information (the seasonal market for croissants, the role of music in establishing the tone of a video game) and sparked new ideas. The individual chapters grew out of, and eventually outgrew their origins as, lectures delivered at residencies of the Warren Wilson College

MFA Program for Writers. During the years I worked on them, I lived in Norway, North Carolina, and Arizona. At Arizona State University a small, trusting group of graduate students engaged in a seminar on puzzles and mystery, and various insights and readings from those discussions and others that followed inform these pages. My greatest debts are to the Warren Wilson MFA program, which has long been receptive to unusual approaches to the discussion of writing, and to the students at both Warren Wilson and Arizona State who not only tolerated what seemed to be (and were) highly digressive discussions but eagerly joined them. Their enthusiasm was encouraging, and their questions, occasional frustrations, and bemusement were instructive.

The two people most responsible for seeing this book completed are my wife, Laura, and my supportive, patient editor, Barbara Ras. Assistance came in various forms from Debra Allbery, Andrea Barrett, Robert Boswell, Richard Gabriel, Allegra Hyde, Cathy Jewell, Charles Ritchie, and Richard Schmitt, among many others. My sense of the forms writing about writing can take has been influenced by many earlier teachers and essayists, from Aristotle to E. M. Forster, from Virginia Woolf to Flannery O'Connor, as well as by contemporary practitioners, most notably Robert Boswell, whose *Half-Known World* is itself richly narrative; Charles Baxter, who has modeled, for many years, a kind of essay that manages to be instructive, playful, and idiosyncratic; Ellen Bryant Voigt, whose essays and lectures are models of passion, clarity, and rigor; and Stephen Dobyns, whose books of essays (which claim to be for poets, but benefit any writer) are extraordinarily lucid and combine close reading and strong opinions with good sense and a generosity of spirit. More generally, my colleagues at Warren Wilson have reinforced the value of never-ending exploration.

Experts in other fields responded to my questions with remarkable magnanimity. They include puzzle master Will Shortz, with whom I crossed paths, serendipitously, at a table tennis club (we didn't play; he would have won), and who introduced me to the puzzles of Thomas "Dr. Sudoku" Snyder and to Michael Ashley; Thomas Snyder, who allowed me to reproduce some of his work here, and whose website is a portal into another dimension; Michael Ashley, who agreed to compose an acrostic with a literary theme on very short notice; master designer of theatrical illusions Jim Steinmeyer, whose books on magic are both entertaining and instructive; and video game designer and teacher Jesse Schell, whose *The Art of Game Design* was an inspiration, and who invited me to meet his students and colleagues at Carnegie Mellon's Entertainment Technology Center, a real-world Wonderland. Ultimately, not much more than a mention of video games made it into this book, but the conversations there informed my views of other puzzles and games, and reminded me that it's possible to do serious work and still have great fun.

Arizona State University and the University of Houston provided funds directly related to this project, and the John Simon Guggenheim Memorial Foundation provided financial support long ago, when I thought this book would focus on "writing as a way of seeing." I came to see it differently, but the foundation, a true patron of the arts, placed no restrictions on the final product.

Finally, I'd like to thank some of the independent bookstores who supported *Maps of the Imagination* and so, in the best way they could, made this book possible: Malaprop's in Asheville, NC; St. Mark's Bookshop in NYC; City Lights in San Francisco; Micawber's Books in St. Paul, MN; Harvard Book Store in Cambridge, MA; the Tattered Cover in Denver; Prairie Lights in Iowa City; Collected Works in Santa Fe; Chapters in Washington, DC; Daedalus Bookshop in Charlottesville, VA; Maria's Bookshop in Durango, CO; Powell's Books in Portland, OR; and Barbara's Bookstore in Chicago. While I discovered Changing Hands Bookstore in Tempe, AZ, after *Maps* came out, I appreciate that the puzzle section there is located behind the podium provided for visiting writers, so gave me frequent reminders of my work while I listened. Here's hoping those booksellers and their kind are around for years to come.

The Contemplation of Recurring Patterns

Michael Korda is quoted from Tracy Daugherty's *Just One Catch: A Biography of Joseph Heller*; Juan Tamariz is quoted from Alex Stone's *Fooling Houdini: Magicians, Mentalists, Math Geeks and the Hidden Powers of the Mind*; Howard Thurston's instructions for the Front and Back Palm are from his 1903 book *Card Tricks*; and all references here and throughout to Marcel Danesi are to his book *The Puzzle Instinct*, an excellent overview of the history of a wide variety of puzzles, their applications to other fields, and their broad appeal.

1. Directions for Attaining Knowledge of All Dark Things

John Le Carré is quoted from an interview in the online Short Attention Span Press; the illustration of books at leisure is *The Card Players*, Jonathan Wolstenholme, 2004, watercolor on paper, private collection, © Portal Painters/The Bridgeman Art Library; Jerry Seinfeld is quoted from "Jerry Seinfeld Intends to Die Standing Up," by Jonah Weiner, in the *New York Times*, December 20, 2012; the image of the Rhind Mathematical Papyrus, written in hieratic script, circa 1650 B.C.E., appears thanks to the De Agostini Picture Library/The Bridgeman Art Library; the first sudoku puzzle is from jolanda85/Shutterstock.com; Benjamin Franklin is quoted from his autobiography; most of the crabby author quotations are from Emily Temple's "The 30 Harshest Author-on-Author Insults in History," originally posted on January 1, 2012, on *Flavorwire*; Flannery O'Connor is quoted from "Writing Short Stories," in *Mystery and Manners: Occasional Prose*; *Butch Cassidy and the Sundance Kid* was released in 1969 by the Twentieth Century-Fox Film Corporation; Joseph Heller's discussion of the origins of *Catch-22* is from Tracy Daugherty's biography; John McPhee is quoted from his essay "Structure," in the *New Yorker*, January 14, 2013; Charles Ritchie's *Night in Three Panels* (2000; watercolor, graphite, conté crayon, and pen and ink on Fabriano paper; sheet/image 4 1/2 x 19 1/8 inches; private collection) and *Night with Terraces* (1995–97; conte crayon, wax crayon, watercolor, graphite, and collage on Fabriano paper; sheet/image 13 x 29 3/4 inches; private collection) are reproduced here by permission of the artist; Bruce Springsteen is quoted from *Springsteen on Springsteen: Interviews, Speeches, and Encounters*, ed. Jeff Burger, Chicago Review Press, 2013; the Emily Dickinson stanzas are from "I dwell in possibility"; Kathleen Spivack is quoted from *With Robert Lowell and His Circle: Sylvia Plath, Anne Sexton, Elizabeth Bishop, Stanley Kunitz, and*

Others; Ross MacDonald is quoted from his book *Self-Portrait: Ceaselessly into the Past*; Milan Kundera discusses his seven-part structures in *The Art of the Novel*; the Don DeLillo quotation in the footnote comes from "Don DeLillo: The Art of Fiction No. 135" in the *Paris Review* 128, fall 1993; T. S. Eliot's "East Coker" is part of his *Four Quartets*, copyright renewed © 1968 by Esme Valerie Eliot, reprinted by permission of Houghton Mifflin Harcourt Publishing Company, all rights reserved; as of this writing, Foldit is still online at fold.it, and the image of one of the puzzles is reprinted with the permission of the Foldit Project, University of Washington Center for Game Science.

SOLUTIONS

THE ONE WHO ALWAYS LIES, THE ONE WHO ALWAYS TELLS THE TRUTH

You point to one of the roads and ask one of the twins, "If I were to ask you if this road leads to town, would you say yes?" If it does, the truth-telling twin will say yes; if it doesn't, she'll say no. Similarly, if the road does lead to town, the liar will say no if asked directly, so she's forced to lie and say yes. If the road doesn't lead to town, she, too, needs to say no. (The more I think about it, the less likely it seems that this question ever appeared on the GRE. No doubt I was introduced to it by my puzzle-loving junior high math teacher, Gordon Culbertson.)

THE GENDER ELEVATOR

After the elevator stops at the fifth floor, it will hold two men and two women.

THE BOY, THE FOX, THE CHICKEN, AND THE BAG OF CORN

The boy takes the chicken across the river (this fox doesn't eat corn), leaves the chicken on the other side, and goes back across. The boy then takes the fox across the river, and since he can't leave the fox and chicken together, he brings the chicken back. Since the chicken and corn can't be left together, he leaves the chicken and he takes the corn across and leaves it with the (crippled? tame?) fox. He then returns to pick up the chicken and crosses the river one last time, vowing to build a bigger raft.

If you haven't solved one of these in a while, it's helpful to build a grid that looks something like the one below.

To see the solution, go to the end of the solutions for this chapter.

		Poet					Drink					Form				
		Edna	Walt	Elizabeth	Louise	Alex	Gin	Apple martini	Malbec	Scotch	Bottled Water	Haiku	Sonnet	Limerick	Villanelle	Sestina
First Book	Two Cheeks, 1985															
	One Moon, 1987															
	My Thoughts, 1990															
	Surging Tides, 1996															
	Mist Shifts in Fits, 2001															
Form	Haiku															
	Sonnet															
	Limerick															
	Villanelle															
	Sestina															
Drink	Gin															
	Apple martini															
	Malbec															
	Scotch															
	Bottled Water															

C	U	B	E
U	G	L	Y
B	L	U	E
E	Y	E	S

WORD SQUARE BEGINNING WITH "CUBE"

This puzzle comes from Martin Gardner's *The Colossal Book of Short Puzzles and Problems*, pages 403–4. One of many possible solutions is shown at left.

4	8	2	1	6	7	3	5	9
5	7	1	9	4	3	6	8	2
9	6	3	2	8	5	1	4	7
1	5	6	8	7	4	2	9	3
8	3	9	6	1	2	5	7	4
2	4	7	5	3	9	8	6	1
7	9	8	3	5	1	4	2	6
3	2	5	4	9	6	7	1	8
6	1	4	7	2	8	9	3	5

ACROSTIC

Readers are invited to submit solutions to the puzzle on pages 28 and 29, created by Michael Ashley for this book. Correct solutions will be chosen at random to win a variety of prizes. For full details visit www.tupress. org/books/a-muse-and-a-maze.

THE FOUR LOGICAL WRITERS

This is a very slight modification of the classic Four Prisoners Problem, which came up during conversation at a lovely pre-wedding dinner out-side of Florence, Italy. It assumes not only that the three people sitting in a row are perfectly logical but that they can rely on each other to be perfectly logical. If there are three writers for whom this is true, I haven't met them. But: if the writer sitting behind her two friends sees that they both have red books on their heads, she knows hers is black; if she sees that they both have black books on their heads, she knows hers is red. If she sees that one has a black book and one has a red book, she knows better than to guess; and the writer sitting in front of her, understanding what her silence means—that he and the first writer in the row have different colored books on their heads—knows the color of his book is not the color of the one he can see in front of him.

The author of Two Cheeks is Alex, who drinks Malbec and writes limericks; the author of One Moon is Edna, who drinks scotch and writes sestinas; the author of My Thoughts is Louise, who drinks gin and writes sonnets; the author of Surging Tides is Walt, who drinks water and writes villanelles; and the author of Mist Shifts in Fits is Elizabeth, who drinks apple martinis and writes haiku.

2. How, from Such Wreckage, We Evolve the Eventual Effect

John Ruskin is quoted from his book *The Elements of Drawing, in Three Letters to Beginners*; the (corrected) larger Franklin Magic Square and a more complete discussion of its remarkable properties can be found under "Franklin's Magic Squares" at mathpages.com; the *Chart of the Gulfstream*, credited to Benjamin Franklin and James Poupard, American Philosophical Society, Philadelphia, 1786?, appears courtesy of the Library of Congress; Raymond Chandler is quoted from his essay "The Simple Art of Murder" from *The Simple Art of Murder*, copyright © 1950 by Raymond Chandler, renewed © 1978 by Helga Greene, reprinted by permission of Houghton Mifflin Harcourt Publishing Company, all rights reserved; Anton Chekhov is quoted from his January 14, 1887, letter to Maria V. Kiseleva and, later, from an October 27, 1888, letter to Alexi S. Suvorin, both reprinted in *Anton Chekhov and His Times*, which also includes the reminiscence by Olga Knipper-Chekhova, "About A. P. Chekhov"; Ross MacDonald is quoted from *Self-Portrait: Ceaselessly into the Past*; the photo of a reproduction of the Turk appears courtesy of its creator, John Gaughan; Vladimir Nabokov is quoted from the transcript of his interview with BBC Television in 1962 and later from a 1964 interview with *Playboy*, both published in *Strong Opinions*; the photograph of Jim Sanborn's *Kryptos* is courtesy of the artist; Teller is quoted from "Teller Reveals His Secrets," published in *Smithsonian Magazine*, March 2012; Sir Arthur Conan Doyle is quoted from his brief and surprising BBC interview of May 14, 1930, courtesy of the Conan Doyle Estate Ltd.; Chekhov's "Criminal Investigator" is in *A Night in the Cemetery:*

And Other Stories of Crime and Suspense. Tim O'Brien is quoted from his essay "The Magic Show," in *Writers on Writing: A Bread Loaf Anthology*, ed. Robert Pack and Jay Parini; Georges Perec is quoted from his "Thoughts on the Art and Technique of Crossing Words," trans. Henri Picciotto with Arthur Schulman, reprinted in the *Believer* in September 2006; Steve Hodges discusses Perec's use of the Knight's Tour in his thesis "The Digital Absurd," available at https://smartech.gatech.edu/bitstream/handle/1853/33950/hodges_steven_201005_phd.pdf; the image of the tour was redrawn by Daniel Thomasson on his site Borderschess .org, which includes various Knight's Tour puzzles; the Perec quotation comes from *Oulipo Compendium*; Matthew Gidley is quoted from his essay "Georges Perec and the Oulipians," in frieze.com, 53, June–August 2000; the image of books playing chess is *Your Move*, Jonathan Wolstenholme, 2003, watercolor on paper, private collection, © Portal Painters/ The Bridgeman Art Library; the 1613 map of Königsberg by Joachim Bering can be found on WikiCommons at http://commons.wikimedia.org/ wiki/file:Koenigsberg,_Map _by_Bering_1613.jpg.

SOLUTIONS

First, a hint for the second cryptogram: the author's name, following the quotation, is two words of nearly equal length.

CRYPTOGRAM

"I wish I could write as mysterious as a cat."—Edgar Allan Poe

SECOND CRYPTOGRAM

"Why do people always expect authors to answer questions? I am an author because I want to ask questions. If I had answers I'd be a politician."—Eugène Ionesco. And if that was too easy: this cipher is based on several key words—specifically, on the titles of four of Ionesco's plays. By writing out the alphabet A–Z, and then writing out the substituted letters in sequence, you should—well, might—be able to identify those plays. Remember, repeated letters are omitted. The play titles are at the end of this chapter's solutions.

By Emily Cox and Henry Rathvon. Copyright © 2002 by American Crossword Puzzle Tournament (www.crosswordtournament.com). Used with permission.

F	R	O	M	E			O	P	E	R	A		M	E	S	H
L	O	C	A	L		S	T	A	Y	O	N		O	R	C	A
I	C	E	R	S		L	O	W	E	S	T		C	R	O	W
C	H	A	M	E	L	E	O	N		S	E	A	C	O	W	S
K	E	N	O		O	I	L	S		S	P	A	R	S	E	
		S	A	R	G	E		S	E	U	S	S				
C	H	E	E	T	A	H		P	O	R	P	O	I	S	E	S
H	E	A	T	O	N		T	H	A	I		N	O	A	H	
A	C	T		S	T	R	O	K	E	S		U	S	A		
S	H	I	P		E	O	N	S		P	L	A	C	E	D	
M	E	N	A	G	E	R	I	E		P	H	O	N	I	L	Y
		R	Y	A	N	S		G	R	E	T	A				
C	E	D	A	R	S		S	E	E	R		C	E	D	E	
A	X	O	L	O	T	L		A	N	T	E	L	O	P	E	S
G	U	L	L		E	A	G	L	E	T		O	N	S	E	T
E	L	L	A		N	I	N	E	T	Y		A	D	O	R	E
S	T	Y	X		D	R	U	M	S		N	A	M	E	S	

1	6	5	9	8	3	7	4	2
8	2	4	6	7	1	5	3	9
9	7	3	2	4	5	8	1	6
4	1	8	7	5	2	6	9	3
3	5	7	4	9	6	1	2	8
2	9	6	1	3	8	4	5	7
7	3	1	5	6	9	2	8	4
6	8	2	3	1	4	9	7	5
5	4	9	8	2	7	3	6	1

MISSING DIGIT?

was created by Thomas Snyder, three-time world sudoku champion and the author of many puzzle books, including *Sudoku Masterpieces*, *Battleship Sudoku*, and *Mutant Sudoku*. For more variations on the form, see his Grandmaster Puzzles at gm-puzzles.com.

WILL SHORTZ'S ALPHABETICAL SETS

1. Tuesday
2. Jupiter
3. Clinton
4. Antarctica
5. Cupid
6. Nickel
7. Esther
8. Scorpio
9. Center field
10. Four of a kind
11. Doc
12. French hens

by Thomas Snyder, at right.

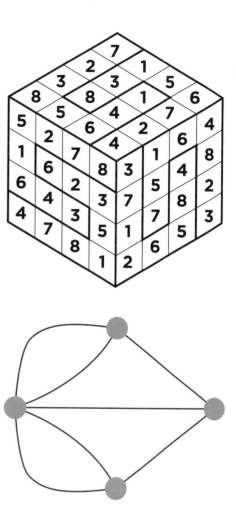

THE SEVEN BRIDGES OF KÖNIGSBERG

That single continuous walk which involves crossing each bridge once and only once isn't possible, but not because of the number of bridges. The key is the number of bridges that attach to each land mass. A graph of the problem would look like the diagram at bottom right.

Mathematicians refer to the bridges, or connections, as edges; they refer to the land, or connecting points, as nodes. Assuming all the nodes are connected, it turns out that, no matter how many bridges and connecting land masses are involved, if zero or two of the nodes have an odd number of edges, the single continuous circuit can be completed; in any other instance, it can't. Since Königsberg's four land masses were each accessed by an odd number of bridges, the walk was impossible.

THE IONESCO CIPHER

is thebaldprimoncsxkgjufqvwyz, which represents *The Bald Prima Donna*, *Rhinoceros*, *Exit the King*, and *Jack, or The Submission*, followed by the six unused letters of the alphabet.

3. Seven Clever Pieces

For more on the history of jigsaw puzzles, see Anne D. Williams's *The Jigsaw Puzzle: Piecing Together a History*; the image of the Spilsbury puzzle is copyright © The British Library Board Maps 188.v.12.; Jan Kjærstad is quoted from *The Seducer*; the screen shots from *Citizen Kane*, originally released by RKO Pictures in 1941, are from the 70th Anniversary Edition; Martin Scorsese is quoted from the article "Within Him, Without Him," by Dave Itzkoff, published in the *New York Times*, September 23, 2011; Tim O'Brien is again quoted from his essay "The Magic Show"; Charles Ritchie's *Twilight* (1999; litho crayon, conte crayon, pen and ink, watercolor, graphite, silver ink, and collage on Fabriano paper; sheet/image 4 7/8 x 30 inches; private collection), *Blue Twilight* drawing (1996–97; graphite, watercolor, pastel, conté crayon, and litho crayon on Fabriano paper; sheet/image 22 x 30 inches; University of Richmond, Virginia), *Blue Twilight* print (2000–2001; dark-manner aquatint on heavyweight Rives BFK paper; image 10 15/16 x 14 7/8 inches, sheet 15 1/4 x 18 1/4 inches; published by Center Street Studio, Milton, Massachusetts), and *Self-Portrait with Night I* (2000–2002; watercolor, litho crayon, gouache, pen and ink, and graphite on Fabriano paper; sheet/image 5 1/8 x 11 7/8 inches; private collection) are reproduced here by permission of the artist; Stephen Greenblatt is quoted from *Will in the World*; excerpts from *The Great Gatsby*, by F. Scott Fitzgerald, are reprinted with the permission of Scribner Publishing Group, copyright © 1925 by Charles Scribner's Sons, renewed © 1953 by Frances Scott Fitzgerald Lanahan, all rights reserved; the photographs of Anish Kapoor's *Memory* appear courtesy of the artist and Deutsche Guggenheim (2008; Corten steel, 4.48 x 8.97 x 14.5 meters; installation view, Guggenheim New York, 2009; copyright © 2014 Anish Kapoor/ARS, New York/DACS, London); the page from *Fun Home: A Family Tragicomic* is copyright © 2006 by Alison Bechdel, reprinted by permission of Houghton Mifflin Harcourt Publishing Company, all rights reserved; James Salter is quoted from *A Sport and a Pastime*; the first two photographs of Markus Raetz's *Head* appear courtesy of Vegar Moen/Artscape Nordland (1992; iron and granite; height 178 cm; Vestvågøy Municipality), while the third image is from a home video (see www.peterturchi.com). Finally, for a related discussion on characterization, see Steven Schwartz's essay "The Absence of Their Presence: Mythic Character in Fiction," in *A Kite in the Wind*.

4. The Treasure Hunter's Dilemma

The iconic 1899 photograph of Houdini in chains is courtesy of the Library of Congress, McManus-Young Collection; Hermann Hesse is quoted from his *Autobiographical Writings*; the poster of Houdini's Death-Defying Mystery is from the Harry Ransom Center, the University of Texas at Austin; most of the information on Houdini, the Proteus Cabinet, and the disappearing elephant illusion are from Jim Steinmeyer's *Hiding the Elephant: How Magicians Invented the Impossible*; the illustrations of the Proteus Cabinet and the elephant illusion are by Allegra Hyde, based on Steinmeyer's originals; Dylan on Rimbaud is quoted from *Bob Dylan: The Never Ending Star* by Lee Marshall; the Thomas Wolfe quotation appears in David Herbert Donald's *Look Homeward: A Life of Thomas Wolfe*; Louise Glück is quoted from *Proofs and Theories*; *The Wizard of Oz* was released in 1939 by Metro-Goldwyn-Mayer; Flannery O'Connor is quoted from *Mystery and Manners*; Bruce Springsteen is quoted in "Bringing It All Back Home," by David Fricke, *Rolling Stone*, February 5, 2009; Joseph Conrad is quoted from "A Familiar Preface, 1912," in *A Personal Record*; the quotations from Charles Ritchie are from personal interviews and the exhibition catalog *Suburban Journals: The Sketches, Drawings, and Prints of Charles Ritchie*; Ritchie's *Erased Self-Portrait* (1983; watercolor, graphite, and pen and ink on Fabriano paper; sheet/image 7 x 4 inches; The Cartin Collection, Hartford, Connecticut) is reproduced here by permission of the artist; *Van Gogh's Chair* (1888) is in the National Gallery, London; *The Empty Chair, Gad's Hill, 9th June, 1870* is by Sir Samuel Luke Fildes, oil on canvas, Rare Book Department, Free Library of Philadelphia/The Bridgeman Art Library; Dorothy Parker is quoted from her review "A Book of Great Short Stories," in the *New Yorker*, October 29, 1927; Ernest Hemingway is quoted from an August 1924 letter to Gertrude Stein that appears in *Ernest Hemingway: Selected Letters, 1917–1961*; the Whitman lines beginning "From behind the screen" are from "So Long"; Charles Ritchie's *Self-Portrait with Paper Whites* (1994–98; watercolor, graphite, and pen and ink on Fabriano paper; sheet/image 4 1/4 x 3 inches; private collection) and *Kitchen Windows with Reflections* (2011; watercolor and graphite on Fabriano paper; sheet/image 4 x 6 inches; collection of the artist) are reproduced here by permission of the artist; Evert A. Duyckinck is quoted from "Melville's *Moby-Dick; or, The Whale*," which originally appeared in *New York Literary World* 9 on November 22, 1851; Justin Kaplan is quoted from his book *Mr. Clemens and Mark Twain: A Biography*; the Twain-Howells letter is quoted by Jonathan Raban in his introduction to the Library of America paperback edition of *Life on the Mississippi*; Jonathan Raban is quoted from same; John Updike is quoted from "The Short Story and I," in *More Matter: Essays and Criticism*; David Shields is quoted from "An Interview with David Shields," *Writer's Chronicle*, May 2004; the reproduction of the poster "Europe's Eclipsing Sensation" is courtesy of Photofest; Ellen Bryant Voigt is quoted from "Song and Story," an interview with Steven Cramer in the *Atlantic*, November 24, 1999; Norman Rockwell's *Triple Self-Portrait*, illustration provided by Curtis Licensing, for all nonbook uses © SEPS, all rights reserved, printed by permission of the Norman Rockwell Family Agency, copyright © the Norman Rockwell Family Entities.

5. The Line, the Pyramid, and the Labyrinth

Wassily Kandinsky is quoted from his book *Point and Line to Plane*; the Ladders to Salvation game board image is taken from WikiCommons, http://en.wikipedia.org/wiki/ File:Snakes_and_Ladders.jpg; John McPhee is quoted from his essay "Structure," in the *New Yorker*, January 14, 2013; Walt Whitman is quoted from "Song of the Rolling Earth"; the image of the game board is by Allegra Hyde; Homer is quoted from the first lines of *The Odyssey*; Rudolf Arnheim is quoted from *Art and Visual Perception*; all the quotations of Tim Ingold, the discussion of reindeer hunters, and the Khanty storytellers are drawn from his book *Lines: A Brief History*; the picture of the garden path is copyright © Derek Fell, reprinted with permission; *St. Jerome in the Wilderness* (detail) is by Albrecht Dürer, c. 1496, engraving, private collection, The Bridgeman Art Library; John Ruskin is quoted from *The Elements of Drawing*; Henry Ernest Dudeney's puzzles appear in *The Canterbury Puzzles, and Other Curious Problems* (1907); "Petie Pete versus Witch Bea-Witch" is from *Italian Folktales*, selected and retold by Italo Calvino, translated by George Martin, copyright © 1956 by Guilio Einaudi editore, s.p.a., English translation copyright © 1980 by Houghton Mifflin Harcourt, reprinted by permission of Houghton Mifflin Harcourt Publishing Company, all rights reserved; the leaping dancer and the following images are from Kandinsky's *Point and Line to Plane*; the image of the Chartres labyrinth is from EcOasis/Shutterstock.com; maze by Dave Phillips, www.dave-phillipspuzzlemaze.com; the drawing of The Man in the Maze is by Allegra Hyde; Alice Munro's "Royal Beatings" appears in her collection *Who Do You Think You Are?*; Michael Ondaatje is quoted from his *Divisadero*; the map of the caves of Crete is taken from *Lines: A Brief History*, was drawn by F. W. Sieber, and is in the Historic Collections, Kings College, University of Aberdeen; and Jonathan Raban is quoted once again from his introduction to *Life on the Mississippi*.

SOLUTIONS

THE PARDONER'S PUZZLE

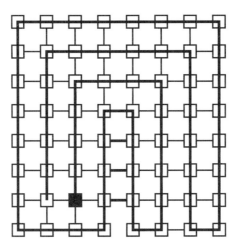

6. The Pleasures of Difficulty

Mark Twain is quoted from the previously mentioned introduction by Jonathan Raban; Chekhov is quoted from his October 27, 1888, letter to

Alexei S. Suvorin, reprinted in *Anton Chekhov and His Times*; "The Miller's Puzzle" appears in Henry Ernest Dudeney's *The Canterbury Puzzles, and Other Curious Problems*; Antonya Nelson's "Strike Anywhere" appears in her collection *Some Fun* and, accompanied by her discussion of the story's evolution, in *The Story Behind the Story*; James Salter is quoted from *Solo Faces*; Charles D'Ambrosio's "The Scheme of Things" appears in his collection *The Dead Fish Museum*; David Jauss's essay "What We Talk About When We Talk About Flow" appears in his collection *Alone with All That Could Happen*, republished as *On Writing Fiction*; Jesse Schell's flow charts are reprinted from *The Art of Game Design*; the two drawings of stepping stones are by Allegra Hyde; the photo believed to be of Buddy Bolden's band is reproduced here courtesy of the New Orleans Jazz Club Collection of the Louisiana State Museum; the sonograph image is reproduced from Michael Ondaatje's *Coming Through Slaughter*; Whitman is quoted from an unpublished introduction dated May 31, 1861; Tony Hoagland is quoted from "Pinsky, Hass, Glück, and the Deployment of Talent," in *Real Sofistikashun: Essays on Poetry and Craft*; Marin Alsop is quoted from her piece on Mahler for National Public Radio on February 9, 2007, available at npr.org; Mahler is quoted from a letter dated February 8, 1911, to Georg Goehler, in *Selected Letters of Gustav Mahler*, ed. Knud Martner; the Herbert von Karajan quote is attributed to him in many places but the actual source is unclear; ditto the later Mahler quotation; Andrew Wiles is quoted from *Fermat's Last Theorem*.

SOLUTIONS

THE MILLER'S PUZZLE

The sacks should be arranged to form 2, 78, 156, 39, 4. Each pair multiplied by its single neighbor equals 156. There are three other possible solutions, but they all require moving more sacks.

THE POETIC LINE

The puzzle is from Martin Gardner's *The Colossal Book of Short Puzzles and Problems*, where he attributes it to Walter Penney of Greenbelt, Maryland. The scrambled quotation, "There is no frigate like a book / To take us lands away," is by Emily Dickinson.

would make twice as much money. Thanks again to Martin Gardner.

SYNONYMS?

This puzzle appeared in *US Airways Magazine*, June 2012, copyright © 2012, reprinted with the permission of Pace Communications.

(1)

stagecoach	beach bum
battle cry	automate
hearing aid	drama teacher
tangent	chieftain
carpooler	warrant
clanking	gavel

(2)

opts	bowl over
Robin Hood	say a blessing
coquette	tower
adverse	at ease
dog race	jingle
tugboat	shutout score

(3)

decimal	Lilliputian
domain	seafood seller
standoffish	searing
atoll	off the old lady
bedroll	often
minuteman	act funny

WORD GOLF

love lave have hate
dirt dart dare bare bate bath

FOUR LETTERS

Also from Martin Gardner's *The Colossal Book of Short Puzzles and Problems*. The consecutive letters *R, S, T, U* will spell "rust" or "ruts."

Peter Turchi's books include *Maps of the Imagination: The Writer as Cartographer*; a novel, *The Girls Next Door*; a collection of stories, *Magician*; a collection of stories; *Suburban Journals: The Sketchbooks, Drawings, and Prints of Charles Ritchie*, in collaboration with the artist; and a limited edition artist's book of his story "Night, Truck, Two Lights Burning," with images by Charles Ritchie. He has coedited, with Andrea Barrett, *A Kite in the Wind: Fiction Writers on Their Craft* and *The Story Behind the Story: 26 Stories by Contemporary Writers and How They Work*; and, with Charles Baxter, *Bringing the Devil to His Knees: The Craft of Fiction and the Writing Life*. Turchi's stories have appeared in *Ploughshares*, *Story*, the *Alaska Quarterly Review*, *Puerto del Sol*, and the *Colorado Review*. He has received Washington College's Sophie Kerr Prize, North Carolina's Sir Walter Raleigh Award, and fellowships from the National Endowment for the Arts and the John Simon Guggenheim Memorial Foundation. For fifteen years he directed the MFA Program for Writers at Warren Wilson College in Asheville, North Carolina; he then directed and taught in the MFA Program at Arizona State University. He currently teaches at the University of Houston and for the Warren Wilson MFA Program. For more information about this book as well as other resources for writers, visit peterturchi.com.

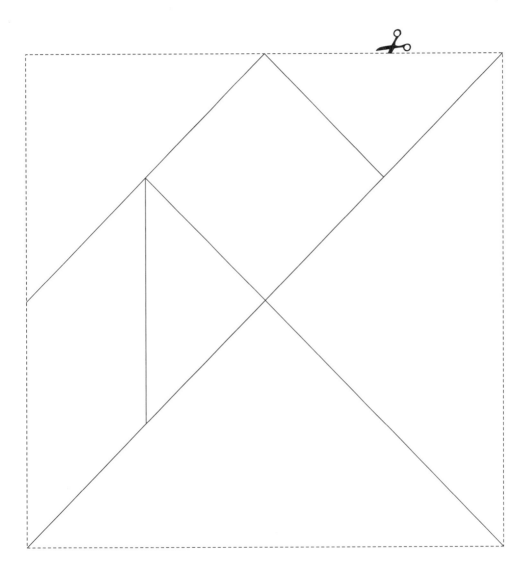